# Power and Principle

*Advancing Human Rights*
Sumner B. Twiss, John Kelsay, and Terry Coonan, Series Editors

# Power and Principle

Human Rights Programming in
International Organizations

Joel E. Oestreich

Georgetown University Press
WASHINGTON, D.C.

As of January 1, 2007, 13-digit ISBN numbers have replaced the 10-digit system.

13-digit
Paperback: 978-1-58901-159-5
Cloth: 978-1-58901-158-8

10-digit
Paperback: 1-58901-159-7
Cloth: 1-58901-158-9

Georgetown University Press, Washington, D.C.

Oestreich, Joel E.
   Power and principle : human rights programming in international organizations / Joel E. Oestreich.
   p. cm. — (Advancing human rights)
   Includes bibliographical references and index.
   ISBN-13: 978-1-58901-159-5 (pbk. : alk. paper)
   ISBN-10: 1-58901-159-7 (pbk. : alk. paper)
   ISBN-13: 978-1-58901-158-8 (hardcover : alk. paper)
   ISBN-10: 1-58901-158-9 (hardcover : alk. paper)
   1. Human rights. 2. International agencies. 3. United Nations. I. Title.
   JC571.O357 2007
   341.4'8—dc22
                                   2006031188

∞ This book is printed on acid-free paper meeting the requirements of the American National Standard for Permanence in Paper for Printed Library Materials.

14 13 12 11 10 09 08 07    9 8 7 6 5 4 3 2
First printing

Printed in the United States of America

# Contents

# Acknowledgments

This book is the result of a long process of research and writing on the issue of intergovernmental organizations, and many people have provided invaluable help along the way. Thomas Biersteker, Craig Murphy, and Nancy Rosenblum all provided support and intellectual assistance while I was doing my early research on the World Bank. Thomas Weiss gave important guidance during early work on UNICEF and the Convention on the Rights of the Child (CRC). The chapter on UNICEF draws heavily on the work of Patricia Smyke, who has written the definitive history of UNICEF's involvement in the early years of the CRC. I am heavily indebted to her research. Where possible, I have tried to confirm her information with my own interviews or a review of the documentary evidence. Michael Tierney was kind enough to read and comment on chapter 1, and he made suggestions that have immensely improved my theoretical argument. Peter Uvin was gracious enough to review chapter 3. Sofia Gruskin gave the same help for chapter 4, and she has been extremely important in helping me refine my understanding of the World Health Organization. I am deeply grateful to Charli Carpenter, Richard Claude, Roger Coate, Julie Mostov, and Kendall Stiles for commenting on drafts of the book and, more important, for their moral support, generosity with their time, and willingness to help. Of course, whatever errors remain are entirely my own fault.

A number of staff members at UNICEF, the World Bank, and the World Health Organization agreed to allow me to interview them. All were very generous with their time and provided me with extremely useful information about the inner workings of their organizations. Thanks are due to all of them for their time and their candor. I promised many that I would not cite them by name, and, just to be on the safe side, I have decided to extend that anonymity to all the interview participants; but they know who they are and all have my gratitude.

At Drexel University, I owe many, many thanks to my friends and colleagues Richardson Dilworth, Kali Gross, Christian Hunold, and David Munns. Their support and friendship have kept me going through numerous bouts of writer's block. Thanks also to Don Stevens and the Drexel History and Politics Department for providing me with much-needed travel funding.

Finally, thanks to my parents, for everything else.

# Acronyms and Abbreviations

| | |
|---|---|
| CEDAW | Convention on the Elimination of All Forms of Discrimination Against Women |
| CRC | Convention on the Rights of the Child |
| IBRD | International Bank for Reconstruction and Development (World Bank) |
| IDA | International Development Association (World Bank) |
| IGO | intergovernmental organization |
| IMF | International Monetary Fund |
| NGO | nongovernmental organization |
| UNAIDS | Joint United Nations Programme on HIV/AIDS |
| UNICEF | United Nations Children's Fund |
| WHO | World Health Organization |

## Chapter One

# Agency and Intergovernmental Organizations

In 1979 the Polish delegation to the United Nations proposed that the international community consider a new charter on children's rights. The Polish proposal came during the International Year of the Child, and it was meant to build on the publicity being generated for children's welfare around the world. The then-communist Polish delegation's proposal for the charter also had overtones of Cold War propaganda; it emphasized the sort of "positive" rights that were favored by socialist states (e.g., the right to health care or adequate housing) and that were used to embarrass those Western states that tended to promote more "negative" rights (e.g., free speech and freedom of religion).

As the process of drafting the charter—the proposed Convention on the Rights of the Child (CRC)—wore on, it followed the usual pattern of such documents, as compromises were made between East and West, and North and South, over its content. By the mid-1980s, however, an unusual factor emerged: A particular UN agency, the United Nations Children's Fund (UNICEF), began to take an interest. By the late 1980s UNICEF had become an important behind-the-scenes force in drafting the CRC. And by 1989 it was running its own campaign aimed at achieving universal acceptance of the CRC.

Intuitively, UNICEF's actions do not seem very surprising. As the UN's "lead agency for children," it ought to have been interested in and supportive of the CRC from the beginning. Yet its decision reversed the standard model of how such agencies work, in which states create international organizations, and those organizations carry out the wishes of their creators. In this case, UNICEF's executive director, James Grant, decided what he wanted, and he then used his organization to push states along the path he desired. Even more interesting, he was initially skeptical of the CRC and concerned about its implications for UNICEF, and he was persuaded to change his mind by UNICEF staff and some smaller UNICEF member states. Eventually his goal went beyond merely seeing the CRC ratified; he wanted to use it as a tool to increase the influence and effectiveness of his own organization. UNICEF was, in a sense, pressuring and cajoling states into handing it greater power to pressure and cajole them in the future.

None of this fits well with standard state-centric notions of international organizations. And it raises some important questions. First, when and how are international organizations able to act with this level of independence? What allows them to reverse the usual model of where power comes from and how it's used in multilateral agencies? And second, what do international organizations want, if not just what states tell them to want? How do they decide on priorities, where do their ideas come from, and how do they go about acting on those ideas? How, in other words, can the actions of these quiet but important players in international politics be understood? Although work on formal modes of organization in international relations has been said to lag behind that done on informal ones (Kratochwil and Ruggie 1986), new theoretical perspectives and an expanding literature on "global governance" have substantially revived the field. Still, the literature on how intergovernmental organizations (IGOs) such as the UN evolve, decide what they want, and go about pursuing it remains underdeveloped.

This study focuses on one area of IGO activity: the promotion of international human rights. Although human rights have always been central to the mission and identity of the United Nations, they have taken on increasing prominence in recent years. When he was the UN secretary-general, Kofi Annan instructed all UN specialized agencies and other affiliated organizations to consider how their work might advance the cause of human rights around the world; many of these bodies have taken this call to heart, and there has been considerable intellectual ferment and some substantive change. As Mertus has written, "UN human rights practice used to happen where the name plate on the door said 'human rights.' . . . This is no longer the case" (Mertus 2005, 3–4). Instead a wide range of IGOs have been incorporating human rights standards into their operations and have more generally been trying to play a more positive role in promoting human welfare. The idea of combining human rights with international economic and social development, in particular, has become an important theme of IGO activities (Alston and Robinson 2005). It is important to understand the ability of IGOs to adopt human rights norms and ideas to improve their own activities, the reasons they do so, and the outcome of that adaptation. Explaining how and why IGOs develop and nurture new ideas in the field of human rights is thus the primary purpose of this book.

At the broader level, this book delineates some of the ways in which international organizations are able to play a positive, independent role within international politics. It adds to a growing body of literature—primarily dealing with the phenomenon of global governance (Rittberger 2001; Diehl 2001)—that seriously considers the question of how international organizations, both formal and informal, assist states in mitigating anarchy and pursuing public goods. Recent research has added nuance to the understanding of how IGOs operate. Still, the viewpoint of these works is state-centric; they primarily seek to explain how and why states use organizations to pursue their goals, and through what mechanisms states can control the work of their creations (Foot, McFarlane, and Mastanduno 2003; Muldoon 2004).

My research parts ways with much, though not all, of the work in this state-centric vein. I focus on the preferences of the *organizations themselves*, and I ask why and how they develop their goals and strategies, at times even against the wishes of their member states. In particular I show that under certain circumstances, IGOs can act as "norm entrepreneurs," developing and promoting ideas in the international system that are not dictated by state preferences and that also cannot be reduced to a matter of simple bureaucratic self-interest. Though state and bureaucratic interests cannot be ignored, the power of internally developed ideas based on principle can at times be extremely strong. The circumstances that allow those ideas to flourish and become institutionalized thus are also examined in the chapters below.

## International Organizations and New Priorities

The work of formal international bureaucracies—such as UN specialized agencies, international financial institutions, and regional security organizations—is all around us. These organizations are created by their member states to coordinate activities, to provide expert guidance in highly technical issue areas, and even, on occasion, to assuage the consciences of wealthy countries. Like other forms of international cooperation—regimes, alliances, and such basic "institutions" as sovereignty and diplomacy—they represent the desire of states to find solutions to local or global problems, to keep the peace, and even to move toward something better than unfettered anarchy in the international realm. In some cases, their formal structure is the result of having sprung from larger formal institutions, such as the UN. In others, they are appropriately structured to manage financial or military operations that require permanent staffs of experts to oversee ongoing efforts or to coordinate work on issues that are too complex to leave to more haphazard organizational forms.

Whatever their origin, there is now quite a number of such international bureaucracies. A glance at the UN's organization chart shows the complex structure of its specialized agencies, committees, commissioners, and other organizational forms; many others, some more loosely affiliated with the UN and some not affiliated at all, dot the global scene. Though some efforts have been made to understand the UN and its agencies as *organizations* with their own agendas, resources, and internal logic (Dijkzeul and Beigbeder 2003b; Reinalda 2004; Ness and Brechin 1988), only now is a literature emerging that ties together organizational analysis with larger questions of international relations theory (Foot, McFarlane, and Mastanduno 2003; Barnett and Finnemore 2004). The goal of this book is to present a systematic analysis of IGOs as independent actors in international relations, taking seriously their nature as highly structured bodies operating in a global environment, by examining their ability to develop, incorporate, and pursue new priorities concerning human rights and other ethically based standards. At the same time, this book also poses an ethical question: Should we *want* international bureaucracies of limited accountability to work in such a morally charged areas as human rights? This question inevitably arises from the research, and it deserves to be examined here.

An important recent development in international relations has been the move by many multilateral organizations to take on tasks with explicitly moral components: promoting refugee rights, providing access to HIV/AIDS medications, or seeking reform in international criminal law. Particular states have always used international forums to chide other nations regarding various moral lapses (Forsythe 2000, 143). And this chiding has often been driven by the interests of certain states rather than by any real moral conviction. In some recent cases, however, IGOs themselves have taken on moral campaigns that are often independent of the wishes of powerful member states. Occasionally, they have even been antithetical to them.

The adoption of these value-laden agendas—here referred to as "principled ideas" (following Sikkink 1993)—raises interesting questions about the workings of IGOs. Research on networks of nongovernmental organizations and other more informal modes of organization has often focused on human rights and other matters related to international ethics, reaching the conclusion that these groups have had an effective and at times profound impact on state behavior and identity (Risse-Kappen 1995; Sikkink 1991). If this is the case where formal organizations are concerned, it suggests an important and overlooked avenue for IGO evolution and adaptation, not to mention agency. The pursuit of ostensibly moral goals in international organizations is a particularly interesting way for such bodies to show their independence, considering the presumption that they would steer clear of contentious or contestable issues. In a world where moral values can vary widely among countries, one might expect international organizations, which by their nature are representative of many states parties, to want to avoid exactly these contentious matters. The fact that they do not suggests that the issue is more complex than it first appears.

Chapters 2, 3, and 4 of this volume examine the adoption (or failure to adopt) of a rights-based policy by three UN-affiliated agencies: UNICEF, the World Bank, and the World Health Organization (WHO), respectively. Each of these organizations has begun to speak of integrating human rights standards into its operations, and they have had varying success in turning this rhetoric into actual policy changes. Significantly, none of the three has been under pressure from member states to adopt these new policies; and it can be assumed that by holding the issue area constant, there is no *substantial* variation in state preferences. (This is not to say that there is no variation at all; e.g., the United States has objected to certain reproductive rights issues that are more salient to some organizations than others.) With state preferences and issue areas largely removed from the equation, it is possible to see variations in outcome as resulting from factors *internal* to the organizations under study. These factors, it is shown below, include a conviction that adaptation will increase institutional effectiveness, a corresponding belief that adaptation will also be the "right thing to do" from an ethical perspective, and strong leadership at the top of the organization. A careful examination of why each organization chose to put human rights on the agenda, and how they have integrated new ideas into their operational mandate, demonstrates the importance of these internal factors in explaining policy outcomes. Thus, the importance of internal factors in explaining IGOs' policy preferences comes more clearly into view.

## Bureaucratic Explanations and Principled Ideas

That IGOs have some room to maneuver is increasingly well established in the international relations literature. IGOs are problem-solving devices, and their intellectual power comes into play when complex international problems require collective action by states. What may be harder to understand, however, is why IGOs choose to champion certain ideas—and why they choose one idea rather than another. As Vaubel (1986) points out, standard bureaucratic explanations of IGO behavior tend to focus on the bureaucratic imperative to increase staff size, budgets, and the other trappings of power and prestige. As with bureaucratic explanations of domestic politics, research on international organizations assumes that the desire to continue and expand the work of their bureaucracy is the primary motivation for bureaucrats. Seen this way, IGOs will use the freedom inherent in their structure and financing for these purposes.

Barnett and Finnemore take issue with this simple assumption, arguing that it is both indeterminate (because there are many ways to achieve such ends) and has "not fared well in the American politics literature where it was created" (Barnett and Finnemore 2002, 2). In terms of IGOs and the adoption of principled ideas, it is shown below that bureaucratic explanations are useful but not complete. Looking at the adoption of human rights standards in particular provides a good way to gain insight into idea creation, because at first glance they seem considerably removed from material needs and desires. Though there is certainly a connection between pursuing principled ideas and expanding IGO powers, the bureaucratic explanation significantly underdetermines how these organizations choose to take principled stances and how they then pursue their principles. Although it is unlikely that an IGO would take a principled stance that actually *weakened* its influence, in the cases under study here the principled position is not one that is best calculated to advance its interests; in various ways, these organizations have chosen to adopt controversial ideas rather than to compromise and reach accommodations with powerful member states.

Along with a desire for self-aggrandizement, two other factors appear to be common when IGOs pursue principled ideas. One issue shared by each case under discussion here is a genuine belief on the part of the IGO, or some group of its staff, that a principled stance will increase the *actual effectiveness* of its operations. This is related to arguing that it will increase the IGO's size and resources, because these are often key elements of program effectiveness. But this is not inevitably the case, and besides, there are other issues involved in program effectiveness than mere size. At the same time that an IGO's interest in principled ideas cannot be explained simply by pointing to the bureaucratic imperative to increase powers, budgets, and the like, it also appears that it cannot be explained entirely without reference to a belief that principled ideas will actually improve the quality of its work. In other words, the bureaucratic explanation is necessary but not sufficient; the organizations under study here were not so cynical as to pursue an issue without some belief that it would actually make them more effective as an organization.

A second issue common to all three cases is the conviction by a single person or small cadre that such a course of action was the right thing to do. In all three cases one or more persons within the organization, and not always at the top of its hierarchy, made the case that pursuing a principled idea, here a broad notion of human rights, was worthwhile from an ethical as well as a practical point of view. The ethical perspective, generally supported from outside the organization by the nongovernmental organization community as well as from within by early "true believers" (as they will be called in this book), was or is both an important early selling point for principled ideas and a key element in convincing others to follow those ideas. Of particular importance, it was never the only selling point; in all three cases it was combined with the argument that these policies would increase program effectiveness, and it seems likely (although there is no way to prove this) that the ethical argument would have been ineffective had there not also been a practical one to back it up. Yet the moral argument appears at key points throughout the transition of each organization from an older to a newer way of solving problems and approaching its responsibilities, and it is never far from the internal discussion. Most significant, in all three cases, groups of true believers banded together to develop and push for their ideas, sometimes in the face of resistance from every direction; they played a necessary, though not by themselves sufficient, role in putting new ideas on the agenda.

Finally, these factors still are not sufficient for the independent adoption of principled ideas without the presence of another factor, namely, strong leadership from the top of the organization. This leadership, it is shown below, provides a crucial determinant in the success or failure of change within international organizations. The importance of leadership in these organizations has received its share of attention (Kahler 2001; Moravcsik 1999; Young 1999). This previous research has tended to focus on the role of "supranational entrepreneurs" in bringing states together in agreement on how to solve transnational problems ranging from environmental protection to economic and political union. The emphasis, in other words, has been on "forum organizations" rather than on those charged with pursuing a particular mandate, such as child welfare or public health. Conversely, Cox (1969) and Haas (1990) have recognized the power of leadership in helping these technically oriented organizations change and adapt to new priorities. In this study, too, the value of leadership and the power of the executive head to set an organization's course are shown to be crucial.

In the cases under discussion here, strong leadership has been at least as important in overcoming *internal* opposition as it has in overcoming *external* opposition. The ability of IGO leaders to broker among the competing interests of member states is certainly an important element of international politics. In all three cases under study, the organization's chief executive has had to fend off demands on his or her attention from states, with varying success; this has been an important determinant in the varying levels of adaptation among the cases. The cases, however, were chosen largely because they did not directly challenge the interests of powerful states and therefore were able to control for varying state preferences. What emerges is a clearer picture of the importance of combating opposition from entrenched bureaucratic interests within the organization itself. This has proved to be a consistent problem across the cases. The determination of a strong leader to push for change in the face of such inertia may be the variable with the highest explanatory power in these studies. Where the executive director was convinced that change was in the interest of the organization and was prepared to expend effort to convince resistant staff, adaptation took place; where the executive director was not willing to make such an effort, change stalled.

Seeing where ideas come from and what does or does not give them traction can help bridge the gap between two types of thinking on the autonomy of IGOs. On the one hand, a number of careful internal studies of adaptation in IGOs, most notably the financial institutions, has shed light on the internal workings of international bureaucracies. They have shown how such bureaucracies pick up new ideas, how they institutionalize them, and the difficulties they encounter translating those new ideas into practical policy outcomes (Jonsson 1996; Kapur 2002; Wade 1997). These studies have, to a lesser or greater extent, taken for granted that the bureaucratic structure of an organization and the personal preferences of those working within it have a meaningful effect on policy outcomes. On the other hand, a renewed interest in principal–agent analysis has refocused attention on IGO agency and the problems of controlling large organizations set up to pursue the interests of states free from day-to-day control by those states;

but this provides only a thin theory for the consequences of principal–agent dynamics in terms of actual policy outcomes. It is hoped that the analysis of the case studies in the following chapters will begin bridging the gap between these two research agendas.

## Agency and Ideas

The institutionalization of IGOs and their development of bureaucratic structures explains the tendency toward IGO independence, at least among those with large professional staffs and mandates as service organizations. In the cases under discussion in this book, the activities of IGOs are significantly similar to those of what Peter Haas and others have termed "epistemic communities." In Haas's terms, an epistemic community is "a network of professionals with recognized expertise and competence in a particular domain and an authoritative claim to policy-relevant knowledge within that domain or issue-area." Epistemic communities share beliefs over normative and theoretical issues within their area of expertise, as well as a "common policy enterprise" with a general conviction that "human welfare will be enhanced as a consequence" of their activities (Haas 1992a, 3). The members of an epistemic community are bound together not by national ties but by professional or principled ones; they are technical experts engaged in a shared enterprise, and they understand that that enterprise requires both a high level of international cooperation and their own efforts to convince states that their true interests lie in collective efforts.

Like members of an epistemic community, the staffs of the IGOs described here view themselves primarily as responsible for promoting a particular issue or set of issues rather than for facilitating any particular state's short-term gains. Their loyalty tends to be to the organization and to a set of principles embodied within it (Verbeek 1998, 22). When the organization's ability to achieve its goals is enhanced, their own position is enhanced as well—members of the IGOs studied here have both personal and professional stakes in seeing their employer succeed. This blending of self-interest and group interest is particularly noteworthy at the very top of these organizations, where the most crucial decisions get made; as Cox (1969) has noted, the executive head of UN agencies can, under the right circumstances, exercise considerable power both within and outside his or her own organization and can be a very persuasive force in framing problems as well as formulating solutions.

This loyalty to the organization and its problem-solving task means that the decisions made by IGOs will often have two separate purposes: to find innovative solutions to the problems at hand, and to enhance the power and independence of the organization itself. At times, of course—likely, in the majority of cases—IGOs will do best by not "rocking the boat" with state members. With some IGOs, the tasks at hand are purely technical and relatively simple, and the IGO will determine that its best course is to work in a purely cooperative way with member states. At other times, however, it may find that challenging the status quo is the most effective way of advancing its own interests and its own view of how best to solve the problems it was set up to address. It is argued below that an IGO can and will do so when the conditions are right—that is, when its leaders and staff believe they can best advance its agenda by doing so.

Epistemic communities are not identical to bureaucracies. In particular, as Haas points out, bureaucracies lack a shared set of "causal beliefs" and a consensual basis of knowledge upon which to make decisions (Haas 1992a, 17). And as the following cases show, IGOs, unlike epistemic communities, have extremely diverse personnel, and by no means can it be said that all agree with the adoption of human rights norms—or any other set of IGO policy goals. It is not at all uncommon for individuals within IGOs to disagree with and even actively oppose the adoption of new ideas, even those that are accepted at the highest levels of management. At the same time each of the cases presented begins with a single individual or small group of individuals—true believers—promoting a new idea or approach *within* the group itself, at a time when others in the IGO are content with "business as usual" or are discontent but unsure of any alternative. Under the right circumstances, these small groups can sway others to their cause and ultimately have real, lasting influence over the bureaucratic culture as a whole.

For the most part the three IGOs under study here speak publicly with one voice. More important, they strive to create an internal consensus, although in each case this process is at a different stage of progress. Unlike with a true epistemic community, this consensus does have to be forged, and at times it will be imperfect; this contrasts with the situation in which experts are actually brought together by their shared set of beliefs regarding a particular issue. The organization can become an advocate for principled issues—in these cases, human rights—and work actively to promote them. Equally important, these issues are not reducible to some set of outside influences on the organizations; nor are they in all cases the path that would most likely lead to an increase in the organization's power. This is a tricky point because it is not always easy to tell whether a principled stance is being taken on moral grounds or because it will increase an organization's influence through moral suasion. For example, in all three cases discussed below, an IGO has chosen to pursue a human rights agenda partly because it felt that framing issues in the language of human rights would increase its organizational influence; at the same time, however, that increased influence was desired primarily in order to pursue a principled agenda (child welfare, economic development, HIV/AIDS treatment) that it felt was not being addressed sufficiently by more traditional means.

## IGOs as Organizations

The primary goal, then, of the three case studies presented here is to examine the nature of IGO agency. The bureaucratization of certain international functions would seem, logically, to lead to greater freedom of action within international organizations. A growing literature has taken on the bureaucratic nature of international organizations—in the words of one analyst, to treat "international organizations as organizations" (Ness and Brechin 1988, 245). One important strand of this thinking that was mentioned above has been to focus on the principal–agent problem in international organizations, viewing states as principals and the staff of these organizations as their agents (Hawkins et al. 2006). This work has tended to focus on the two aspects commonly identified in such principal–agent relationships: the control of agents over information not available to the principles, and the divergence of

interests between principal and agent. Various aspects of the relationship—for example, whether or not multiple principals agree or
disagree over institutional goals, or the degree of trust built up between principals and agents—are identified as affecting the independence of agents. The bureaucratic imperatives of international
organizations have also been examined: survival and the expansion
of the organization's influence and resources have been identified
as primary possible bureaucratic goals, although as Verbeek (1998)
points out, there are problems with this approach, which tells us
little of how specific policies are formulated and is often able to explain any policy outcome in retrospect. As the case studies below
indicate, there is reason to believe that while these interests are certainly important, they are not paramount. International organizations certainly do care about their survival and scope of action, but
they also care about carrying out their mandate, as they see it.

This strand of thinking about international organizations as
organizations draws on research on the relationship between bureaucracies and elected officials (Dijkzeul and Beigbeder 2003a).
In specifying a particular type of principal–agent problem, that
which arises in government bureaucracies, it reduces the problem
of controlling bureaucracies to the simple problem of conflicting
interests and to a couple of very basic variables, notably inequality
of information. The contention here is that this approach leaves
out several other factors that can give a more nuanced understanding of how IGOs and member states interact.

A starting point for examining the organizational nature of international organizations is provided by work done on the theory
of the corporation. *The Modern Corporation and Private Property*, a
landmark study of the growth of the modern corporation by Adolf
A. Berle and Gardiner C. Means (1932), suggests one way to view
the effects of the bureaucratization of certain international institutions. Berle and Means were writing on the trend, still relatively
new at the time of publication, toward a separation of ownership
and management in large publicly held corporations. At one time,
they argued, the owner of a business enterprise was usually the
manager as well; he would run it in a self-interested way to maximize his own profits and would take a personal interest in all aspects of its operations. This tended to make management a fairly
easy task for a variety of reasons; most relevant here, it meant that

a single person could understand with relative ease all the various aspects of an organization's activities, and it removed the principal–agent problem, which suggests that those hired to pursue another person's interests (in this case, making a profit) will usually act to advance their own interests rather than the interests of the person who hired them. Conversely, it tended to limit the growth of corporations, because of the limited ability of a single person to oversee complex operations and the tendency of owners to focus on short-term profits rather than long-term plans.

The movement to publicly held corporations with professional managers responsible to stockholders meant important changes in the dynamics of such firms. Berle and Means identify two important dynamics that tend to make managers independent from stockholders and to increase the range of their discretionary powers. The first, and more important to Berle and Means, is the diffusion of stock ownership in large corporations. Larger corporations demand ever larger quantities of capital, requiring them to turn to the public for investments from both individuals and institutional investors such as insurance companies and pension funds. With no single stockholder owning a large stake in a company, "the position of ownership has changed from that of an active to that of a passive agent" (Berle and Means 1932, 66). This means that the professional managers of a corporation are freed from having to answer to any single investor, or a small group of investors, who may have particular opinions about the way a company ought to be managed.

The second dynamic identified by Berle and Means is more relevant here: the tremendous size and wide-ranging influence of the largest corporations, and the difficulty small stockholders have in understanding and influencing corporate policy (Berle and Means 1932, 8–46). By the early twentieth century, it simply was no longer possible in the largest organizations for shareholders to exercise constant control over the operations of a large bureaucracy or to keep up with and understand all the problems and issues that face the corporation on a day-to-day basis. In such a case, according to a seminal book on managerial discretion by Oliver Williamson, "stockholders are seldom in a position to exercise decisive control over a large firm. Their demands, more often, take the form of a minimum performance constraint" (Williamson 1967, 13). As long as the corporate body appears to be fulfilling the basic goals set for it by the owners, they will see it as neither practical nor profitable to involve themselves in the day-to-day operations of the firm. It is a corresponding feature of modern organizations that their managers are now thought of as professionals (Heald 1970), with both the attendant duties of a professional and a need for special skills and training. The diffusion of ownership and the growing importance of large corporate bodies means that "new responsibilities towards the owners, the workers, the consumers, and the State thus rest upon the shoulders" of the new managerial class (Berle and Means 1932, 6). This new professional class is imbued with greater discretion; and as professionals, they see themselves as having responsibilities beyond merely serving the short-term interests of shareholders (Koehn 1994, 144–53).

This same dynamic—the separation of management from "ownership," which in this case means the member states of UN specialized agencies—is at work in UN-affiliated organizations and is an important factor in giving these organizations far more freedom of action than is generally supposed. The sort of agency that is of interest here applies less to UN bodies that are essentially forums for discussion—what Cox and Jacobson (1973) term forum organizations—than to those that are bureaucracies tasked with pursuing particular, usually complex or technical, goals—"service organizations." Given the premise that this freedom of action follows largely from these two dynamics identified by Berle and Means—the separation of management and ownership, and the size and complexity of modern, highly bureaucratized organizations—it is likely that certain factors will lead to greater IGO freedom of action:

- Larger organizations—with larger staffs, more extensive responsibilities, and greater financial resources—are likely to exhibit greater managerial independence than smaller organizations. Confronted with the sheer size of a substantial bureaucratic organization, and with a large number of different operations going on at the same time, the "owners" of an IGO will have two choices: to increase their oversight staff and the amount of time spent actually following the organization's operations, or to accept that the organization will operate most of the time on its own. Martin suggests that the size of an organization measured by its budget may be a better indicator in this area than the size of its staff (Martin 2002, 46).

- Along with the size of the organizational structure itself, the *complexity* of the issues involved in organizational operations will tend to remove the work of managers from the regular supervision of owners. Those charged with the oversight of IGO operation will be willing to defer more to managers when dealing with highly complex, highly technical issues. Barnett and Finnemore point out that a substantial source of IGOs' power is their ability to organize complex information and knowledge (Barnett and Finnemore 1999, 710–11). This will be less true in organizations that serve as a forum rather than those with a technical mission to perform, although as Young (1991) and Cox and Jacobson (1973) have shown, the secretariat of forum organizations can also play an important and independent role in forming regimes.

- The professionalization of the given bureaucracy—the degree to which its managers view themselves as holders of arcane knowledge with responsibilities to use that knowledge for the betterment of society rather than for narrow gain—will be a third factor in separating management from ownership (Greenwood 1983). Well-established, highly organized bureaucracies with long traditions of activity and little fear of being eliminated will be more likely to have a sense of being engaged in an enterprise in which long-term goals, combined with standard operating procedures, will take precedence over the short-term interests of owners.

- When organizations are overseen by a collective principle, meaning in this case multiple states that contract with an IGO, policy outcomes will not be the same as the preferences of the largest states (Lyne, Nielson, and Tierney 2006). This will mean that less powerful states can form coalitions that will sway IGO behavior. It also means that where no single state has a powerful incentive to monitor IGO behavior, there will be less oversight and more room to maneuver. As Berle and Means were cited above as noting, the diffusion of ownership enhances the principal–agent problem when no single agent has the time and resources to oversee all actions of an agent, or when collective action problems lead to the perception of a limited ability to assert authority over the organization in question.

- Krasner (1981) suggests in a study of regional development banks that institutions have greater freedom of action when their operations are considered peripheral to the major donors. That is, the primary contributors of funds are less likely to interfere in operations and policy when they are not directly affected by the way those funds are used. Other studies have made the same point more generally (Hazelzet 1998, 28). It stands to reason that the most important states parties are less likely to supervise the day-to-day operations of an organization that does not operate in an area they consider of primary security or power concern.

Elements of all these factors are present in the cases examined here, although not always to the same degree. Taken together they help to explain how IGOs, having determined to pursue new agendas not suggested by member states, might nonetheless be able to develop and adopt those ideas. Of course there are plenty of reasons why states might also object to the development of new ideas and resist. In the case of WHO in particular, state resistance was strong and decisive; without a determined voice for change at the top of WHO, the organization failed to "stand up to" the protesting states.

This list represents, in a sense, a background condition for the remainder of the present study. The factors identified above all contribute to the independence of international organizations, and a substantial body of theory has begun to be built up behind them. But where IGOs' preferences come from, once they have been able to carve out a range of independence, remains the primary question here.

## Moral Responsibility and Principled Ideas

Along with the question of why IGOs turn to principled ideas, it is important to ask whether it is a good thing that they do so. The international relations literature on the development of principled ideas—on environmental issues; on the elimination of odious practices such as colonialism, slavery, and apartheid; and on the taboos against the use of certain weapons or force itself—has been surprisingly free of any such questioning of the moral standing of these ideas. This gap, it seems fairly clear, results from the fact that most research in this area has focused on what one would more-or-less unanimously consider good ideas, such as those listed just above. For example, when examining why the international community declared itself against the trade in human chattel or the use of nuclear weapons, there was no need to consider whether it was a good idea for it to have done so—history had already answered that question.

When the question of the source of principled ideas comes up, however, and particularly when the issue is IGOs as the source, there are reasons to be cautious. First, though the literature on ideas in international relations generally has tended to focus on positive ideas, history suggests that there are as many bad ideas as good ones floating around international society. If the Anglo-American concept of "embedded liberalism" (Ruggie 1983) seemed a positive model for a postwar economic regime, it took a world war to replace it with the Nazi alternative, as spelled out in Hirschman's *National Power and the Structure of Foreign Trade* (1945) (a fact that Ruggie himself recognizes). Support for proxy wars by both sides during the Cold War was once seen as an acceptable way to do business, and much ideological ink was spilled justifying the practice. Concern has been raised recently that a new norm of "preventive war" might be popularized by recent U.S. action, with potentially negative results (Crawford 2003). Generally speaking, the literature on bad ideas is poorly developed.

Second, whether ideas are good, bad, or indifferent, it is important to consider what sorts of organizations *should be* making morally laden decisions and carrying out policies with a clear normative content. The internationalization of moral ideals is fraught with danger: Standards differ from country to country, interpretations of even the most universally accepted norms can vary, and modes of application (e.g., through legislation, the courts, community education) appropriate in one context may be ineffective or counterproductive in another. Thus there may be widespread acceptance that human rights are important and that human rights standards should be spread; but, for example, is the World Bank really the best organization to champion such ideas? Should development projects themselves be required to serve the goal of rights protection and promotion when this might mean a reduction in their ability to serve other goals (e.g., increasing national gross domestic product, relieving food shortages)?

Yet the general arc of "progress" in international ethics has been exactly this gradual internationalization of moral issues once considered entirely within the realm of domestic sovereignty. The very concept of human rights as a matter of international concern and international instruments is based on this process of opening domestic affairs to scrutiny by international bodies of some—at least presumed—impartiality. It certainly seems desirable to involve the entire UN system in the promotion and protection of human rights, and the decision by the UN secretary-general to task all UN agencies with human rights responsibilities has not raised general criticism. What is needed, clearly, is a way of determining the proper scope of such activities—both breadth (What rights should be included, and how should they be interpreted?) and depth (How much power and influence should be given to these new rights protectors?). A better understanding of how these organizations view and respond to human rights and other principled ideas will help to clarify the desirable limits of their action in this field.

## A Note on "Human Rights"

The concept of human rights is referred to regularly in the following pages, and it is worth clarifying how this term is used here. The term "human rights" has been much abused in the literature on international politics, and the intention here is not to add to this abuse.

The concept of "rights" is often used in very unspecific ways and often seems designed to justify any agenda with a moral or values-based component. At one level, of course, international human rights are what international instruments say they are. A large and growing body of international instruments lay out various rights, and states are free to sign onto these or not as they like. A party to the UN Convention Against Torture accepts that freedom from torture as defined by the convention is a right of citizens. Of course, there are problems with this approach. The main human rights documents are not a certain guide; none has been accepted by every UN member, many are only "declarations," and many contradict each other and sometimes even themselves. Beyond these documents, what one considers a human right depends on everything from one's philosophical position (e.g., are rights strictly negative, or can so-called positive rights be given the same respect?) to the exigencies of power politics. Some academics, politicians, nongovernmental organizations, and ordinary citizens often defend as rights various positions that few would agree on, and in doing so they seriously demean the entire concept of human rights.

In other words, the concept of a right gets used quite a lot in world politics, often with little or no precision and little agreement on what counts as a right. It is not the intention of this book to add to the current confusion or to do more violence to the concept of rights. It is not possible to define here what is or is not a human right, and it does not seem necessary in the current circumstances to critique how the concept is used by IGOs. Each of the study's three case studies devotes a section to examining how the particular IGO defines the concept of human rights. For the most part, not surprisingly, they define the concept loosely, and in a way that fits their own organizational mandate and strengths. To a large extent, they also define rights—or, more accurately, a "rights-based approach"—in a way that makes it very similar to ethics or an ethical approach. To think about human rights in this context becomes largely thinking about whether policies are morally defensible and whether they help individual people.

For the present purpose, it is enough to accept the idea of rights as it is used by IGOs. The important point is to understand how IGOs think about what rights mean for them, not to critique the philosophical underpinnings of that definition. The fact that rights, in this context, often come close to meaning simply a concern with ethics is itself significant, for it shows how organizations seek simple, universal concepts to frame solutions to their problems. This study aims only to show how the concept is used, adapted, and interpreted by IGOs, and to examine why they choose (or do not choose) to make rights language part of their daily lexicon. Thus the terms rights and rights-based approach are used quite a bit in the following pages, and they mean what IGOs believe they mean. The process of reaching that definition is an important part of the story. Whether IGOs *should* have the leeway to define rights as they like is an important question addressed in chapter 6.

## Research Design and Case Selection

The three organizations under study here—UNICEF, the World Bank, and WHO—were not chosen randomly. They were selected exactly because they exhibit varying outcomes in their efforts to turn themselves into rights-based organizations. UNICEF is a "special organ" of the UN; the other two are specialized UN agencies. The specialized agencies were established under Article 57 of the UN Charter and were brought into relationship with the Economic and Social Council (ECOSOC) through Article 63. They are, in the terms of one analysis, "highly independent and autonomous" within this structure (Williams 1987, 18). UNICEF, conversely, was created by the UN General Assembly under Resolution 57(I) of 1946. It is funded differently from the specialized agencies (the World Bank, of course, is also funded differently, raising its capital in a variety of ways), relying on contributions from member states and other sources rather than on the regular assessments that fund WHO. Its relationship with the ECOSOC is more direct than that of the specialized agencies.

The specific means by which states oversee each agency differ in some ways. The World Bank is ultimately answerable to a board of governors that meets on an annual basis and uses weighted voting and also to a smaller number of executive directors appointed by members of the board. WHO is overseen by the World Health Assembly (which does not have weighted voting) and by a smaller executive board "to give effect to the decisions and policies of the Health Assembly" and "act as the executive organ of the Health Assembly," among other duties, as stated in the WHO Constitution, Articles 28(a) and 28(b). UNICEF is overseen by a thirty-six-member executive board, with no universal membership body above that (except to the extent that it takes guidance from the ECOSOC and the General Assembly).

As Williams points out, the similarities are more important than the differences here; there are an executive board to represent the interests of members, with or without a universal assembly above that, and a permanent executive staff, managed by an appointed executive head (Williams 1987, 18). There is one crucial legal difference, in that UNICEF has the more direct responsibility to the UN through its relationship with the ECOSOC. This has ramifications for the interpretation of UN human rights instruments, for it appears to make UNICEF more directly bound to follow and advance the human rights provisions of the UN Charter.

Although there are differences in the management structures and legal status of the three organizations, they are not different in a way that ought to significantly change the practical level of independence of each organization. Each has a formal relationship with the United Nations, each reports to a body made up of instructed representatives of member states, and each has an executive head appointed by those members. It is generally assumed that they serve the interests of member states and that the members can, if they have sufficient power themselves or can form coalitions with others, restrain or redirect the activities of the organizations. The World Bank in particular has a certain level of funding independence, given its ability to raise money through international capital markets; and UNICEF raises a substantial portion of its money on its own, through direct grants from governments, individuals, and other entities; yet neither could survive long without support from key member states, any more than could WHO, which lacks substantial outside donors. Given the assumption that international organizations serve member states and are controlled by those states, there is no reason to assume that the variation in the exact structure of institutional oversight or funding mechanisms should lead to differing outcomes.

In each case study the factors that went into successful or unsuccessful adaptation are traced and examined. In chapter 1 and again in chapter 5, some common themes are extracted and examined. Because there are only three cases, with somewhat different results, there is no reason to assume that *every* factor present in IGO decision making can or will be sufficiently analyzed. It is unlikely that any study could accurately delineate all the various factors that go into decision making in an extensive set of large and complex organizations. The key here, however, is not to determine a definitive list of such factors but to demonstrate the importance of looking at the internal workings of such organizations if we are to fully understand policy outcomes.

## Plan of the Book

The next three chapters present the empirical material concerning the approach of IGOs to human rights issues. The material is organized into three case studies, on UNICEF, the World Bank, and WHO. In the manner of "structured, focused comparisons," each study attempts to trace the interest of the organization in pursuing a human rights agenda. Each case asks two separate questions: Why did this organization choose to put human rights at the center of its operational paradigm? How does the nature of the organization shape the way it interprets rights norms? The decisions made by these organizations are tied to the various forces acting upon them—by their member states, by their own mission, by bureaucratic imperatives, and by international civil society (which will be defined later in the book), among others. The goal is to delineate which of these forces were the most powerful, and why.

It is important to note up front that in each case, a UN-affiliated agency chose to incorporate ethical standards into its operations *before* Secretary-General Kofi Annan directed all UN bodies to do so. Each is a case of a decision coming from within the particular organization, and thus it best highlights the organization's internal workings. Although each organization is not at the same stage of policy development, these differences help to illuminate the process of organizational change.

The three examples have been chosen for their similarity with one another, rather than as a random sampling of UN-affiliated agencies. To posit that international agencies are capable of independent action, and that their internal preferences and organization are important determinants of policy outcomes, it is not necessary to prove that *all* international agencies do so *always*. Thus, the accusation that this work "stacks the deck" by choosing only those organizations that have shown a capacity for independent action in this area would not pose a relevant criticism. At the same time, it is the purpose of this book to identify those elements—some of which have been mentioned above—that do seem conducive to independent agency. It might be helpful to identify some cases of agencies that do not show such a capacity and to compare why they fail to do so. In several instances, comparisons of that sort are made. But there is no separate study of such a case developed into a single chapter. This is partly because such a case would not make for terribly interesting reading (or research!) but, more important, also because it raises the problem of the dog that does not bark—there are presumably any number of reasons why an organization might simply do as it is told by member states, and besides, no study would definitively prove that it would not do so in the future.

The final two chapters of the book deal consecutively with the two main themes presented: Why and how do IGOs choose to adopt principled ideas such as human rights as operating paradigms; and what moral questions do their actions raise? Chapter 5 reviews some of the factors that led to successful or unsuccessful adaptation. What led IGOs to redefine their mission and to choose new strategies? How do IGOs overcome resistance from member states, and from their own staffs? What strategies do IGOs follow to maximize their own power and influence? How do IGOs choose from among competing policy priorities, rather than merely acting as filters for various exogenous forces?

Chapter 6 focuses not on empirical but on normative questions. The question of authority is a key point. Once it is established that IGOs make decisions that affect people, that they are actors in their own right, it is relevant to ask what authority they have to make their decisions. In purely technical areas, this authority will come either from their specific mandate (e.g., UNICEF has been charged by the United Nations to undertake child welfare activities such as providing safe drinking water and educating parents on healthy eating habits for children) or from their expertise in certain areas. This sort of "epistemic authority" (De George 1985, 27) is most effective in areas that require scientific knowledge or a command over complex facts—areas in which bureaucratic organizations excel, for the most part. It will be less effective where choices need to be made among issues or priorities of contested value.

To anticipate the argument of chapter 6, the movement of IGOs into areas like human rights has shown the difficulty of separating technical from ethical issues. The very definition of development, for example, has evolved over time, and it has done so because of moral concerns raised over what initially appeared to be purely economic concerns. Thus the power of international agencies is both in their ability to use their resources to influence state behavior (most notably in the case of the World Bank and "conditional" lending) and also in the realm of ideas, where they have considerable discretion over definitional issues. The nature of an organization—for example, the extent to which it is accountable to states parties for its actions or the extent to which it resembles either a private corporation or a government agency—will have a great deal to do with the amount of authority we wish to grant it over issues with ethical implications. Thus the case studies, and the distillation of the primary components of independent action, help in evaluating their moral responsibilities.

The ultimate goal of the ensuing chapters is to create a more complete picture of the role of IGOs in international relations. Although some recent work, such as that cited at the beginning of this chapter, has started to look at these organizations from differing and constructive viewpoints, much remains to be done in this vein. It builds on earlier research, suggesting that IGO agency exists and has meaning. It takes as self-evident the simple fact that for millions of people, the actions of WHO, UNICEF, and the World Bank do indeed have tangible effects and therefore that it is important to understand why they do what they do. Also, although the book of course seeks the broadest possible conclusions, it is not intended as a general theory to cover all international organizations. Appropriate comparisons are made, but the premise of the argument—that the organizational structure of these bodies affects their decision-making capacity—presupposes that bodies with other structures will have different capacities. How these differ, and how other structures affect outcomes, is left for a future work.

## Chapter Two

# UNICEF, Human Rights, and Children

Although the Convention on the Rights of the Child (CRC) has taken a central role in the way that the United Nations Children's Fund (UNICEF) perceives and pursues its mission, the convention itself was not UNICEF's idea. It was originally viewed with some indifference as a concept by UNICEF. When initially proposed by the Polish delegation to the United Nations in 1979, during the International Year of the Child, the proposal was not taken very seriously by Western governments (Cohen 1993, 11), and it was greeted with suspicion by UNICEF's director, Jim Grant. By the time it was adopted by the UN ten years later, UNICEF had not only thrown its full support behind the document and lobbied states to accede to the convention; it had also managed to carve for itself an official role in the promotion of children's rights. UNICEF has progressively, albeit sometimes haltingly, turned the CRC into the central document in UNICEF programming: It is now a requirement of all UNICEF operations that they be directed toward implementation of a human-rights-based approach to development. This turnaround in UNICEF attitudes toward the CRC is an important example of how a UN agency can come to see the language of human rights as an important institutional tool and a source of both guidance and power in the pursuit of its interests.

## Adoption

The United Nations International Children's Emergency Fund, the original name for UNICEF, was founded in late 1946 as an offshoot and successor organization to the United Nations Relief and Rehabilitation Administration (UNRRA). Like the UNRRA (and also like the International Bank for Reconstruction and

Development [IBRD], the original component of the World Bank Group), UNICEF was intended to be a temporary organization, with the specific mandate to assist war-torn countries in Europe. According to Maggie Black, UNICEF's historian, UNICEF itself, led by its founding executive director, Maurice Pate, lobbied intensively for the organization's continuance (Black 1986, 81–83). This was done against the initially firm intention of the United States and its primary UN allies to see the organization disbanded when its initial mandate was fulfilled. As the IBRD would do, UNICEF fought against its redundancy by shifting the focus of its operations from war-torn Europe to the underdeveloped countries of Asia, Africa, and Latin America.

Thus, in its earliest years, UNICEF showed a capacity for independent action and established a tradition of strong-willed executive directors motivated by principle. It also conformed to the general rule that organizations, once established, tend to be difficult to get rid of and to resist their own demise. Yet Pate seems by all accounts to have been motivated largely by his own humanitarian impulses rather than a desire for self-aggrandizement; he had begun his career in public service by working with Herbert Hoover aiding Europe during and after World War I and had impeccable credentials as an organizer of international humanitarian assistance (Black 1986). He had also had a successful life as a businessman in the Midwest and thus by the late 1940s had a limited need to enhance his status through international service.

If UNICEF's initial mandate—to provide relief in emergencies—was tightly constricted, so too were the means at its disposal. In Europe, UNICEF's operations were limited to operating feeding programs for hungry children and providing immunizations and medication for common diseases, particularly tuberculosis and syphilis (which was often passed from parent to child). In both cases, UNICEF provided not only the materials themselves but also equipment such as milk dryers and pasteurization machines, as well as technical assistance with such activities as coordinating vaccination drives and helping with the storage of medicines.

In these operations of UNICEF and in its relationship with the World Health Organization (WHO)—in which UNICEF was willing to defer to WHO on many health-related issues, so as not to appear to be duplicating the other agency's operations (Black 1986,

51)—UNICEF continued to fulfill a basic mandate as a technical organization, built to provide a particular type of service and expertise deemed necessary by the UN and its member states. Once given a set of instructions, however, UNICEF almost immediately began improvising in ways not originally foreseen by its founders. One example of this was UNICEF's move into education, a field not at all intended when the original UN emergency fund was set up. This move, the idea for which came from the UNICEF executive director and his inner circle of advisers (Black 1986, 202), continued the expansion of UNICEF activities, gradually including into the organization's purview both new territories and new categories of child welfare. Though UNICEF had been created by the UN and tasked with protecting children, UNICEF's management continued to push outward on the strict limits initially imposed on their activities.

Other changes occurring outside the UNICEF structure were also leading to an expansion of UNICEF's mandate. In 1950 a draft Declaration of the Rights of the Child was presented to the Social Commission of the UN. This declaration was consciously modeled after an earlier Declaration of the Rights of the Child, adopted by the League of Nations in 1924. In response to the draft, the Social Commission "expressed the view that although there was a close relationship between the draft and the Universal Declaration of Human Rights, the special needs of the child justified a separate instrument" (United Nations 1951, 597).

By the time a draft declaration came before the Economic and Social Council in 1959, it was being subjected to the same Cold War treatment that other human rights instruments had undergone: The U.S. delegate complained that it was not concise enough, while the Soviet Union and its allies argued that it needed to specify more specific duties of governments toward child welfare (United Nations 1960, 193–95). The final document is concise, with ten points expanding on the more general themes of the Universal Declaration of Human Rights. UNICEF was named by the UN General Assembly as an organization that could help in promoting the declaration's goals. It does not appear that UNICEF was directly prodded into expanding its scope of activities by the declaration; but as part of a general move to place more emphasis on child welfare in developing countries, UNICEF was simultaneously considering how it could take a more holistic view of child develop-ment, particularly by becoming involved in education (Black 1986, 200; Smyke 1990, 2). In this case, the desire to expand the scope of operations of UNICEF was part of a larger trend to include child welfare, particularly in the developing world, in the concerns of international organizations.

By the time a binding convention on children's rights was first proposed to the United Nations—in 1979, by the Polish delega-tion—UNICEF had further expanded its base of operations, ac-cepting the Declaration of the Rights of the Child as an important document but not as a specific guideline. (The Polish delegation had also originally proposed a Declaration of the Rights of the Child in 1960. Poland has had a long tradition of championing children's rights in international forums, and it had a strong connection both to Pate—whose first wife had been Polish—and to Ludwik Rajch-man, a Polish citizen and key figure in UNICEF's foundation and early years; Black 1986, 30–32.) The focus of the organization was still on traditional areas of service provision to needy children. Jim Grant became UNICEF's executive director in 1980 and soon was speaking of a "child survival revolution," based on a small number of simple, cost-effective interventions; this would supplement and focus the wide range of activities that UNICEF had taken on in the interim, including work in education, water and sanitation, health care provision, and food supplements. In the United States and around the world, UNICEF was one of the most highly visible and respected UN agencies. As an organization, it had continued to ex-pand its reach and scope of activities, and it had done so with a sur-prising degree of effectiveness—it was considered by many within the UN development system as a model for effective action.

UNICEF was initially reluctant to embrace the idea of a new children's rights convention, despite the possibility that it would advance the agenda of child protection. It is noteworthy, or at least suggestive, that while the Polish delegation pushed for a new con-vention with backing from most of the Eastern European nations, a number of Western countries expressed reservations about this idea (LeBlanc 1995, 20–21). Some nongovernmental organizations (NGOs) expressed reservations as well; as LeBlanc points out in his study of the CRC, "in its earliest stages, the drafting of the con-vention on the Rights of the Child did not enjoy very broad-based support, but . . . it did not face strong and sustained opposition" (LeBlanc 1995, 24). UNICEF itself remained on the sidelines during its early days. In a substantial study of UNICEF during this period, Patricia Smyke notes that UNICEF's attitude appeared to many observers to be one of "benign neglect"; she quotes a participant as noting that "UNICEF had . . . a low profile in the early stages" and that "[one] had to force UNICEF to make a statement and then they almost never did. . . . UNICEF seemed so passive" (Smyke 1990, 15). She explains, and interviews with UNICEF staff have confirmed, that UNICEF was initially extremely wary of the notion of human rights for fear that it would politicize the organization and involve it in controversial issues, and this might weaken UNICEF's ability to work in a pragmatic and cooperative way with states. This opinion was common throughout the UN development family (Smyke 1990, 6). Smyke quotes one source that described UNICEF as "frightened . . . to death" of any specific talk on rights (p. 13)!

In a pattern repeated in the other two case studies to follow, UNICEF first began to change its attitude toward human rights issues largely because of pressure from NGOs, which perceived rights as being important for both moral and pragmatic reasons. NGOs had been active in pressing for a draft children's rights convention, and they were active in drafting it from the beginning (LeBlanc 1995, 41–42). From the earliest days, they had had some relationship with UNICEF, and UNICEF is mentioned as having provided some facilities for NGOs, such as meeting rooms, travel money for visiting experts, and other logistical support. As the drafting process moved forward, the NGO representatives began to enlist support within UNICEF, most notably Marjorie Newman-Black (later Newman-Williams), UNICEF's NGO liaison officer in Geneva. Newman-Black, in Smyke's words, "began to grasp the importance of the Convention for children and thus for UNICEF" (Smyke 1990), or, to put it without the benefit of hindsight, began to consider the usefulness of a convention and how it might tie in with UNICEF's work.

At the same time, other forces were also encouraging an interest in a children's rights convention. UNICEF was then involved in developing a new strategic priority, focusing on what are called "children in especially difficult circumstances" (CEDC). This new issue area redefined UNICEF's role toward children in situations of armed conflict or natural disaster, children who were sexually exploited, working children, children with disabilities, and other children who found themselves particularly at risk. It was an important departure from the traditional UNICEF role of helping children through the first few years of life. In this case the pressure actually came from UNICEF's executive board, which, in response to the child survival revolution, began to worry about an "excessive narrowing" of UNICEF's operations (Smyke 1990, 20). The board asked UNICEF to consider ways it could help children in especially difficult circumstances (UNICEF 1984, 2–3). It also suggested that UNICEF would become more involved in less tangible issues— legal reform, for example, and the creation of national programs to assist working children (UNICEF 1986a, 28–29).

These were just the sorts of issues that Grant feared a children's rights convention would raise—yet they were becoming issues that he would have to address in any case. A meeting of experts on children in armed conflicts in early 1985 brought up the opinion that the new CEDC policy in fact would mesh well with a children's rights approach (UNICEF 1986b). Grant was present at that meeting, and he suggested an in-house meeting in July 1985 to review UNICEF's policy toward the convention (Smyke 1990, 24). This meeting, which successfully convinced the executive director to involve UNICEF in the drafting process and to embrace children's rights, focused on the potential of the new convention as an advocacy and social mobilization tool for future UNICEF's activities, and its potential to support country-level legislative action in the CEDC area (UNICEF 1985).

This decision to become more actively involved in drafting the CRC, and to move toward accepting it as a central document in UNICEF programming (although there was no talk at this stage about a specific UNICEF role in implementing children's rights), resulted from the congruence of a number of forces, both internal and external. Externally, the process of creating a children's rights convention was going to proceed with or without UNICEF participation. It is easy to see why NGOs were surprised that UNICEF was not taking a more active role in the early years, in light of the direct impact such a convention would have on UNICEF and its work. Surely, they thought, the organization would want to shape such a document. NGOs began pressuring UNICEF to take a more active role, even after UNICEF did offer the logistical support mentioned above (Smyke 1990, 7–8). A particularly important conduit of information was Newman-Black, who "began to grasp the importance of the Convention for children and thus for UNICEF." She and a handful of others would form "several isolated cells of interest in the Convention within UNICEF," largely converted and motivated by this outside pressure (Smyke 1990, 9, 22).

Internally the decision of the executive board to push for a wider UNICEF scope of operations, and the subsequent development of a CEDC agenda, was also an important factor in motivating UNICEF's interest in the CRC. In 1986 the executive board went further, specifically asking UNICEF to participate in the drafting process of the convention (UNICEF 1986c). Once the true believers within the organization found that the CEDC agenda reinforced their own argument in favor the CRC and UNICEF involvement, a solid core that could muster both moral and practical arguments began to press for change within UNICEF. Smyke puts it this way: "Continuing NGO and governmental pressure, solidifying support from individuals within the organization, linkages between children's rights and CEDC, the 1985 in-house meetings. . . . All of these, combined with the 1986 board decision, created a distinctly different climate. . . . It was obvious that Mr. Grant was warming up to the idea" (Smyke 1990, 29–30). Certainly the decision of the executive board—and member state influence—was an important element, but it was only one, and not really the most important. It asked only that UNICEF take an interest in the process, and to assist in the drafting with its technical expertise. It stopped short of a full endorsement or a directive to put the CRC at the center of UNICEF's operations.

Instead the impression given is of a focus on convincing Grant to guide UNICEF toward adopting the convention and an interest in human rights as a way to expand UNICEF's influence and visibility. Once he had made this decision, the true believers within the organization began to find themselves not marginalized but placed in important strategic positions; and Grant put himself "at their disposition, saying, 'Okay, tell me what I have to do'" (Smyke 1990, 39). From being opposed to the notion of the CRC, Grant made its adoption a key component of the overall UNICEF strategy: He mobilized UNICEF staff in New York and also in field offices to advocate for the adoption of the CRC, making it a goal of UNICEF that the CRC approach universal ratification. This was going far beyond anything that the board had asked UNICEF to do and, for that matter, beyond what the NGO representatives and the CRC working group had wanted or expected. As chapter 1 notes, the example of a UN specialized agency mobilizing itself on a worldwide scale to persuade governments to support and ratify a human rights instrument was an intriguing reversal of the usual model in which member states direct a UN agency to perform certain tasks. Once Grant became convinced that the political nature of the CRC would help rather than hinder UNICEF in pursuing its mandate, the CRC became a key strategic priority.

It is important to reiterate here that Grant became convinced of exactly that: that the CRC would empower UNICEF to more effectively protect children and contribute to the ongoing child survival revolution. Recall that it was exactly the fear that the CRC would work against UNICEF—by placing it in confrontational, political situations vis-à-vis states parties—that originally scared off UNICEF and other UN agencies. By 1987, that fear had evaporated and UNICEF had determined that the CRC was instead a potentially powerful advocacy tool—that it not only justified many of the things UNICEF was considering undertaking in the CEDC area but could also add legitimacy to its more traditional operations. This was a decision made by Grant in consultation with his advisers; and once the decision had been made, Grant himself was able to mobilize UNICEF support for the CRC. Grant's vision of the role of the CRC in the activities of UNICEF was limited; it would fall to others to move the rights agenda to the center of UNICEF's operational paradigm.

## Definition

The process of defining what human rights means to UNICEF is not simple. It involves determining the content of relevant human rights law, deciding what other standards are appropriate beyond those contained in the most important international documents, and discerning how these laws and standards translate into actual policy ideas. This process is ongoing and not uncontroversial.

*Basic Documents*

Unlike the other organizations discussed in this study, UNICEF began its interest in a rights-based approach with two documents that specifically addressed rights in the context of its programming: the CRC and the Convention on the Elimination of All Forms of Discrimination Against Women (CEDAW). (Because UNICEF considers the health and welfare of mothers to be a central determinant of the health and welfare of their children, it sees CEDAW as an important add-on to the CRC, although UNICEF feels free to pick and choose which CEDAW articles it will try to implement.) Like other human rights documents, the CRC was drafted by states; and like other documents, it represents a compromise, with its terms determined at least as much by political and practical considerations as by moral or philosophical ones. Thus, for example, the matter of the age below which children could be drafted into the military was heavily influenced by the practices of certain states participating in the drafting process, and the question of when life begins (and therefore if or when human rights attach to a fetus) was avoided entirely, on the understanding that a common definition was a political as well as philosophical impossibility (LeBlanc 1995, 66–73). CEDAW is similarly the result of political negotiations.

Coming as it did during the child survival revolution, the CRC was initially seen by UNICEF less as a departure from its previous practice than as an enabling tool for pursuing what it did best. This is not to say that there were not some immediate changes; in particular, the CRC and CEDAW strengthened and sharpened UNICEF's definition of operations in the area of CEDC and, subsequently, both enabled and impelled a widening of the scope of these efforts. For example, Article 35 of the CRC, which deals with the problem of child trafficking, practically mandated that this area be added to the definition of children in especially difficult circumstances and brought UNICEF action in this area. The same is true of children in armed conflict, or those subject to torture or brutal punishments. Yet the heart of UNICEF operations in such basic, survival-oriented areas as proper sanitation or access to medical care, as well as access to basic education, remains the same more than a decade after adoption of the CRC; what has changed is how these actions are framed and defined.

UNICEF considers the *entire* CRC as coming under its purview (though it is more selective in the case of the CEDAW); the UNICEF "Implementation Handbook," for example, does not prioritize various CRC articles (Hodgkin and Newell 2002). Implementation issues for both survival rights, such as adequate nutrition or health care, and for more political rights, such as freedom of expression or assembly, are given equal prominence. By taking on the CRC as a sort of "central document" for the organization, UNICEF had committed to a substantial expansion of its mandate and agenda. This in itself has had two important effects. First, it has required UNICEF—almost without wanting to—to consider a variety of new issues, such as children's rights to free speech and to religious freedom, which before would have been deemed outside its mandate. Second, it has meant that there is less room than before for *prioritizing* certain interventions. Whereas before the CRC certain survival issues were considered of paramount importance, now all issues relating to children, or at least all covered by the CRC, are rights and therefore nonnegotiable. Though in practice there is still an understanding that some rights are more important than others, or that the achievement of some is premised on the prior achievement of others, it has made it more difficult to actually ignore those issues that may not be central to survival and basic development.[1]

Thus the CRC has meant a considerable and somewhat complex expansion of UNICEF's mandate. The positive result of this expansion is a more complete view of children and UNICEF's place in protecting then and promoting their interests. "The Convention's most fundamental impact on UNICEF," notes an early study, "is that it broadens the framework for analysing the situation of children and it stimulates new thinking about effective strategies" (Newman-Black 1991, 7). UNICEF consistently argues that it now takes a more "holistic" approach to children in need, looking at all their needs, rather than narrowly focusing on survival and basic development.

Central to UNICEF's view of children as rights holders is Article 3(1) of the CRC, which states that "in all actions concerning children, . . . the best interests of the child shall be a primary consideration." As interpretation of the CRC evolved, the "best interest" principle became one of four foundation principles in UNICEF planning documents, and it remains the most general and comprehensive of the identified core components (Bellamy 1998, 12–13). It forms a powerful element in the rhetoric of children's rights, implying as it does that the best interests of the child take priority over other considerations—despite the fact that, as UNICEF recognizes, the best interest principle is described in the CRC as "a primary consideration" rather than as *the only* primary consideration (Bellamy 1998, 12). The various rights then enumerated in the CRC, and in CEDAW, suggest the various areas in which the best interests of the child must be considered by states parties (UNICEF 2003a, 237).

## Defining a Rights-Based Approach

It is one thing to recognize key principles inherent in a document like the CRC, such as the best interests of the child. But it is more difficult to discern what it means to actually implement a human right. What, in other words, would UNICEF and states parties (acting together with UNICEF taking an advisory and assisting role to the state, which was the primary holder of human rights obligations) have to do to actually live up to the standards of the document?

The problem of defining "implementation" was among the earliest questions UNICEF asked itself. Given its successes in the 1980s, it was natural for the organization to ask what a rights-based approach added to its operations. More important, the question of what it means to implement a human rights document like the CRC is also of crucial interest to UNICEF because of its highly practical, "can-do" tradition and orientation. UNICEF sees great value in its decentralized structure, local presence, and focus on results (Oestreich 1998). Its personnel often distinguish their agency from others that they feel focus more on politics than on local programming. This attitude was reinforced by the results of the child survival revolution, with its strategic emphasis on finding a handful of interventions with the highest payoff in helping children, but it reaches back to UNICEF's earliest years as well.

As early as 1991, according to UNICEF, its regional offices were "examining the implications of this Convention for the work of the organization. They [were] attempting to define, in terms of practical action, what impact the Convention [was] likely to have on UNICEF programmes of cooperation" (Newman-Black 1991, 5). Among the earliest steps taken was stressing the notion of "empowerment," a development concept already in common use at UNICEF by the time the CRC was ratified. In general, empowerment is used in development studies to mean "the expansion of freedom of choice and action . . . increasing one's authority over the resources and decisions that affect one's life" (Narayan 2002, 19). It is helping people to increase their well-being by taking control of the assets available to them and maximizing their own capabilities. In this context, empowerment came to be a key concept distinguishing the rights-based approach from earlier work, which was characterized as mere provision of services. According to one of the earliest studies of the CRC's implementation, it "transforms charity-oriented approaches to providing services for children into national obligations to give meaning to their rights" (Newman-Black 1991, 7). Another early document analyzing one aspect in particular of UNICEF operations notes that "the empowerment of parents with knowledge about the advantages of vaccination . . . is the surest way to ensure that they will seek, demand and assist in making immunization widely available" (UNICEF 1989, 12). To help children achieve their right to immunization differs from simply providing immunization by placing it in a political context where children and their mothers become empowered to understand the need for such services and to demand them from the primary obligation holder, the government.

Closely connected with this is the principle of requiring the participation of children and their caregivers (usually mothers) in program design. As one key document puts it, "a programming approach that is guided by CRC [*sic*] and CEDAW should explicitly seek to create conditions that allow women and children to participate more fully in community life and in the development of policies that affect them" (Bellamy 1998, 20). Enhancing participation of children and their caregivers, both in program design and in politics in general, is considered a key component of "empowerment" and therefore of the move from service delivery to rights implementation. Planning documents within UNICEF speak of the decentralization of service delivery and other political changes as being necessary to encourage local participation in project planning and implementation (Lewin 2000, 19).

UNICEF thus argues that the difference between what it had traditionally been doing in the health care sector, for example, and implementing a "right of the child to the enjoyment of the highest attainable standards of health and to facilities for the treatment of illness and rehabilitation of health" lies in this distinction between empowerment and mere service provision. The distinction is not always entirely clear or even entirely relevant, although it is significant in its own way. What is interesting here is that it *does* add a political element to UNICEF's rhetoric and actions, despite UNICEF's repeated insistence, during the drafting of the CRC, that it did not want to be pulled into political debates that might reduce its ability to work cooperatively with states.

A further political issue raised by the idea of rights-based programming is equity. Nondiscrimination is mentioned along with the best interest of the child as a key principle of the CRC—as well as, of course, of human rights in general. "We must," notes one study, "look at whether national laws protect all children and women equally or whether in the application of laws there is inherent discrimination" (UNICEF 2003b, 232). An analysis of the results of rights-based programming concludes that "[the human-rights-based approach to programming] moves programmes to pay even greater attention to marginalized groups in society. . . . Strengthening accountability and participation, by itself, is not sufficient to ensure equality and inclusion and to challenge discrimination" (Theis 2004, 31).

Human rights programming requires that attention be paid to differences across groups, including male/female discrimination but also including, for example, attention to underserved minority groups. So, for example, a rights-based approach means looking to see not only how many children are being helped but also whether there is a hidden form of discrimination at work causing some groups of children to be neglected. This priority, significantly, is often combined with the concern for empowerment and participation rather than held as a separate category. A study of Latin America, for example, concludes that "the reality . . . demonstrates strongly interrelated structural limitations, such as social exclusion and anti-democratic social relationships, that makes it difficult to comply with the basic principles of the convention and the rights set forth therein. A move towards a more inclusive, universal-type model of development is imperative if the enormous social divisions and inequalities are to be mitigated" (Lewin 2000, 19).

A rights-based approach, then, is defined as one that seeks social change, not mere service provision. The problems that cause poor child health and welfare, including social discrimination, poor government, and powerlessness, are part of the background condition of poverty and must be considered as part of the same problem. If the source of the problem is not attacked, then the paradigm remains one of mere service provision and not rights protection.

## Political Implications of Rights-Based Approaches

As early as the mid-1980s, the question was raised whether UNICEF would want to be names as a monitoring body of the CRC, but it was quickly decided that the organization could in no way accept such a role. It was felt that UNICEF would go only so far in politicizing its position—the term used was that UNICEF needed to retain its "specific personality" (UNICEF 1987, 2). There was also a decision to accept a designation in the CRC of UNICEF as the "lead agency for children" (although UNICEF would not actually seek such a designation). In fact, UNICEF is mentioned in the CRC along with "other United Nations organs," giving it specific recognition as having an implementation role but excusing it from any particular function. With such recognition, however, the question of what implementation would entail was all the more pressing.

The more political nature of UNICEF work can be fit roughly into two categories. In the first place, the widening scope of issues now considered under the UNICEF umbrella—including the situation of working children, child trafficking, child soldiers, disabled children, and the like—means that UNICEF must take an interest in issues that require much more political action than traditional work in education, nutrition, sanitation, and so on. The highly political nature of some of the reforms mentioned in the previous section should be obvious; empowering the poor, tackling inequality, and promoting social change are all far more controversial than what UNICEF had previously concerned itself with.

It would be inaccurate to say that the CRC alone is responsible for this increased political sensitivity: Recall that UNICEF
was already showing an interest in children in especially difficult
circumstances even before its engagement with the draft CRC in
the 1980s. But it is certainly true that a rights-based, CRC-oriented
approach to child welfare dictates direct engagement in a wide variety of issues with social causes and that require political solutions. A first step in assessing the situation in a program country
now includes "the degree to which national laws and, where applicable, customary laws do or do not provide children and women
with legal safeguards. . . . In other words, UNICEF must know
and understand how legislation, public policy and national institutions impact on the realization of children's and women's rights"
(UNICEF 2003a, 242). The CRC itself requires changes in national
law: "As a legally binding instrument," UNICEF notes, "the Convention can be used in many countries to strengthen existing laws
and regulations. . . . In some cases, there are ambiguities or incon-
sistencies between this international instrument which need to be
resolved" (Himes 1993, 7).

The other way in which the CRC has made UNICEF more politicized is that it has very consciously become an advocacy tool
for UNICEF to use on behalf of children, to force change in states
parties. Of the three organizations under study here, UNICEF is
by far the most eager to use rights language as a tool to get its
way, and therefore to help it fulfill its operational mandate. "States
voluntarily acknowledge and accept obligations when they ratify
human rights treaties," notes a key training document. "In doing
so they agree to implement these treaties and to be accountable
for meeting the rights and providing for the needs of the people
within their jurisdiction" (UNICEF 2003a, 234). Where necessary,
UNICEF in other words will be prepared to use the CRC to remind
states of their obligations.

There is a close tie-in here with the concept of implementation
of human rights: If rights empower children and women to demand services, then the ultimate obligation falls not on UNICEF,
it argues, but on states to provide those services. In a rights-based
approach, "it is accepted that the State is normatively required to
work consistently towards ending denials or violations of human
rights, and that the empowerment of rights holders is in itself an

important result of various processes" (UNICEF 2003a, 234). To speak of human rights in development requires that states cooperate and, therefore, also requires that UNICEF be sometimes confrontational. Rights are a tool to be used by UNICEF to make sure that states are acting in ways that UNICEF deems in the best interest of the child.

It is worth pointing out again that, though UNICEF has made some strides toward defining human rights in practical, programmatic terms, it is still only in the early stages of doing so. Thus most UNICEF planning documents still define a rights-based approach in relatively abstract terms, along the lines of the "best interests" principle. Here UNICEF defines rights as more of a background condition than an actual goal in itself—as something that informs and shapes activities whose focus remains on practical matters. An important example of this sort of thinking centers on the issue of nondiscrimination. Article 2 of the CRC states that "States Parties shall respect and ensure the rights set forth in the present Convention to each child within their jurisdiction without discrimination of any kind, irrespective of the child's or his or her parent's or legal guardian's race, colour, sex, language, religion, political or other opinion, national, ethnic or social origin, property, disability, birth or other status." In the context of UNICEF, nondiscrimination has become not only a right in itself (that of equality) but also a guiding principle in programming for other interventions. To implement the right to nondiscrimination, UNICEF must take steps to eliminate both overt and hidden discrimination in its programs and those it supports.

This emphasis on equality does take one particularly concrete step, and that is in UNICEF's work for the equality of women in society. This is both more specific and more prominent than any talk of "equality" for children, which is not in fact mentioned in the CRC. Children have rights, but they are not "equal" to adults. (This is not to dismiss that the CRC does insist that children deserve equal treatment and regard with one another.) Conversely, the right to equality for women is a key element in UNICEF programming and an issue that the organization lobbies for as strenuously as it can. It has become a matter of unquestioned principle within the organization that the rights of women and the welfare of children are inextricably linked. In the realm of nondiscrimination, this means that a key element is preventing discrimination against the girl child in the areas of health care, nutrition, and especially education. More generally, improving the status of women in society is now a primary goal in all countries, with the understanding that women, as the primary caregivers for children, are the key to making sure children receive the care they need. Hence CEDAW is approached as a general background condition for any talk of human rights in UNICEF programming and of the rights of women in general as a key strategic element.

It was noted in the first section of this chapter that the problem of politicizing UNICEF's mission was a concern from the beginning of discussion of the CRC—it was a primary reason Grant was initially wary of the CRC. This concern has not entirely faded, and it is something that is raised almost whenever new interventions are considered. Staff remain wary of promoting new policies, or changing existing ones, in ways that appear to violate the sovereignty of states or that risk so angering states that they will curtail cooperation with UNICEF. There remains a sense of there being a fine line between those CRC aspects that will actually help UNICEF pursue its goals and those that will ultimately undermine its ability to work cooperatively with states. This will be a common theme among the various cases under study here, and it is worth highlighting here. Although human rights, particularly those specifically contained in the main international legal documents, have considerable standing in the international system, their application is hardly uncontroversial, and states are not always accustomed to having them promoted by agencies that traditionally focused on more politically neutral interventions.

*New Issue Areas*

Along with the changes described above, the CRC does add new rights-related issues to UNICEF's view of its own mission. The definition of human rights, from UNICEF's standpoint, therefore includes a number of issues enumerated by the CRC. For one thing, the CRC provides justification and rhetorical power behind those issues contained in the CEDC agenda, including disabled children, street children, children caught in the criminal justice system, and children in war zones and refugee camps. UNICEF's documents also now refer to its obligations to work toward such goals as respect for the views of children, the existence of "education, leisure and cultural activities" for children (UNICEF 2003a, 247–48), combating the illicit trade in children (Hodgkin and Newell 2002, 521–30), and any number of other issues that are covered in the CRC, including the rights of refugee children, working children, and child soldiers.

Some of these issues, of course, are more central to the UNICEF mandate than others, and some receive more attention—UNICEF is not unwilling to skim over issues (family planning and freedom of religion are commonly cited examples) that it deems too hot to take on or to claim that others are legitimate but simply too far outside its scope of expertise to do much other than general advocacy. In a central document on UNICEF's relation to children's rights, Carol Bellamy dedicated only two sentences to the issue of the "views of the child," even though she identified that concept as being one of the CRC's four foundation principles along with the best interest principle (Bellamy 1998, 12). Foundational it may be, but it is also another political land mine that UNICEF would rather avoid. The organization, in fact, has shown considerable latitude in choosing which elements of the CRC it wishes to pursue and which it deems to fall outside its mandate. They all receive rhetorical support, but only those deemed to be both central to UNICEF and politically viable are actually incorporated into program planning.

"Rights based programming," according to UNICEF, "does not mean that everything we do must change. In fact, the policies and programmes of co-operation supported over the last 20 to 30 years are very largely consistent with what the CRC and CEDAW mandate. Adopting a human rights approach simply means that we look for the 'value-added' that the general principles and specific standards of the Conventions can provide" (UNICEF 2003a, 30). Rights are seen as "a crosscutting aspect of all areas of programme support" rather than as a programming area in and of their own (UNICEF 2003b, 5). Rights remain primarily a way of talking about practical matters while shifting great responsibility on to governments; of "empowering" children and women to demand for themselves what they need for their survival and development.

UNICEF, then, defines rights as having both a strategic factor—the notions of empowerment and state obligations—and a functional side, with a list of new issues that ought to be addressed by UNICEF. But both these factors remain rather vague in terms of their actual impact on UNICEF programming, and for good reason: The CRC (and CEDAW) were supported initially by UNICEF because of what they could do to help it carry out its core mission; and their interpretation also depends on what the organization feels does and does not improve its operations and leverage with states. The most accurate way to look at UNICEF's relationship to rights is to view rights language as a tool with which to pursue its more general mandate, that of protecting children and aiding in their development. This clearly perpetuates Grant's initial vision of the CRC as a way of leveraging UNICEF's power in host states. He saw in the CRC, and in the careful enumeration of children's rights, a way of raising the profile of his organization and the issues it addressed. The concept of rights was to be a tool that UNICEF could use to pursue an organizational mandate.

## Implementation

Among the organizations under study here, UNICEF has gone the furthest in actually integrating human rights into its operational agenda. Rather than seeing rights as an additional goal to be pursued by the organization—that is to say, rather than adaptation in Ernst Haas's scheme of organizational development—UNICEF has set for itself the desire to learn from the CRC. Under such situations, according to Haas, "behavior changes as actors question original implicit theories underlying programs and examine their original values" (Haas 1990, 14). Grant intended that the CRC would become a foundational document for UNICEF, and that it would increase UNICEF's effectiveness as well as its reach and power. He pursued this organizational goal aggressively during the latter part of his tenure with UNICEF, and he made it clear that this was a permanent feature of the organization's way of doing business.

Seventeen years after the CRC came into force, the process of transformation within UNICEF has not yet been completed.

Though there have been some notable advances in changing both UNICEF's organizational culture and the operational paradigm of its various program departments, there has also been a countervailing tendency toward inertia. Programming areas that were relatively new—most notably, those dealing with CEDC issues, and those created specifically to address new issues raised by the CRC—have made the most progress. The process of determining just what the CRC means in, for example, the sanitation or education fields, has made less progress. UNICEF's commitment to reform remains fairly strong, and the process appears to be irreversible, but the successes and failures of this learning process make clear the challenges in all such transformations. What does remain clear is the need for dedication among the top management to creating such change. When this dedication has appeared to waver, the learning process has itself wavered; when it has remained firm, learning has progressed.

*Early UNICEF Efforts*

The first programmatic change made by UNICEF—Grant's push for universal ratification of the CRC by states—was made before the CRC had even been approved by the UN General Assembly. Grant's decision to endorse the CRC has already been discussed; and he also understood that its effectiveness as an advocacy tool would be increased as it neared universal ratification. In 1987, therefore, Grant committed UNICEF (against the recommendations of some of his advisers) to push governments to ratify the CRC (Smyke 1990, 34). He set a target date of 1989, which would be ten years after the CRC had been proposed, as part of the International Year of the Child, for completion of the convention and its approval by the UN General Assembly. A task force was created at UNICEF headquarters in New York, coordinating with the Geneva office and with NGO partners, to begin working for ratification around the world.

The significance of this effort should not be underestimated. It was, once again, Grant's own decision that pushed UNICEF to work for ratification, supported by the same true believers who had urged him to support the CRC in the first place and to give rights a central place in UNICEF thinking. UNICEF's decision was certainly a noteworthy one, more so because it was not directed by the UNICEF executive board. And the success of this effort should not be underrated; the CRC quickly became the most ratified human rights document in the world, with near-universal acceptance. (At present, only the United States and Somalia have failed to ratify the CRC.) Though it is easy to say that this is because the object of the CRC, the protection and development of children, is something no nation could be seen opposing, one might say the same thing about the Genocide Convention, which has fewer signatories. The worldwide drive for ratification was clearly a success.

Within UNICEF, however, there was no clear and simple transformation of the organizational culture from tradition to rights-based programming. By the early 1990s, Grant had done a good job convincing top UNICEF management that the CRC made sense for UNICEF as a political position and as a way of leveraging UNICEF's power and influence. Yet he was content to leave the issue there. In part, this resulted from Grant's own abilities as an innovator: The child survival revolution he had initiated had been a notable success, and he himself, along with most top staff at the time, questioned whether the CRC would add to that success. His primary interest was in seeing the CRC ratified and placing it as an important rhetorical and political tool for UNICEF; with this accomplished, he was content to relegate the CRC to a role supporting UNICEF's primary activities. Because he had committed UNICEF to a series of survival and development goals based on the child survival revolution (and embodied in the goals set by the 1990 World Summit for Children), it appears that he simply had little time or energy left to nurture the CRC and its strategic implications. Though the true believers continued to advocate a rights-based approach, they remained relatively junior staffers within UNICEF, and their influence went only so far.

As with the other organizations under study here, UNICEF also faced the problem of convincing staff with technical backgrounds and extensive field experience of the importance of adopting a new paradigm. This has proven to be a serious problem across the board. It was not enough that a core of true believers and other managers were willing to consider the importance of rights-based programming; to effect organizational change, it is necessary to convince personnel at all levels. It is worth examining why UNICEF has been more successful than other organizations at creating effective change. Though pressure from the top has been important, it is also particularly useful to analyze the intellectual development of a rights-based paradigm, which was instrumental in developing support at all levels of the organization.

The first substantial shifts within UNICEF regarding rights-based programming were not organizational but intellectual: There was an early recognition that more specifics were needed concerning what the CRC and other rights documents actually meant to UNICEF. To convince technical staff, a moral argument had to be connected to what will be called in this book the "argument from effectiveness"—that is, an argument based on careful analysis that human rights concepts can actually improve programs and outcomes. In this effort, UNICEF was fortunate to be able to turn to the Innocenti Research Centre (formerly the International Child Development Center) in Florence, which had been working on the issue of rights since its establishment in 1988 (Himes 1993, 3). In 1991 the Innocenti Centre began publishing a series of studies on various aspects of the CRC, and in particular what the CRC would mean for UNICEF operations. Many of those who had been instrumental in drafting the CRC, or who had been among the early true believers in it along with Grant, were affiliated in the years after 1989 with the Innocenti Centre and helped work toward a better definition of how to implement it. The Innocenti Centre remains to this day an important resource and a place where rights experts from UNICEF and elsewhere contribute to the problem of CRC implementation.

Further intellectual stimulus was provided by the UNICEF field offices operating around the world. UNICEF takes seriously its decentralized mode of operation and the limited interference from headquarters in New York in the activities of its field representatives. It considers this to be a key component of its success, because it operates around the world and recognizes the need to adapt to local conditions, customs, political climates, and the like. As early as 1989 UNICEF field offices were instructed to consider how the CRC would affect their operations and to build rights-related issues into their country programming. This was done *before* there were clear guidelines from New York on exactly what such programming would mean (Newman-Black 1991, 5). To a

large extent this was done on the initiative of the field offices themselves, with little or no direction from New York—including little
direction from Grant. Offices in Bangladesh and Mali, for example,
moved ahead with considering how the CRC would affect their operations and included rights-based programming in their planning
documents; "about ten" offices did likewise while others paid only
passing attention to the CRC.[2]

In New York, however, the clearest sign of what the CRC initially meant was reflected in organizational change—or the lack
thereof. The only significant change to the structure of UNICEF at
the time was the creation of a children's rights unit in the public
affairs division of UNICEF; rather than creating a line of authority
over programmatic issues (either in the program division or sepa-
rately), the issue was handled as one of public relations. New York,
at that time, was perceived to be particularly heavily populated with
doctors and others with degrees in the health professions, and they
were resistant to the notion of a rights-based agenda in programming.[3] As with the other cases under review, the effort at organizational change was challenged by the technical training of staff,
who considered rights-based issues "fuzzy" and outside their area
of expertise, as well as of limited usefulness (if not actually harmful
to programming effectiveness).

With Grant's fading interest in the CRC, with resistance from
staff in New York and elsewhere, and without a clear organizational line of authority to push the agenda, what rights work was
being done in the period 1990–97 was largely confined to the field
offices, on a haphazard basis. It was being undertaken by the true
believers, some of whom had left New York or Geneva to work in
the field. It was in the field offices that there was finally palpable
organizational change, where resident representatives began to appoint "protection officers" to pursue rights-based programming,
often built around the issues of the CEDC agenda. These were
often lawyers, free from the technical prejudices of the medically
trained personnel but also often misunderstood or marginalized
by their colleagues. They were appointed by resident representatives in the field to begin thinking about how rights might affect
programming.[4] Rights-based language also began working its way
into the annual reports and planning documents being prepared
in the field. Local operational plans began speaking of "providing

children with their rights" as part of the UNICEF mission, and they speculated, often with little or no directive from New York other than the influence of the Innocenti Centre and those connected with it, on how rights might affect areas from CEDC to the traditional program areas such as education and nutrition (e.g., UNICEF 1994).

The next major change in UNICEF occurred early in 1997, as a result of a change in UNICEF's top leadership. James Grant died in 1995, not long after resigning as director of UNICEF, and his successor was Carol Bellamy, another American. Bellamy signaled a changed in direction in UNICEF early in her tenure with an organizational shakeup; she brought Marjorie Newman-Black, one of the original CRC true believers from Geneva, in from a field office to be deputy director of the Program Division in New York. Working against the resistance of some in UNICEF who remained skeptical of the usefulness of a rights approach, Newman-Black prepared for Bellamy an "Executive Directive on Human Rights and UNICEF," which was issued to staff in early 1998 (Bellamy 1998).

Further signaling a change of emphasis, UNICEF moved responsibility for human rights into the heart of the program process, appointing a human rights adviser in the office of the director of the program division, the heart of policy development within UNICEF—thus moving the intellectual center of rights-based programming back from its exile in Florence. Perhaps even more significant were changes mandated by Bellamy in the field offices. Although some field offices had been among the most progressive voices for human rights programming in UNICEF, this was an uneven development, and many others ignored or marginalized rights issues. This was particularly noticeable in the creation of numerous child protection officers, often with legal backgrounds, to deal with some rights- and CEDC-related issues separate from the main work of the office. This was often seen as a way for an office to appear to have a rights-based program without actually changing its main work. The most significant change was to create rights advisers in regional offices but to give them a mandate covering all UNICEF activities—in essence, to make rights less a marginal issue and instead to create an atmosphere where rights were to be considered in all programming decisions.

By the late 1990s the second stage of the transformation of UNICEF was well under way. The 1998 "Executive Directive" was followed up by a report to the executive board in 1999 further laying out the rights-based approach (UNICEF 1999), and by the hiring of further staff with legal or similar backgrounds in order to build the capacity in rights-related issues that was lacking in UNICEF's traditional staffing priorities. Acceptance of the CRC has also been built into a "management excellence program" now ongoing at UNICEF, to further inculcate UNICEF staff on the need to consider rights-based programming priorities.

A recent study of UNICEF's current strategic direction concluded that "it is evident that the application of a human rights based approach to programming . . . has been uneven. So far roughly one half of all UNICEF-assisted country programmes show good or adequate application of the approach" (UNICEF 2004, 20). This report notes that a lack of capacity and bureaucratic inertia, as well as lingering skepticism among staff, have contributed to this uneven progress. Nevertheless, changes have been undertaken to effectively implement a rights-based approach, and they accelerated under Bellamy's leadership. These changes are discussed in the following sections.

## Programmatic Changes

It is useful to divide the programmatic activities of UNICEF field offices—the actual changes to UNICEF practice—into three categories: changes in the rhetorical approach (the way UNICEF speaks with and deals with host governments); the new program areas added since 1989; and changes in traditional programming areas such as health, education, or sanitation. Rhetorical changes are worth focusing on to gain insight into how UNICEF justifies its other operations and thinks about its overall mission. Also, the political risks of the CRC have been a continuing concern for UNICEF, and the way UNICEF uses the concept of rights to prod governments and influence public opinion remains a source of both strength and a concern. Rhetoric can have a power in and of itself, independent of actual activities on the ground.

## RHETORICAL CHANGES

As a UN specialized agency, UNICEF can do few things by it-self; rather, it must work though the governments of host states, promoting and assisting with programs that they then carry out. All such agencies operate at the sufferance of host states and must understand the political climate where they operate; persuasion and alliance building are at least as important as service provision and programming, if the agency is to be effective. Building and maintaining coalitions can be complicated in environments where corruption is endemic, where there is intense competition for scarce resources, and where governments are often little accountable for their actions. In such situations it is often necessary to mobilize grassroots support for programs, yet at the same time this is problematic exactly because of the authoritarian nature of governments, which will resent this effort to circumvent their authority.

UNICEF field offices now frame their programs of cooperation with reference to the CRC. This is of course not surprising, considering that the CRC was always valued for its political useful-ness as a way of prodding host governments into action. By insisting, as UNICEF does, that all activities directed at child welfare should be and can be directly related to the realization of human rights, UNICEF is able to reframe all its activities as rights related. Thus, for example, a study of UNICEF's rights-based activities in Latin America mentions "establishing and maintaining relations at the highest political level of decision-making" as an important strategic element in a rights-based program; and, more important, "placing important issues on the political agenda" and "systematic and permanent communication about child rights" become prominent strategic goals in and of themselves (Lewin 2000, 20–21). An important internal guidance document on children's rights also stresses their universality: "All human rights and fundamental freedoms are indivisible and interdependent. Equal attention and urgent consideration should be given to [their] implementation" (Pais 1999, 7).

Any number of UNICEF field reports prominently display their efforts to bring to the attention of national leaders the terms of the CRC and other rights documents. From Mali it is reported that officials "frequently mentioned their efforts to become more fluent

with the HRBAP [human-rights-based approach to programming].
. . . The Ministry of Health prepared PowerPoint presentations on
the integration of the CRC and CEDAW in the health sector" (Rios-
Kohn 2003, 37). A cynic might question the sincerity of this deep
interest in the details of rights-based programming on the part of
the Health Ministry, but clearly UNICEF's field office placed great
stock in it.

The effort to use the CRC as a tool for influencing policy is not
limited to interaction at the highest level of government. Efforts to
spread the word on the CRC, and to drum up support at the grassroots level, is as old as Grant's initial campaign for universal CRC
ratification. One of the first steps UNICEF took to move for universal ratification was the preparation of handbooks on the nature
of the CRC, which were to be distributed in all program countries;
and the UNICEF public affairs office made a concerted effort to
contact journalists worldwide and to mobilize goodwill ambassa-
dors on behalf of children's rights (Smyke 1990, 46). It was always
Grant's intention to pressure governments for ratification by using
the public relations value of the CRC—a particularly high value
given the emotional power of a children's rights convention. The
NGO community was also enlisted, and it continues to be an important ally in the effort for public education.

In general, there has been a concerted effort to move the terms
of debate away from traditional notions of providing services and
toward the issue of rights and duties. The Tanzania office, for example, notes "a shift away from activities that could be labeled 'service delivery' with more emphasis put on 'advocacy' and 'capacity
building'" (UNICEF 2002, 5). In all country offices, the principles
of the CRC have been given a central place in the master plan of
operations (MPO) that governs UNICEF activities for five-year periods. The Tanzania office reports that the government there was
particularly receptive to talk of human rights but also that other
countries might not be so receptive; the study of experiences in
Latin America notes that "resistance, political frustration and over-
reaction are easily provoked when external actors press for change,
express viewpoints or become involved in what is considered internal affairs" (Lewin 2000, 47). Initial concerns over the impact
of the CRC were that they would make exactly such provocation
more likely. Interviews with current UNICEF staff continue to

show a keen appreciation for the balancing act necessary when rights-based language and programming are used, which can be seen as particularly intrusive to a country's internal affairs. Though UNICEF expresses satisfaction that it has avoided provoking confrontation, this danger continues. Yet the perceived benefit of using the CRC as an advocacy tool continues to outweigh the dangers, and all UNICEF planning documents and MPOs continue to include references to the CRC and other rights documents.

### NEW PROGRAM AREAS

It has already been noted that UNICEF's interest in the CRC coincided with a gradual expansion of its mandate. In particular, the CEDC agenda—moving UNICEF away from its core mission of simple health, survival, and education interventions and toward a wider definition of child protection—seemed to fit well with the holistic picture of child welfare presented by the CRC. The CRC justified this move while also giving it both a specific reference point and an overall picture of child welfare toward which UNICEF might progress.

In some areas where the CRC raises controversial issues of children's rights—for example, those touching on a child's right to choose his or her religion, or anything to do with family planning—UNICEF has tended to argue that these rights are outside its purview and therefore not relevant to its operational goals. Where there are fewer such considerations, UNICEF has been more willing to take on new priorities. Thus UNICEF has used the CRC to justify an expansion of its mandate while also recognizing the need for political expediency. In other words, UNICEF itself, not its member states, has directed its expansion, albeit while it keeps in mind what is and is not in opposition to the wishes of powerful member states.

UNICEF argues that the evolution of its mandate has been a gradual, not sudden, process: "This evolution is a very natural transition for an organization so active in development activities and so concerned with the situation of children and women" (Pais 1999, 1). The view of human rights as interrelated suggests that "all human rights, civil, political, economic, social and cultural are inherent to the human dignity of every person. . . . Human rights must inform both national policies and international cooperation"

(Pais 1999, 1). There is very little talk in UNICEF documents even of prioritizing rights—of suggesting, for example, that survival rights might take precedence over political ones. This has caused considerable internal debate in certain situations, such as emergency relief efforts, with some staff members arguing that basic survival rights come first and others arguing that all rights were equally important. In most situations, however, such arguments either are not made or are made quietly; UNICEF is officially committed to pursuing a wide range of rights with equal fervor, and a number of new issues arise in its country programming documents.

A few new program areas deserve particular attention. One of these is the broad notion of legal reform to protect children's rights. In some countries this has taken a fairly wide definition, involving UNICEF in a great variety of children's rights issues. In Costa Rica, for example, UNICEF supported the creation of a Child and Adolescent Code approved by the government in late 1997; UNICEF lobbied successfully for the adoption of a similar code in Venezuela, reaching success in 1990; and in Brazil UNICEF was active from the mid-1980s (i.e., before the completion of the CRC) to effect legal change on the status of children (Lewin 2000, 23–29). Similarly, in Mali a new Protection Code was adopted to help the government implement the terms of the CRC, and the 1998–2002 Mali MPO states that "the UNICEF contribution [to the plan of operation] . . . is aimed at strengthening the legal framework, supporting the promotion of human rights as well as actions that aim to reduce the vulnerability of children and women that need special protection" (Rios-Kohn 2003, 5). Such wide-ranging involvement in constitutional and general legal reform marks a very broad involvement by UNICEF in national politics—one that is quite unusual for a UN specialized agency and certainly a far cry from UNICEF's original mandate. It also marks a substantial increase in UNICEF's operational scope and power.

More specifically, UNICEF has involved itself in particular legal changes to improve the situation of children in the countries where it operates. These include changing laws to deal with street children in Latin America, for example, and seeking the regulation of child labor practices (if not outright abolishment) in various parts of Asia and elsewhere. UNICEF has also recognized a specific responsibility to intervene, legally if necessary, to eliminate harmful traditional practices such as female genital mutilation, child marriage, and the systematic disenfranchisement of women, through legislative change and other means (UNICEF 2003b, 241). Each of these issues is carefully related back to provisions of the CRC or CEDAW, and each has been taken up with host governments in any number of cases. UNICEF has suggested that traditional behavior in host countries can have both positive and negative consequences for children's health and for the health of mothers but that legal analysis is necessary to assist in change where the impact is negative. "The administrative and legal frameworks that govern the relations between women, children and the State are important determinants of rights. . . . National legislation and, increasingly, decentralized government structures also need to be looked at for their compliance with CRC and CEDAW" (UNICEF 1998, 22–23).

UNICEF has at times intervened more directly. In Guatemala, for example, it has quietly assisted in a lawsuit with the state on behalf of street children. There was concern that this was too direct a confrontation with the government, but it has not had a noticeable negative impact on UNICEF's operations or relationships.

Another new function of UNICEF that deserves mention here, although not considered itself a programmatic area, is supporting the process of administrative change and particularly of administrative decentralization. The idea of decentralizing government in developing countries to promote human rights is common in current thinking, and central, for example, to the World Bank's agenda on governance, to be discussed in chapter 3. Though UNICEF, unlike the Bank or the International Monetary Fund, lacks the financial muscle to really push for government reorganization, it has made a decision to support the decentralization process. Putting authority in the hands of local government agencies, which are presumably more sensitive to the needs of children in their own jurisdiction, was a central strategic goal of the World Summit for Children, which took place in 1990 in conjunction with the approval of the CRC. Decentralization of authority, UNICEF argues, "fuel[s] local demand for coordinated social development, and for more coherent approaches to social service provision, especially at the point of delivery . . . and reinforce[s] a sense of social responsibility for children" (UNICEF 2006).

According to the rights-based program document for Nepal, "Strengthening decentralization and local systems to be more transparent and responsive to people through participation [and the community action process] were the central strategies towards promoting accountability" (Prasada 2001, 19.). The Nepal plan included a process of "Decentralized Planning for the Child Program" intended to "strengthen local planning processes to holistically address issues surrounding child survival and development" (Prasada 2001, 23). In Tanzania, "Local Government Reform is seen as one of the most important political and administrative reform processes. . . . The aim is to bring decision-making 'closer to the people' in order to enhance democracy and good governance" (UNICEF 2002, 13). Such involvement with local government and with host-country planning would have been unthinkable to UNICEF before the CRC but is now considered central to the CRC's implementation, and it means that UNICEF potentially may be taking part in highly charged political activities.

One other important area where UNICEF has expanded into new programming is its relationship with the Committee on the Rights of the Child. The committee was set up by the CRC to receive reports from states parties and to otherwise promote compliance with the CRC and international cooperation toward CRC implementation. When the CRC was being drafted, the possibility was raised of mentioning UNICEF specifically as a treaty-monitoring body. Grant and others within UNICEF decided against this role, determining that it was too political and would jeopardize UNICEF's ability to work cooperatively with member states. However, UNICEF has seen the CRC reporting process as an important way of leveraging its influence within host-state governments. A key document notes that "UNICEF must . . . find effective ways through the programming process to link its situation assessment and analysis in programming with the State's process for reporting under its treaty obligations to children and women" (UNICEF 1998, 14).

It is UNICEF policy to inject itself in each stage of the reporting and compliance process—to assist states in preparing their reports to the Committee on the Rights of the Child, to assist the committee with expert advice in evaluating the reports, and to offer its assistance to states to rectify those problems identified by the reporting process. Most country MPOs now include details about how the country office is planning either to help a country prepare its submission to the committee or to carry out the committee's suggestions for rights implementation. The approach to the committee is in many ways calculated to avoid political conflicts; once again, UNICEF is cognizant of the potential problems. So, for example, UNICEF is quite circumspect about the specific help it provides to states when they are preparing their reports to the committee. The overall goal of UNICEF is to become a key but quiet part of the process, injecting itself into the implementation of norms but through cooperative channels.

## CURRENT PROGRAM AREAS

As important as the CRC has become to UNICEF—and as much as it requires UNICEF to involve itself in issues and programs it has not traditionally tackled—the bulk of its work remains in what might be considered the traditional programming areas of health and nutrition, water and sanitation, education, and other areas related to child survival and development. Here, the impact of the CRC has been more ambiguous than in the newer programming areas. Though the CRC directs UNICEF into some new operational areas clearly promoted by rights-based thinking, it is harder to recognize exactly what a rights-based approach might be to the distribution of nutritional supplements, to the construction and equipping of schools, or to the promotion of immunization or early childhood development. This remains an ongoing project— and one in which resident representatives and others in the field have been able to innovate with limited guidance. New documents are now being created in New York, as well as at the Innocenti Centre, that clarify the meaning of the CRC in the technical areas of operations. Much of the work remains ad hoc, although progressively more is being done.

What a human rights approach means, primarily, is placing traditional programming areas within the context of the larger political and social themes of the CRC, as it is interpreted by UNICEF. UNICEF has focused on the need to bring concepts such as empowerment, equality, and voice to traditional water and sanitation, education, or nutrition. A first step, for example, involves linking UNICEF programming areas to a much more explicitly political agenda of policy setting at the national level. "The rights approach," according to one report, "requires UNICEF to play a vital role in working with national partners to improve policy"; this includes paying attention to "the links between a given policy and the realization of rights . . . [and] the degree to which a given policy is consistent with the human rights principles, including the best interests of the child, non-discrimination, participation and survival and development" (Rozga 2001, 4). There is also greater emphasis on working with other civil society partners (beyond national and local government) to help form a policy environment that is conducive to helping UNICEF with its work in its traditional policy areas. A rights-based approach means not only being able to work but also making UNICEF's priorities part of the national policy landscape.

Thus rights-based programming requires political change. A plan devised for Mali, for example, touts the legal changes made at the national level, including legal commitments in the areas of health care, nutrition, and education (Rios-Kohn 2003, 19–20). This process was to be enabled by a "transfer of power to the local level" in order to allow "local populations [to] assume control of their development and the satisfaction of their needs; . . . ultimately, decentralization would facilitate rights-holders to claim their rights" (Rios-Kohn 2003, 23). This situates the provision of traditional services within the larger framework of empowerment and the recognition of human rights. In a theme that will be repeated in discussing the World Bank, UNICEF sees a rights-based approach to traditional operations as one where citizens are empowered to make political demands that lead to better service provision and to the sort of situation where citizens can provide services for themselves. For example, a rights-based approach to sanitation is one where citizens themselves are able to demand and to some extent design and implement a sanitation project rather than waiting for government to do it for them. UNICEF cites a project in Brazil that specifically links participatory programming to the larger question of increasing democratic participation in Brazil (Theis 2004).

Similarly, a rights-based approach to traditional programming is one that pays attention to matters of equity and discrimination. Because the principle of nondiscrimination within the CRC requires UNICEF, under the new paradigm, to work with states to address problems on inequality, this principle also needs to be built into specific programming guidelines. So programs that fail to "reach the unreached" fail the test of implementing human rights, however successful they may be in the overall terms of increased service delivery. "Under a rights approach, the organization gives priority to the most disadvantaged children in the countries in greatest need. Issues of disparity and injustice are central concerns and programmes work towards ensuring that the marginalized, remote, or excluded have equal access to their rights" (Rozga 2001, 6). To help with this, the collection of disaggregated data remains a central priority; and these data are to be used to guide UNICEF operations and thus ensure that the unreached are brought into the mainstream.

UNICEF's overall joint health and nutrition strategy also moves rights to the center of programming in a technical area. Primarily, the strategy emphasizes those areas where UNICEF has traditionally been effective: access to nutritious and adequate foods, maternal care and education, effectiveness of health care provision, and a data-driven strategic basis, among other factors, to increase effectiveness. But the strategy also emphasizes the need to "reach unreached, marginalized, discriminated against and excluded children, . . . build capacities and empower rights holders, . . . [and] increase and monitor the performance of duty bearers and build their capacities as needed" (UNICEF 2005, 8). This requires more extensive data gathering and an attention to the political context of development. The strategy also helps to define more concretely what empowerment means in the specific context of health and nutrition: "This will include recognition of danger signs and improved care- and seeking behaviours, as well as improved behaviours and practices for a number of key maternal, newborn and child survival interventions" (UNICEF 2005, 14). Along with this effort, "UNICEF will promote, support, and strengthen national, subnational and community-based monitoring processes," again to increase community control over interventions and make government more accountable (UNICEF 2005, 15). The strategy of empowerment also includes working with new partners in civil society to enlist greater community resources.

Other more specific areas of health care also deserve mention. UNICEF has been at the forefront of developing the integrated management of childhood illness (IMCI) approach to health care delivery. This is intended as an integrated or holistic approach to childhood health care emphasizing preventive services, a few major health risks, and primary care. IMCI also focuses on strengthening community health care systems and on improving the responsiveness of local health care providers. It also emphasizes education for families, both to teach them how to take care of their own health (e.g., by taking steps to reduce risk factors in the home) and to help them demand better services from local health care providers. Like WHO (which also helped develop the IMCI approach), UNICEF considers this an element of a rights-based approach to health (or survival) programming and has begun to portray it as such in country programs (UNICEF 2002, 13).

Other programming areas, as they adapt to the needs of the CRC, are considering similar issues as the health and nutrition sectors. The CRC is not, for the most part, perceived as requiring a major overhaul in what UNICEF is doing in the more traditional, technical work sectors. If anything, there appears to have been some backing off from the idea of radical change. Much of this is the result of UNICEF's focus on achieving the Millennium Development Goals, a set of UN-determined development objectives to be reached by 2015. The effort to meet these benchmarks has, in the estimation of some, led to a reemphasizing of UNICEF's traditional core strengths at the expense of other objectives. Still, the CRC has permeated even those sectors whose staffs had initially been reluctant to consider new ways of operating, bringing to them a set of political and social goals to be integrated with older, more traditional measures of success.

## Conclusions

Seventeen years after the final draft of the CRC was presented to the UN General Assembly, the transformation of UNICEF's activities from the service-provision model to a rights-based approach remains incomplete. Interviews with UNICEF staff confirm that many within the organization remain unconvinced of the usefulness of the CRC at more than the rhetorical level, and top management still must contend with a certain passive resistance from staff at all grades. Yet UNICEF has made the most dramatic change of the three organizations here, in bringing human rights to the center of its operations. It has faced many of the same hurdles as others but has overcome them with greater success.

The most noteworthy issue regarding UNICEF's relationship with human rights has been the importance of individuals in advancing the agenda. It is true that in the mid-1980s some events at the level of the UNICEF executive board were preparing the way for an acceptance of the rights issue. These included both indirect and direct encouragement. The new emphasis on CEDC issues was one factor. The 1986 executive board directive to Jim Grant to take an interest in the CRC also cannot be ignored. Combined with the pressure from within UNICEF and from NGOs, it clearly spurred Grant to become involved in the drafting process. Still, the specifics of this action were clearly Grant's doing, as was the aftermath—in particular, the drive in the late 1980s to push for universal CRC ratification.

What was at stake for the various actors involved at this time? For the UNICEF executive board and particularly for Anwarul Chowdhury, a Bangladeshi who was chairman and a vocal advocate of the CRC, it had far less to do with specific instructions from host states (the CRC could hardly be said to be a top priority of states, particularly as the Cold War waned and its propaganda potential faded) than with matters of principle and expediency.[5] Chowdhury had been heavily lobbied by UNICEF true believers and NGOs and was convinced by them, rather than by his government (Newman-Williams 1999). The real direction of UNICEF involvement was set by those within the organization—both the executive director and those who were able to sway him to their line of thinking.

What was at stake for UNICEF? The initial interest by those in Geneva, and also by Chowdhury, appears to have been an actual matter of principle—rare enough in the international realm but not unheard of. There is no reason to suppose that UNICEF staff members such as Marjorie Newman-Black and others were motivated by anything more than a desire to see UNICEF help children as effectively as possible and by a belief that the CRC would help it to do so.

Grant's motivation is more complex. A great deal can be learned from the way he came to strongly support the CRC and to work hard for its ratification worldwide but then was content to set it aside and treat it as little more than a rhetorical device. For him, the CRC potentially served to increase the power of his organization: If there were universal ratification of the CRC, UNICEF would be in a stronger position to advocate change in program countries. What he did not want was to actually have the CRC dictate the nature of UNICEF's operations, particularly not while it was working on a set of goals (those arising from the Special Session on Children) to which it was committed.

The UNICEF executive board also played a role in moving this process forward. The role of the board in initiating interest has been noted already. After 1989, the board came to insist that MPOs refer to the CRC—at first looking to see if countries have ratified the CRC, and later checking that the CRC was being used in programming. One person intimately familiar with Grant's relationship with the board describes his attitude toward it as "a nuisance preventing full realization of his magnificent vision" and able to ignore them in pursuing his own goals.[6] The board itself is not entirely united in its support for the CRC, and the United States remains skeptical of its usefulness, considering it a distraction from more important issues. While the board has been interested in seeing a change at UNICEF, it had little ability to force change while Grant was in charge. There is also little the board can do in the short term about staff resistance to rights ideas. Indeed, Grant's resistance to the board's desire for fuller CRC implementation highlights the difficulty of managing UNICEF: It took a change in management, not the board, to move the CRC from rhetorical status to full programmatic integration.

After Grant pushed for universal ratification and made the CRC an important rhetorical tool, the next major change came when there was a change at the top, that is, the appointment of Carol Bellamy as director. Bellamy had a better, more cooperative relationship with the executive board but was of her own mind when it came to the CRC. The board did not change significantly in the mid-1990s; it was the UNICEF management that changed. Nor did the United States or other major states become noticeably more in favor of the CRC than in the past. Bellamy's decision to change UNICEF's strategic direction again came from her own interests, and not from the board, and the hindrances she faced had a great deal more to do with bureaucratic inertia than meddlesome states. She was no less aware than Grant of the potential pitfalls of a rights-based approach, and UNICEF planning documents repeatedly refer to the risk of damaging relations with states. But the benefits are seen to outweigh the risks.

Even before Bellamy's decision to integrate the CRC more fully into UNICEF programming, the process of CRC adoption was being driven primarily by internal forces, often far away from New York. So, too, was the process of actually interpreting how UNICEF would define rights. Whether in Dhaka or Florence, UNICEF was able to put its own "spin" on what the standards of the CRC would mean. Clearly it felt constrained by outside pressure; the avoidance of matters regarding family planning is proof of that. But it was also able to move to the center of its interpretation those issues from which it felt it got the most benefit, particularly the "best-interest principle," and to use other issues, such as nondiscrimination, to advance its interest. It is also important to see the imprint UNICEF's internal culture had on its definition of rights: The problem of how to implement rights, so important to a culture that focuses on decentralized planning and effective solutions, was vital in determining what rights actually meant in the UNICEF context.

UNICEF's interest in the CRC cannot be easily reduced to any single cause. Grant was convinced by the mid-1980s that the CRC would expand his power and help continue the child survival revolution; this was more important in shaping his approach than executive board activity or any bilateral relationship with member states. When he felt the CRC had reached the limit of its usefulness, he consigned it to the Public Affairs Department. Yet this was not the end of the concept; in a decentralized organization, there was plenty of opportunity for individuals, acting on principle or conviction, to work with the CRC, an activity accepted so long as it did not contradict the core UNICEF mission. A change of leadership also entailed a change of focus, as Bellamy brought her own calculation of what would make UNICEF most effective.

Though it's true that Bellamy, an American, was not exactly acting against the wishes of the American representative to the executive board, she was not exactly acting according to those wishes either. She was instead acting as any organizational director might, in the way she believed best pursued the organization's mandate and expanded its influence.

## Chapter Three

# The World Bank: Pushing at the Boundaries of "Economic"

Human rights issues present a particularly complex and troubling set of concerns for the World Bank. On the one hand, the general concept of human rights would seem to be tangential to the official mission of the World Bank, which is supposed to provide financing, in a strictly neutral way, for development projects. Although economic development and human rights are certainly connected, the missions of the United Nations Children's Fund (UNICEF) and the World Health Organization (WHO) would seem to be more directly related to making the lives of individuals better. On the other hand, the World Bank and its sister institution, the International Monetary Fund (IMF), have been more directly and stridently criticized for their human rights records than any other UN-affiliated bodies. "You can only hear people chanting 'fifty years is enough,' for so long," a Bank staff person was once overheard remarking, "before you figure you have to do something about it."

Technically the "World Bank" refers to the International Bank for Reconstruction and Development (IBRD) and the International Development Association (IDA), which in reality are not literally separate organizations but the names for the Bank's two lending "windows," or facilities; IBRD loans are made to middle-income and creditworthy poor countries, and IDA loans are made to the poorest countries in the world. Bank staff members are Bank staff members, not IBRD or IDA staff members. The "World Bank Group" includes these two organizations and three actually separate agencies, the International Finance Corporation, the Multilateral Investment Guarantee Agency, and the International Center for the Settlement of Investment Disputes. In terms of budget and influence, the Bank dwarfs the other two institutions under study in this volume. In 2004, for example, UNICEF spent $1.6 billion while the World Bank group made lending commitments of more than $20 billion. The same is true regarding the importance that the United States and other large Western countries place on the Bank's activities. Though the work of WHO and UNICEF can have important symbolic meaning for the major industrial states (e.g., around family planning issues or HIV/AIDS), the Bank has both a direct and indirect impact on their financial well-being. Given the volume of criticism directed at the Bank and IMF, few other international organizations feel the same pressure from civil society to reform their practices.

It is not easy to sort out all the things that contribute to decision making at the Bank. But it is clear that many powerful factors, both internal and external, press on an institution with this level of visibility and influence. The Bank's history, one of change and evolution, reinforces this impression. Yet any number of studies of the Bank have attempted to reduce its policymaking to a single causal factor. It is not unusual to read that the Bank's policies are dictated to it by the U.S. government, by the demands of global capital, by the intellectual dominance of U.S. and British universities, or by sheer inertia. To be sure, all the UN institutions have had the same things said about them, but the Bank and IMF are generally held up as the prime examples of how these forces come into play.

An analysis of Bank policy, therefore, presents a particularly good opportunity to study the capacity of international organizations to change and set their agenda. Many of the factors that might lead to organizational independence—such as size and complexity, professionalism, and independent funding sources—are present in the case of the World Bank. Conversely, the Bank more than UNICEF or WHO directly affects the preferences of powerful states, and it is involved in an issue area where strong regional preferences are also at work. As the Bank has grown and evolved, its top managers have struggled to assert their independence from member states in day-to-day operations, and they have seen this independence as vital to the organization's success. As will be discussed below, this need for independence from state pressures has at times been cited as a reason *not* to develop a more assertive human rights policy. This position argues that rights are inherently political and that therefore getting involved in their promotion would open the Bank to charges of political manipulation. Despite this concern, the Bank has begun to think seriously about its obligations toward international human rights standards. In doing so, it has responded to civil society pressures, to the preferences of its own staff, and to the concerns of member states. The successes and failures of this evolution say a great deal about how decisions are made in a large international institution.

## Adoption

Although WHO can trace its genesis to the Sanitary Conferences of the nineteenth century, and UNICEF can point to initial interest in children's rights during the League of Nations era, the form and function of the World Bank (initially just the IBRD facility) were almost entirely set during the Bretton Woods conference of 1944 and in its immediate wake. Rather than building on a previous, incomplete idea, the IBRD was invented from whole cloth to fill a gap in the international financial architecture. The IBRD—conceived at the same time as its sister institution, the IMF—was intended to form part of the structure of a new, more stable postwar economic system. Like the IMF, the Bank has evolved over time and changed its mission to suit new conditions and new needs in the international system.

The general goal of the IBRD's designers was a very practical one: to overcome essential market imperfections that had hampered the growth and stability of international trade. At the same time, the Bank served a humanitarian purpose, as it was designed first to aid with the reconstruction of war-ravaged Europe. The idea of a more general development policy, once Europe was back on its feet, was also implicit in the organization's founding, and the early IBRD did take loan applications from such countries as Chile, Mexico, and Iran (Kapur, Lewis, and Webb 1997, 71–77).

The evolution of the World Bank from its original reconstruction role in the 1940s to an organization dedicated to international development provides important insight into the ability of international organizations to evolve and to set their own priorities. More so than the other two institutions under study here, the story of the Bank, and later the World Bank Group, is one of regular change and redefinition. As Kapur and his colleagues point out, the process of development and how to define it was at best understood only vaguely in the 1940s (Kapur, Lewis, and Webb 1997, 67). As the role of the Bank changed from reconstruction to development, it was inevitable that the Bank and its board of directors would have to give a great deal of thought to what its strategies and mission would be. Thus, to understand the Bank's approach to human rights, it is important to grasp both its understanding of development and its ability to change this understanding over time. Both issues play an important role in the way the organization views its range of options.

The question of a human rights policy was not directly considered in the Bank's early years. This is hardly surprising, given that both the Bank and the concept of international human rights were then in their infancy. A key factor that remains a defining feature of its human rights considerations is the guarantee of political neutrality written into its charter. The mandate of the central components of the World Bank, as written in the Articles of Agreement of the IBRD and IDA, are strictly to assist in the *economic* development of borrowers. The IBRD's Articles of Agreement (World Bank 1989a), for example, give its mission as "assist[ing] in the reconstruction and development of territories of members by facilitating the investment of capital for productive purposes . . . and the encouragement of the development of productive facilities and resources in less developed countries" (Article I[1]), and "assisting in raising productivity, the standard of living and conditions of labor" in developing or recovering countries (Article I[3]). IDA, the Bank's other main lending "window," has a similarly limited mandate, formulated when it was added to the IBRD. Article I of IDA's Articles of Agreement (International Development Association 1960) makes no mention of any political goals, although, as one observer notes of both institutions, "neither [one's] Articles define the term 'development'" (Bradlow 1996b, 53). In other words, although politics is expressly excluded from the Bank's deliberations on lending, the definition of development leaves room for many considerations that might infringe on the political.

More to the point, the IBRD Articles of Agreement contain a clause stating that "[t]he Bank and its officers shall not interfere in the political affairs of any member; nor shall they be influenced in their decisions by the political character of the member or members concerned. *Only economic considerations shall be relevant to their decisions"* (Article IV[10]; emphasis added). The IDA Articles of Agreement contain almost identical language (Article V[6]) This language was inserted to ensure the neutrality of the Bank toward member countries, and to prevent it from using its financial clout on behalf of some members in order to interfere with the internal affairs of others. Early Bank presidents saw this as being vitally important for the Bank's financial soundness, because it ensured that it would stick to financially sound policies and not allow politics to lead it into bad investments (Shihata 1991). Otherwise, it was feared, the institution would not be able to raise money on the world financial markets, because investors might fear that a politicized agenda at the World Bank would lead it to make poor lending decisions. Politicizing the Bank, it was argued, would also jeopardize its fiduciary responsibility to its stockholders, a responsibility the Bank takes as seriously as any private corporation (Mikesell 1972, 70). The IBRD and IDA Articles of Agreement thus set out the purposes for which loans can be used, and how projects are to be evaluated for financial soundness.

Two examples are widely cited as challenging the Bank's statutory and actual neutrality regarding politics. During the 1960s the UN General Assembly passed resolutions prohibiting the Bank from giving financial assistance to South Africa or Portugal, in South Africa's case because of the apartheid regime, and in Portugal's because of its failure to grant independence to its colonies. The Bank's legal department strongly resisted both the idea that internal politics ought to affect lending decisions and also the supposition that the Bank is bound by UN resolutions (Brown 1992, 127–50; World Bank 1967). As it happened the Bank soon found other reasons to deny loans to these two countries. The controversy also led to an official statement that political concerns *might* be relevant *if* they had an impact on a state's financial soundness (Shihata 1988, 44), suggesting that there was some room to accommodate the wishes of the General Assembly in the future.

As the Bank's mission itself has evolved, so has its approach to interpreting its Articles of Agreement. Its early focus on the primary definition of development as expanding gross domestic product in borrower countries was changed largely by the strong presence of Robert McNamara, who as president shifted its focus to poverty alleviation and a focus on social development (George and Sabelli 1994, 37–57). Ayres in particular notes the degree to which this change was brought about by McNamara's own convictions and managerial discretion rather than by member states (Ayres 1983, 66). In the 1980s the Bank similarly evolved through the early years of structural adjustment toward a greater focus on human development and, by the 1990s, a concern for social safety nets.

The Bank also has been expanding its interpretation of what is an economic matter, and therefore relevant to lending decisions, almost from the time of the decisions on South Africa and Portugal. As the Bank expanded its operations to include issues of poverty, for example, it was forced to make judgments "about who the poor are and who the relative winners and losers in [Bank projects] ought to be" (Bradlow 1996b, 56). The adoption of an antipoverty, people-centered paradigm has led, among other things, to a substantial effort to incorporate sociological factors in the design of development projects, both as means and as ends to development (Cernea 1985). Such changes were of course occurring elsewhere in the development establishment, although the Bank, as a key intellectual leader, was important in setting the overall tone. In the same way that distributive issues required the Bank to rethink its Articles of Agreement in the 1970s, in the 1980s structural adjustment lending also required the Bank take up political issues and to create new policies. But, notes Shihata, "in doing so, . . . [the Bank] has been careful not to depart from explicit requirements in its Articles and not to act outside its legally authorized powers." The Bank's legal department decided that adjustment lending, and its overtly political components, could be justified under Article III (4[vii]) of the Articles of Agreement, allowing the Bank to make loans in special circumstances that depart from the strictly neutral, project lending originally envisioned by the Bank's founders (Shihata 1991). With program loans justified under this clause, the definition of what was an economic factor in lending decisions could be considerably expanded.

The Bank's strategy, therefore, has been to widen the scope of what can be considered an economic issue, without actually departing from its insistence that it considers only economic factors and creditworthiness when approving a loan. "To date," Bradlow says, "the distinction the Bank draws between 'economic' and 'political' factors has been based on the impact the particular factor has on considerations of efficiency and economy. On this basis, the Bank has defined an economic factor, within the meaning of the Bank's Articles of Agreement, as any factor that has a 'direct and obvious economic effect relevant of the [Bank's] work'" (Bradlow 1996b, 59). This allows the Bank both to expand its definition of development (e.g., to include poverty reduction or gender issues) and the tools it uses to promote development (e.g., civil service and legal reform) without changing its mission from an ostensibly economic one and—just as important for present purposes—without threatening its fiduciary responsibility as a lender bound by prudent business practices. Much of the discussion about extending the scope of the Articles of Agreement has centered around the promotion of human rights (Marmorstein 1978), although other areas have also been revised.

This expansion of what might be considered economic has had important effects on the way the Bank plans and designs development projects. As the Bank developed a greater social conscience during and after the McNamara years, it equally came under growing criticism from a global civil society more aware of the effects of Bank projects and more mobilized to push for change where these projects were considered to have negative social consequences. For example, the Bank began to speak seriously about the protection of indigenous (or tribal) peoples in 1982, with its policy guidelines on "Tribal Peoples in Bank-Financed Projects" (Operational Manual Statement 2.34), largely in response to public criticism of the effects on indigenous peoples of Bank-financed projects. These included timber plantations in India, which displaced the Muria people; the displacement of indigenous peoples in Amazonia and the disruption of their traditional ways of life, caused by various development projects; and the planned flooding in the Philippines of land owned by the Kalinga and Bontoc peoples (Griffiths and Colchester 2000). On the basis of earlier research done under the Bank's auspices, the new directives in 1982 recognized the greater vulnerability of indigenous peoples, as well as their unique way of life and connection to the land on which they lived, and set out guidelines for how they were to be protected in the course of Bank-financed projects (Davis 1993, 3). Though this was not a rights policy per se, it had elements of one—in its emphasis on protecting individuals, increasing political participation by the disenfranchised (an aspect of Bank guidelines toward indigenous peoples from early on), and particularly the need to consider social as well as economic factors in development planning. These policies were revised and expanded in 1992 (largely in response to concerns that the 1982 guidelines were being ignored) and again were revised in a process culminating in 2005.

Similar to protections for indigenous peoples, the Bank also has recognized the need to incorporate policies to protect people forcibly displaced by development projects, particularly those involving dam construction. Once again this recognition was forced on the Bank by public relations disasters and the ensuing outcry from global civil society. The Bank instituted its first policy in 1980—around the same time as the indigenous peoples policy—with similar goals, to ensure that the rights of affected people were taken into consideration by Bank planners and member states (Fox 1998, 304). As with its indigenous peoples policy, its policy on involuntary resettlement was reviewed and later revised, after it became clear that Bank staff and borrower countries were failing to live up to its requirements (Fox 1998, 309). This policy, like that on indigenous peoples, was not forced on the Bank by its member states; though some supported it, others (particularly borrower countries) opposed it, because it meant greater restrictions and outside oversight in development projects, and even those that supported it were hardly decisive in their influence. These outcomes were the result of the Bank bowing to outside pressure and of institutional concern about the limits that might be placed on the Bank's effectiveness in the future if it did not work to repair its image within international civil society.

## The World Bank and Women

Probably the World Bank's most explicit set of human rights standards for its lending operations is its policy toward gender and development. This policy, known as Women in Development (WID), has become, at least rhetorically, an important and pervasive component of World Bank strategic thinking; the Bank has had an official WID adviser since 1977, and it has had a growing interest in the issue ever since (World Bank 2001b, 2). By 2003 the Bank employed approximately 115 gender experts (Zuckerman and Qing 2003, 18).

Once again both internal and external pressure helped push the Bank to create an explicit policy toward women in development. In the most comprehensive description of the policy's early years (and an excellent examination of the Bank's evolution), Josette Murphy (1995) notes the impact of the decision by the UN General Assembly to designate 1975 as International Women's Year. This was acknowledged by the Bank's president, Robert McNamara, who said that "in connection with the international Women's Year designation, . . . the Bank is reviewing its activities, particularly in the field of education, to make a more direct and effective contribution toward improving the situation of women in the developing countries" (Murphy 1995, 26). There had been an internal Bank "working group" on women's issues as far back as 1973, created by a group of women employees as an "informal WID lunch group." These women were in turn "influenced by the Washington-based women's circles advocating attention to women's issues," and their objective was "to promote WID issues within the Bank" (Razavi and Miller 1995, 33). By 1974 a few Bank field staff had, largely on their own initiative, built consideration of some gender-oriented issues into specific lending decisions (Murphy 1995, 26).

Concern over women's role in development, and about the effects (too often negative, but potentially positive) of Bank lending on women, did not originally develop within the Bank. These issues were picked up by Bank staff from outside, where the topic of women in development was gaining prominence. Though one study of this issue has suggested that nongovernmental organizations (NGOs) were too focused on the effects on women of structural adjustment to advocate effectively for WID in general (Razavi and Miller 1995, 29), it is clear that the Bank and its staff were drawing on the more general movement within both the UN and the NGO community to give more consideration to women's issues, and it is hard to see how the Bank would have made the changes it did without such outside sources of ideas and pressure. Still, though the women's movement had been criticizing the Bank since the mid-1970s, it was "markedly slow," in the words of one report, "in its response to the concerns of women's movements" (O'Brien et al. 2000, 42). Twenty years later the Bank's Operations

Evaluation Department (OED), now called the Independent Evaluation Group, also noted that the Bank had been slow to react to pressures from both the U.S. executive director, who in 1975 asked for periodic progress reports, and also the United Nations, which requested that the Bank contribute to the international conference on women planned for Mexico City that year (Murphy 1995). These requests, however, clearly indicate that by the 1970s women's concerns were beginning to permeate the development community, which in turn was putting pressure on the Bank to come to grips with the issue of gender in development. The events around and just after the Mexico City conference led the Bank to create its first WID advisory post in 1975.

During the 1975–85 period (between the Mexico City conference and the Beijing Fourth World Conference on Women), the Bank gradually increased its attention to women's issues, although without great change in its overall operations. The clear picture that develops from this period is one of multiple sources of concern—pressure from the U.S. government and the Bank's executive board in general, from civil society groups (notably NGOs), from the UN, and from within the Bank itself. Murphy's study notes, interestingly, the importance of pressure from Bank managers' wives "for whom seminars on WID issues were offered during annual meetings" (Murphy 1995, 34). Ideas, in other words, were coming from diverse sources, including internal true believers not dissimilar to the UNICEF staff members in Geneva who became early advocates for the Convention on the Rights of the Child. Despite these pressures, however, this first decade of concern for women was marked by extremely limited actual progress within the organization and little or no real results in programming. The job of WID adviser was largely limited, by all accounts, to being an apologist for the Bank's failure to develop a more comprehensive policy (Kardam 1991, 77), and little was accomplished during this period beyond the rhetorical (World Bank 2005b, 2).

The development of a more comprehensive WID policy within the Bank accelerated in the second half of the 1980s, following the Beijing conference; there was a steady institutionalization of gender expertise as well as a development of the rationale for a WID policy. Yet "[the] problem of inadequate resources for the gender equity concern within the Bank, and a lack of effective powers over

Bank policies and processes, has plagued . . . efforts to 'mainstream' a Women in Development focus in the Bank's work" (O'Brien et al. 2000, 43). The original WID adviser had resigned in 1985 after complaining about the lack of resources devoted to that issue, as well as the lack of authority over Bank personnel. Barber Conable, who took over as Bank president from McNamara in 1986, brought a number of changes to highlight the issue of women. The WID office was (slightly) expanded at this time and given a new institutional home within the Population and Human Resources Department. Conable further signaled his interest in pursuing WID issues. More important, as the OED report describes it, Conable began working closely with the Bank's executive board, which in 1990 had expressed concern that WID was progressing too slowly, and he asked for more regular updates (Murphy 1995, 45). Thus the Bank's experience with women in the early years again parallels UNICEF's work with the Convention on the Rights of the Child, where the interests of the board and of the organization's management develop in parallel as new development priorities are incorporated.

The impetus to develop a WID policy came from a number of sources, both within and outside the Bank. It is also fair to say that the actual shape of this policy was a collective, and often ad hoc, effort. As late as 1999 an internal Bank study complained that the Bank's overall gender policy could be determined only after piecing together various policy statements and operational directives, and that there were several important gaps in the policy, whether the policy was intended to focus on all countries or only those showing a high degree of gender disparity. It also notes that the key official statements on Bank policy—an Operational Manual Statement in 1984 (2.20) and an Operational Policy (OP 4.20) in 1994, which has since been revised several times (World Bank 2005b, 3)—remained vague and uncertain in where and how they are applicable to Bank projects. Institutionally, progress has been halting, although the trajectory has been clear enough. By 1990 the senior vice president for operations had instructed regional offices to appoint WID representatives; the Bank's 1993 reorganization further buttressed the position of WID within the organizational hierarchy; and a Gender and Development (GAD) unit was created in 1997 as part of the Bank's reorganization (World Bank 2005b,

51–55; Murphy 1995, 49). The creation of the GAD unit was intended to replace a more piecemeal approach, with a broader emphasis on gender issues stretching across Bank operational areas. It was located within the Bank's new Poverty Reduction and Economic Management Network, to emphasize the close link between gender issues and the Bank's core mission of poverty reduction (Zuckerman and Qing 2003, 17).

## Governance

Perhaps the most rights-oriented of all recent World Bank policy developments was the move in the 1990s to incorporate a governance agenda into Bank thinking. The concept of governance, more so than any other set of policies, spurred some members of the Bank's executive board to question whether the institution was beginning to violate its commitment to remain nonpolitical, and it also triggered a variety of publications on the Bank's relationship with human rights. In recent years the Bank's concept of good governance has become somewhat less comprehensive, focusing in particular on anticorruption strategies and an enabling environment for economic development at the expense of the more wide-ranging agenda identified in early years. Yet it is still an official part of Bank development planning and an important overarching theme in the Bank's view of sustainable development.

The Bank's initial interest in promoting good governance in borrower states was primarily a result of the controversies arising from the structural adjustment programs of the 1980s (Davis 2004; Miller-Adams 1999; Marquette 2003). Two distinct factors deserve mention. On the one hand, the evident failure of these programs to produce consistent results in economic development led to a reevaluation of the role of the state in managing economic change and a new focus on the importance of institutional arrangements (Burki and Perry 1998, 1–7). At the same time, the terrible social costs of structural adjustment seemed to run counter to the most basic goals of the World Bank and led to calls for a reassessment of the balance between purely economic matters and the Bank's responsibility to address the social situation within a country (World Bank 1990). This, too, led to a new interest in the institutional environment within countries.

The Bank's official interest in governance begins with *Sub-Saharan Africa: From Crisis to Sustainable Growth* (World Bank 1989b). This report notes that "Sub-Saharan Africa now has witnessed almost a decade of falling per capita incomes and accelerating ecological degradation" despite the efforts of donors to encourage debt reduction and restructuring (p. 17). The study does not criticize adjustment programs directly, although it notes that "responsibility for Africa's economic crisis is shared," and that "governments and donors alike must be prepared to change their thinking fundamentally in order to revive Africa's fortunes" (p. 2). And in fact, the report covers a large number of reasons for Africa's economic decline, ranging from unfavorable international terms of trade to deteriorating railways. It does conclude that "underlying the litany of Africa's development problems is a crisis of governance" (p. 60); "by governance is meant the exercise of political power to manage a nation's affairs. Because countervailing power has been lacking, state officials in many countries have served their own interests without fear of being called to account. . . . At worst the state becomes coercive and arbitrary" (pp. 60–61). *Sub-Saharan Africa: From Crisis to Sustainable Growth* suggested that a country's political culture—not just the policies it followed but also the manner in which they were determined and carried out, and the political climate in general—was a key factor in development and could not be ignored by those providing external development assistance.

In 1992 the Bank further refined the concept of governance with the publication of the booklet *Governance and Development* (World Bank 1992b). In his preface to this essay, President Lewis Preston wrote that "efficient and accountable management by the public sector and a predictable and transparent policy framework are critical to the efficiency of markets and governments, and hence to economic development" (p. v). Focusing on specific "institutional characteristics for managing development" (p. 9), the essay divided the general concept "governance" into four categories:

1. Public-sector reform, with a primary emphasis on strengthening the effectiveness of public agencies and the quality of their personnel.
2. Accountability, by which the Bank means "holding public officials responsible for their actions" (World Bank 1992b,

13). Most important, this means combating corruption and the "capture" of government by narrow, self-interested groups, but it also includes holding public officials accountable for poor performance through more careful monitoring and, presumably but not explicitly, some level of democratic choice.

3. The "legal framework for development," especially a set of legal rules known in advance by those engaged in business and applied in a fair and impartial manner.

4. Information and transparency, so that those engaged in business can make informed and rational decisions, and those attempting to hold public officials accountable are not kept in ignorance of government activities.

The World Bank's new emphasis on governance involved it in exactly the sort of political questions that its charter forbids it to consider, prompting the legal department to go to considerable lengths to determine where it must draw the line between allowable and unallowable activities. "It is perfectly clear," wrote Ibrahim Shihata, the Bank's chief legal counsel, "that the Bank's purpose is not to substitute itself for the peoples and governments of its borrowing member countries in deciding how these countries are to be governed" (Shihata 1991, 80). Yet the concept of governance was broad enough to raise fears, or hopes, of the Bank doing exactly that. If nothing else, the very breadth and ambiguity of the governance concept makes it difficult to know where the line can be drawn between economic and political decisions, as the Bank itself well knows (Shihata 1991, 80).

In her excellent study of the governance concept within the Bank, Michelle Miller-Adams (1999) notes the influence of "internal advocates" in the concept's development, as well as the relatively cooperative approach taken by states, even those in Africa most directly criticized by Shihata's 1991 report. Adams describes a relatively organization-driven process throughout the early 1990s, when a number of study groups and task forces were created to develop the new ideas surrounding the importance of government reform in development (Miller-Adams 1999, 112–14). Clearly, there were also external forces at work; as Heather Marquette shows, a focus on the nature of regimes in developing countries, and in particular a focus on such issues as transparency, participation, and even democracy, had gradually been working their way into the intellectual mainstream among development experts (Marquette 2003, 40–50). By the mid-1990s several Western nations, including the United States, were also advocating a greater emphasis on governance issues within the Bank and were supporting lending in this area. The United States made it clear that such issues as corruption and transparency were now vital development priorities, and they became integrated into bilateral U.S. development support as well.

In a process very similar to that seen in UNICEF, Miller-Adams describes the development of specific ideas regarding governance reform in Bank lending as taking place in regions well removed from the organization's headquarters. In particular, the Africa region "was engaged in its own institutional exercise exploring how to apply the governance issues that had been raised in the [Sub-Saharan Africa study]" (Miller-Adams 1999, 113). This is a surprising observation, perhaps, given the more centralized structure and organizational culture of the World bank compared with UNICEF, but it indicates the importance (repeated, to a lesser extent, in WHO's own experience with change) of intellectual ferment at the periphery of the organization acting on a center that was increasingly open to new ideas. Again, it also emphasizes the internal learning process that characterized the new interest in governance; this process particularly stemmed from the Bank's failures in Africa, although the internal process was helped along by the larger international environment, which supported change in this area.

Ultimately, however, it is important to emphasize leadership from the top of the institution in explaining the elevation of governance to a key Bank development strategy. Marquette in particular describes the hesitance of Bank staff to engage in this "new" area outside their expertise; as is shown below, bureaucratic inertia has been as powerful a force at the Bank as it has been at WHO and UNICEF, and it plays a key role in this story. Though a number of internal advocates at various levels pressed for a governance-based approach to development, James Wolfensohn's appointment as the Bank's president in 1995 was a key moment. Wolfensohn also put his unique mark on the governance issue, emphasizing the anticorruption aspect (Marquette 2003, 76; Miller-Adams 1999,

120). His refusal to place the same emphasis on other parts of governance as on anticorruption has left some feeling unsure about the future of human rights within the governance agenda, because they are unsure about other rights-based initiatives; though there is clearly an appreciation of the rights-related importance of governance (and for that matter, of protection for minorities, the forcibly displaced, etc.), the bureaucratic resistance to these new emphases in the Bank's programming has never been fully overcome. As the remainder of this chapter shows, progress toward an integrated rights-based programming agenda has been halting. Nevertheless, without the direct interest of Wolfensohn, it is likely that even less would have been accomplished. What is not clear at the time of this writing is how the new Bank president, Paul Wolfowitz, will help or hinder progress in this area, because staff remain uncertain as to his intentions regarding the rights agenda in general.

## Definition

Despite the World Bank's statutory prohibition on considering "political" issues in its lending decisions or project development, it has in fact recognized the need to think about human rights issues and other social concerns and to consider how they are affected by lending decisions. It has done this by both changing its management structure and altering the paradigm within which it undertakes development. Though the Bank is an institution dedicated to promoting development, that very concept is difficult to define, and as it has evolved, room has opened up within Bank operations to consider various priorities that tend to support rights concerns. The Bank, in other words, is able to redefine the border between political and nonpolitical in development. This has given it leeway to consider issues that have important political implications.

The official attitude of the World Bank toward its positive human rights responsibilities for some time has been to argue that in the course of pursuing its mandate—that is, to promote development and alleviate poverty—it is in fact working to support a variety of human rights goals. A straightforward version of this argument was made in 1991 by Shihata, largely in response to the interest in human rights that arose from the institution's new

governance policies. Despite the legal restrictions on its operations, he noted that "the Bank certainly can play, and has played,
within the limits of its mandate, a very significant role in promoting various economic and social rights" (Shihata 1991, 109). The
rights promoted include (109–32):

- The right to development, as adopted in United Nations
  Resolution 41/128.
- The right to be free from poverty, as stated particularly in
  Article 11 of the International Covenant on Economic, So-
  cial, and Cultural Rights (ICESCR).
- The right to education, as contained in Article 13 of the
  ICESCR.
- The right to health, from Article 25 of the Universal Decla-
  ration of Human Rights.
- The human rights of women, addressed in the Convention
  on the Elimination of all Forms of Discrimination Against
  Women, as well as other documents.
- The rights of refugees.
- Environmental rights, following the 1972 UN Conference
  on the Human Environment's "Action Plan."
- The right not to be subject to involuntary resettlement with-
  out compensation and other safeguards, now a part of official Bank policy for projects that will potentially displace
  peoples.

Each of these rights stems from the more general mission of
the Bank to promote development. Thus building schools as part of
a general development program promotes the right to education;
protecting the environment to better use its resources promotes
the right to a healthy environment; and so forth. In this approach
political rights are secondary concerns; according to a 1994 World
Bank report, "Although human rights are in a larger sense indivisible, the World Bank . . . deals with those aspects of human rights
relevant to its mandate" (World Bank 1994, 53).

At first glance this might seem a rather self-serving attitude. If
the Bank is indeed contributing to the promotion of these rights,
it could appear to be only accidentally doing so, rather than deliberately. Peter Uvin (2002) has—entirely rightfully—criticized this

reasoning as a sleight of hand, which merely repackages old policies in more rhetorically acceptable ways. To be fair, however, the Bank's "people-centered" human development approach—which was institutionalized in response to the debt crisis—has been accompanied by a noticeable shift in actual lending policies. Lending commitments in social sector categories (human development; social development, gender, and inclusion; and social protection and risk management) totaled $6.67 billion in 2005 (including both IBRD and IDA lending) out of total lending commitments of $22.31 billion, making up about 30 percent of total lending (World Bank 2002d, 56–57). In 1990 only about 12 percent of Bank lending went to education or to health and nutrition programs, and there was no "social protection" sector, as there is now (World Bank 1991, 179); ten years before, that figure was about 5 percent. Whether 30 percent is large compared with what it once was, or small compared with what it ought to be, is a subjective question; but it does represent a real shift in institutional priorities and, more important, in the day-to-day operations of the Bank. Lending of this type, of course, is not itself a human rights policy per se, but it does show that resources have moved into program areas with some implications for rights promotion—the link between social spending and human rights, as the Bank sees it, which is discussed below.

## The Bank's Safeguard Policies

The most straightforward example of human rights policies accepted by the World Bank are its so-called safeguard policies. (It should be noted, however, that the concept of safeguard policies was not articulated by the Bank until 1997, bringing institutional order to what had been an ad hoc process; Davis 2004, 24.) Although the Bank has a number of such policies, ranging from cultural property to pest management, the two most relevant here are those related to indigenous peoples and to populations subject to involuntary resettlement. These policies, as noted above, were largely stimulated by the public relations disasters surrounding a number of large-scale Bank projects, such as the Sardar Sarovar Dam in India.

The key safeguard policies discussed here are designed to prevent the (accidental) violation of basic human rights by Bank-funded projects. In this respect, the policies represent an effort to prevent the Bank from violating international human rights treaty law—not the same thing as a policy to actively promote human rights. To further clarify that this was not a rights policy, early documents on indigenous peoples, for example, actually relied heavily on the argument from effectiveness, making a case that the protection of indigenous cultures was important in the economic development process because of the local knowledge they can provide or the intrinsic value of tribal lands—in other words, this was an effort to play down still further the rights implications of what was clearly intended as a rights-oriented policy. The argument from effectiveness makes the case that an ethical policy is in fact justified by purely practical matters rather than by ethical considerations.

A closer look at the Bank's indigenous peoples policy, however, reveals a recognition of the need to take steps towards defining the rights of indigenous peoples, and, more important, a respect for both so-called negative and positive rights. The Bank's rewritten operational directive on indigenous peoples states this clearly: "This policy," it begins, "contributes to the Bank's mission of poverty reduction and sustainable development by ensuring that the development process fosters full respect for the dignity, human rights, and cultures of Indigenous Peoples" (World Bank 2004c). A Bank-sponsored study of the development of the indigenous peoples policy draws a direct connection between the protection of indigenous peoples and the wider effort to promote participation and social development. "This policy," the study puts it, "is more in keeping with current international thinking on the rights of indigenous peoples, as well as . . . recognizing the social and economic rights of poor and marginalized peoples throughout the world" (Davis 1993, 14). Galit Sarfaty, writing in the *Yale Law Journal*, makes the connection more directly between the indigenous peoples policy and human rights: "International organizations," she writes, "particularly the financial institutions, are becoming central players in promoting compliance with human rights norms . . . by adopting operational policies on issues like indigenous peoples, involuntary resettlement, and environmental assessment, the World Bank has emerged as an important actor in the interpretive community for public international law" (Sarfaty 2005, 1792). She goes even further, suggesting that the Bank is an effective force in convincing states to recognize and protect indigenous peoples' rights themselves: "Once its indigenous peoples policy was adopted, the Bank began to apply the policy to borrower countries to encourage them to internalize indigenous rights norms" (1812).

The actual terms of the Bank's new OP 4.10 on indigenous peoples, adopted in 2004, retains language noting the need to respect the rights of indigenous peoples, although the degree to which it represents an improvement over the earlier Operational Directive (OD) 4.20 remains controversial. The central controversy with the new rules, as with the old, was over the amount of participation that indigenous peoples will have in decisions that affect their lives. Many indigenous peoples' groups and their supporters pushed for incorporation of the rule of "free prior informed consent" over development projects that affect indigenous peoples. The previous rule, OD 4.20, had mentioned only "informed participation" and a process of "direct consultation" with affected groups. OP 4.10, which works concurrently with the related Bank Policy 4.10, uses the standard of "free prior informed *consultation,*" which one analyst describes as a "culturally-appropriate and collective decision-making process subsequent to meaningful and good faith consultation and informed participation regarding the preparation and implementation of projects" (MacKay 2005, 81; emphasis added). It pointedly is not a "veto" power given to indigenous peoples, which the "free prior informed consent" would have been; the notion that indigenous peoples would have such power was strongly resisted by a number of executive directors, who found it contrary to both the Bank's Articles of Agreement and the principle of sovereignty (because it would undermine the ability of national governments to set development policy) (MacKay 2005, 78–79). In this respect, the updated policy represents a step forward, but not nearly as large a step as many advocacy groups had hoped for.

Similarly, the Bank has updated its safeguard policies regarding those subject to involuntary resettlement. Here, too, the policy has come under substantial criticism for some of its substantive content; for example, by covering only "direct economic and social impacts" that result from Bank projects rather than taking a broader view of the costs of resettlement. The policy is also weaker than that on indigenous peoples in terms of guaranteeing that those affected by projects will share in the benefit stream of the project. Still, the resettlement policies are a recognition of the rights of those negatively affected by Bank-financed projects. The rights recognized here are, for the most part, negative in scope; they cover the right not to be deprived of property without just compensation, the right to political participation (to the extent that people can at least have a say in the decisions that directly affect their lives), the right to health care and similar services (to the extent they are damaged by resettlement plans), and the right to have protection for cultural assets, for a "way of life." They might be summarized as a right to be protected from unwarranted government-caused long-term hardship, impoverishment, and environmental damage.

An important part of defining the rights of these groups—both indigenous peoples and those subject to involuntary resettlement—is the turn by the World Bank in the past couple of decades to the work done by sociologists on marginalized groups. It was the recognition by champions of environmental causes and sustainable development that certain groups of people in developing countries faced challenges due to their vulnerability that helped drive the need for protections policies. The idea became, in essence, that the impact of development had to be defined more broadly than its mere economic result—and that certain groups, such as indigenous peoples, and those needing to be relocated due to projects, were more likely to be hurt than helped by such projects.

More important, sociologists and other social scientists began to suggest that the damage inflicted on these groups by some projects could not be mitigated merely by moving them elsewhere or pointing out that new economic opportunities existed to replace the old (Cernea and Guggenheim 1993). Thus the true rights being recognized by these protection policies, in a sense, are a particular type of protection from negative impact by Bank projects. This is not to say that there is a blanket protection of this sort; the Bank does not, for example, have policies for any person who loses a job or is otherwise hurt because of funded projects. Rather, it is the right of the vulnerable not to have their way of life taken away, whether through displacement or cultural intrusion (Oestreich 1999). It is a "do no harm" principle that encompasses several other recognized human rights standards, for the most part without specific reference to them.

## Social Development and Human Rights

Beyond the argument that the World Bank works toward a "right to education" by financing school construction or a "right to health" by underwriting nutrition and sanitation programs, there is the implicit belief that economic development itself helps to fulfill these rights. The argument is not just that the Bank (through its partners) builds schools but also that expanding economies and especially increasing the income of the poor makes it possible for people in recipient countries to provide these services for themselves. This is integral to the notion of "sustainability," now a standard concept in all development planning. It argues that in the long term, services cannot simply be provided from above. Instead, the argument goes, people must be empowered (another ubiquitous concept) to provide these services for themselves (Streeten 1994, 148). The concept of development "empowering" those citizens it serves has become a central tenet of the Bank's social development efforts, and it needs to be examined closely here. At times, the Bank has gone so far as to *define* social development as "transforming institutions to empower people" (World Bank 2005a, 1).

By the early 1990s there was an "emerging consensus" within the World Bank and development community in general regarding the need to address "the impacts of development projects on people" (Davis 2004, 6). Many of the issues enumerated above—spending on education, health care, and other human development categories, as well as protection for minorities, indigenous peoples, and other vulnerable groups—gained greater prominence in Bank planning and implementation. They were joined by another Bank priority at the time, which emphasized greater participation by civil society in designing and implementing Bank projects. Together, these elements have been placed under the general rubric of "social development" and are often treated as if they formed a coherent, if limited, policy to protect human rights. One highly placed Bank staff member has stated that "we [the social development staff] are very much in alignment with other agencies in terms of looking at what might be a rights-based approach," although she would, she said, rather refer to it as "ethical public policy" (Advocacy Project 2002). In a few cases—for example, respecting the cultural integrity of indigenous peoples—there seems a clear connection between Bank policy and international human rights law; in other cases—for example, arguing that efforts to eliminate poverty are a rights-based strategy—the connection is less clear. One must certainly keep in mind Jack Donnelly's caution that development and rights are often linked only through a tautology that defines development as rights promotion, and vice versa (Uvin 2002). However, many Bank staff members consider social development an important rights-oriented policy, and the connection is worth examining at length.

The actual definition of social development as the Bank uses it is not easy to summarize. It includes the two basic protection sectors already noted—indigenous peoples and those subject to involuntary resettlement—and in that respect involves basic respect for the rights of individuals. Beyond that, social development includes a number of strategic principles designed to introduce, in the Bank's words, "a person-centered approach," which starts "from the perspective of poor people, their families and communities" (World Bank 2005a, 2). The basic assumption is that development projects will be more effective if they are designed to empower those they are supposed to help. By "more effective," the Bank means *both* that they are more likely to succeed in their goals and that those goals are more likely to be in line with the core mission of reducing poverty and improving the lives of individuals. Thus social development becomes a way of both setting priorities and achieving those priorities.

Key strategies grouped under the rubric of social development include creating "inclusive societies" to "promote equal access to opportunities"; resolving social problems and promoting peace (including in postconflict areas); and creating accountable, transparent institutions (World Bank 2005a, 8). The ultimate goal is to improve the Bank's efforts to reduce poverty and, by extension, to create more equitable and just societies. In one of the more unambiguous statements on the role of human rights in Bank operations, James Wolfensohn explicitly tied these goals to the promotion of rights: "[If] we continue to exclude the disenfranchised—women, indigenous peoples, the disabled, street children—from playing their rightful role in society, and if we ignore their human rights, we will not have sustainable development" (World Bank 2005a, 11). The same document also argued that this strategy was connected to the larger international effort in the rights field.

"Participation" and "empowerment" are certainly desirable ends, and the Bank makes a fair case that they will ultimately enable citizens to demand more specific legal rights, but by themselves they do not represent human rights in any traditional legal sense. (This will be discussed in greater depth in the section on governance.) The same might be said of poverty reduction, another area where Bank staff and publications insist that there are rights-related advances; reducing poverty empowers citizens by giving them greater resources and therefore more leverage against the government. The same documents that point to these advances often also mention efforts by the Bank to address and ameliorate social inequalities, directing aid at the poorest and most excluded groups, and tout this as addressing equality rights. For the Bank to argue that it is protecting or promoting human rights through such a constellation of policies is certainly to stretch the definition of rights, although not perhaps to the breaking point. The Bank, to be sure, does not claim to have a rights-based programming agenda, as UNICEF does; but the Bank certainly does claim, when challenged, that rights are an important influence in its programming and that it is a positive force in this area.

The Bank, then, is surely guilty of using the concept of human rights in a very broad way when it discusses social development. Yet however vaguely or inaccurately the Bank might define rights, it does consider itself to have a rights policy in this area, which is surely significant in itself. There is a legitimate argument to be made that the Bank's preferred policy on development strategy is more likely to contribute to the achievement of so-called second-generation rights than are more traditional development policies. Nevertheless, this remains a highly selective reading of the content of human rights, focusing as it does on the economic side. If the Bank is to be taken more seriously as having a policy to promote human rights, then the first-generation rights cannot be ignored.

## Women and Human Rights

Essentially from the beginning of the WID policy in the mid-1970s, the World Bank's policy toward women has had a substantial social component, which might be considered as stretching its policy of political neutrality. From the beginning, a gender-sensitive policy was supported within the Bank not on ethical or moral grounds but by the argument from effectiveness; the landmark 1979 study *Recognizing the "Invisible" Woman in Development: The World Bank's Experience* (World Bank 1979), for example, made the case that the exclusion of women from development projects could hamper success, and that success itself needed to be defined as including a project's impact on women as well as on men.

The 2002 study *Integrating Gender into the World Bank's Work: A Strategy for Action* begins with a chapter titled "The Business Case for Mainstreaming Gender" (World Bank 2002b). "Integrating Gender" forms the basis for the Bank's updated rule on gender and development (OP 4.20) and thus is a particularly important updating and restatement of Bank policy. As one might expect, "Integrating Gender" again presents an economic—rather than moral—rationale for a gender focus in Bank work. "Gender inequality," according to the report, "retards economic growth and poverty reduction" (World Bank 2002b, 4). Attention to women is presented as having an instrumentally valuable effect on development efforts: "Educated, healthy women are more able to engage in productive activities, find formal sector employment, and earn higher incomes and greater returns to schooling than their counterparts who are uneducated or suffer from poor nutrition and health. . . . Better-educated women are more able to profit from new forms of technology and the opportunities presented by economic change than are less educated women" (World Bank 2002b, 5). Educated women have fewer children and thus slow population growth; and they raise healthier children. Giving women property and other economic rights reduces economic inefficiencies and improves the allocation of labor and capital.

This instrumental argument for focusing on women—the argument that this has a positive, even indispensable, role in development—can be used to justify a number of interventions with far-reaching social implications. One general issue that the Bank approaches, and that the other organizations under study also use as a starting point in their rights policies, is the simple question of equality. Just as UNICEF understands the Convention on the Rights of the Child as requiring it to look for inequities in how children are provided for and empowered, and WHO now considers whether minority groups get equal access to health care, the World Bank now considers gender equity a cross-cutting operational priority, involved in all lending decisions. New policies must be gender sensitive, and staff must determine that "impacts . . . are equitably beneficial for both men and women" (World Bank 2002b, 14). This in itself, of course, is not necessarily a "human rights" issue—one can certainly be in favor of equity without casting it as a rights issue—but it has important political implications in the way it is actually implemented.

One of these important implications is the need for legal reform to guarantee equitable access. If women are to reach their productive capacity and play an important part in development projects, legal reform is needed to guarantee them adequate protections and powers. As with the more general "governance" notion of fair and predictable legal systems, the gender policy requires reform to guarantee equality of justice and rights. "Modifying the legal framework to eliminate discrimination and equalize opportunities for women and men is an important goal for public policy at the national and international levels. A supportive legal environment is also vital for other aspects of public policy that have a direct bearing on the opportunities available to women, such as regulations affecting the formal and informal sectors" (World Bank 1995a, 45).

The gender policy then begins to move the Bank away from purely economic matters and into more technical matters. The notion of equal rights, and not just equal access or opportunities, is unavoidable. "Systemic obstacles . . . stand in the way of translating into reality what appears to be a national commitment to gender equality," notes one study (World Bank 2001a, 12). As a standard of reform, the study mentions the Convention on the Elimination of All Forms of Discrimination Against Women, proposing it as a model for national legal reform. (The study, it should be noted, is a research report rather than an official policy document, but it is explicitly mentioned in the revised OP 4.20 as a foundation of the new gender policy.) Mere talk of gender equality, the study continues, does not necessarily translate into policy outcomes; only a commitment to internationally recognized rights, with the backing of an international legal framework, can guarantee women equality.

Closely tied to this is the concept of "empowerment," already discussed in other contexts. Women, too, need to be not just helped but empowered to take charge of their own economic fortunes. At one level, this is related to the larger social development agenda of participation in the development process; one report notes that "in [the social development] context, addressing gender concerns is relevant for promoting participatory approaches, better identifying stakeholders, and better integrating social factors into Bank work" (Murphy 1997, 15). Women are expected to be helped to achieve control over their own economic fortunes and to play a positive role in planning. There is, however, a more clearly political aspect to this policy as well, as women are to be encouraged to participate in official decision-making structures, that is, in the process of governing.

Some efforts in this area have gone still further toward expanding away from participation issues and into a broader set of responsibilities. Although the steps have been small and, so far, largely outside the mainstream of Bank activities, the Bank has supported efforts to stop violence against women, and it has explicitly accepted this as something that falls within the strictures of its mandate (World Bank 2000, 16). The Bank has also taken a wider view of how legal reform might improve the status of women in society, and looked, for example, at possible changes in family law and other aspects of the legal code to improve women's status within society (World Bank 2001a, 241). In other words, the gender and development policy of the Bank argues that nothing less than a change in the legal, social, and political situation of women will be necessary for full development effectiveness.

Does the focus on gender represent a human rights policy? A recognition of the sweeping nature of this policy appears in a recent report on gender programming, which states that "from the point of view of Bank staff, not only is work on gender permissible under the Articles of Agreement, but is also required by the policy framework of the institution" and notes that the "changing needs of the Bank membership" require new interpretations of the Bank's

charter (World Bank 2005b, 2). In other words, while gender policies do have important development implications and the Bank is
therefore justified in having them, they have political implications
as well. As noted in other contexts, concepts like "empowerment,"
"equality," and "participation" are concepts that, however instrumentally they are used to pursue development goals, overlap with
generally accepted international human rights. In the case of gender, however, the connection is drawn more explicitly. "Ensuring
that women and men have equal rights is an important development goal on its own," notes one study; "establishing equal rights
between women and men creates an environment of equal opportunities and power, critical elements of achieving gender equality
in other dimensions" (World Bank 2001a, 299). The goal remains
primarily development, but the importance of rights remains a
central operating principle.

## Governance and Human Rights

It was noted above that none of the new development priorities
taken on by the World Bank over the past twenty years has been
linked to the promotion of a human rights agenda more than public-sector and governance reform. The very notion that the Bank
would consider the quality and nature of government and administration in a borrower country raised more controversy with the executive board than any other set of reforms. It has been suggested,
when this was largely a theoretical concern rather than a fully integrated development priority, that a focus on governance would
involve the Bank in making decisions based overtly on the nature
of a state's political system, a clear contravention of the Bank's Articles of Agreement.

Both the Bank's executive board and outside observers saw that
the question of governance reform potentially involved unambiguous human rights issues: the "quality of government" might mean
the transparency of government decision making and the elimination of corruption, but it also seemed to mean accountability to
citizens in the larger, democratic sense, or even the way government treated citizens and saw to their needs. Thus it is somewhat
ironic—though perhaps not actually surprising—that this area has
seen less direct advance in actually implementing a rights-based

approach. Governance issues are the more explicitly focused on negative, political rights rather than on those that are more positive and social/economic, and therefore the furthest from the Bank's primary mandate and organizational culture. Governance is also the area where Bank staff must be most circumspect about what they do and do not approach in terms of programming.

A good portion of what has been written on the Bank's responsibilities toward human rights has focused on the governance agenda (Crawford 1995; Landell-Mills 1992; Lawyers Committee for Human Rights 1995; Williams and Young 1994). The concept of good governance as a key development priority was developed within the Bank during the Wolfensohn presidency, and it is clear that Wolfensohn considered governance to be intimately tied to the promotion of human rights (Brodnig 2001, 7). Early statements on governance included an interest in freedom of speech, political voice, elections, freedom of association, and a "sound judicial system" as being among the elements of a governance program (Miller-Adams 1999, 128). It was the turn to governance, more than any other intellectual change by the Bank, that prompted its general counsel to discuss at length its legal status regarding human rights.

Governance issues are considered to be "cross-cutting" throughout the Bank's work; the Public Sector Group is one of four "families" within the Poverty Reduction and Economic Management network. It is itself divided into five themes:

- Legal institutions of the market economy
- Anticorruption
- Decentralization
- Administrative and civil service reform
- Public finance

The first three of these are most often considered part of a larger agenda to introduce rights standards. Each focuses on reforming how power is wielded and controlled within developing societies.

Officially, the Bank does not hide the connection between governance and rights promotion, but it denies that rights are its primary concern. Still, many governance issues have obvious implications for human rights. The Bank's argument for legal reform projects is that a modern legal system is vital to creating an environment conducive to investment and risk taking. "Abstracted from the voluminous definitions and interpretations of the concept of rule of law come the objectives of stability, predictability, and elimination of governmental arbitrariness, which are preconditions to economic development. This, in turn, makes the rule of law a legitimate concern for the Bank as a developmental institution" (World Bank 1995b, 15). But the reforms grouped under this category are wide ranging, moving far beyond the commercial sector. A summary of legal reforms notes that "the rule of law prevails where (1) the government itself is bound by the law; (2) every person in society is treated equally under the law; (3) the human dignity of each individual is recognized and protected; (4) justice is accessible to all. . . . Legal and judicial reform is a means to promote the rule of law" (World Bank 2004a, 3). This is particularly true for at-risk groups, such as women and indigenous peoples (Dakolias 1996, xiii), suggesting that protecting the rights of such groups (already recognized elsewhere by the Bank) is a key legal reform issue. An important study of governance notes that "the poor continue to lack legal rights that empower them to take advantage of opportunities and provide them with security against arbitrary and inequitable treatment. Discriminatory or arbitrarily enforced laws deprive individuals of the individual and property rights, raise barriers to justice and keep the poor poor" (World Bank 2004a, 2).

The Bank's stated goals of fostering accountability and participation in projects also has self-evident political implications, which are linked to human rights as enumerated in international law. Article 21 of the Universal Declaration of Human Rights contains those rights often referred to as "participation": to have a voice in the government of one's country, and to be recognized as the basis of legitimate authority. David Forsythe rates participation as the second most important right, after the "broadly understood" right to life; participation "guarantees" the right to life and makes possible both equality of rights and some measure of financial equality (Forsythe 1989, 40). Participation is not synonymous with democracy; although it has been suggested that there is an "emerging right to democratic government" (Franck 1992), this is at best speculative. There are levels of political participation that fall short of outright democratic government, however, as is clearly recognized in the Universal Declaration.

Often, however, governments see in the notion of participatory development the seeds of a larger demand for political participation. Governments have at times resisted the Bank's participatory approach for a variety of reasons; governments worry about losing control over the development agenda, losing control over economic benefits, and generally losing control over the political process. An early Bank study points out several cases where such concerns were raised, for example, in Ecuador, where "the government's initial interest in using a participatory approach [in a rural development project] was based on seeking financial and labor contributions from beneficiaries, rather than on achieving more meaningful participation" (Reitbergen-McCracken 1996, 4–5). The first two concerns might be seen as technical issues; the first, in fact, is widely shared *within* the Bank as well. Interviews suggest that many Bank staff feel that participatory development removes control over projects from Bank experts and places it in the hands of local, untrained people, and in the worst cases in the hands of special interest groups that seek to control projects for their own benefit. The third issue—that there is an inherently political implication to participatory development—is potentially the most serious, because it is not just about development practices but also about the nature of the Bank's role in society.

It should be noted that "democracy," however defined, is not yet a recognized human right. Donnelly (1999) believes it important for those in the development field in particular to remember that there is no necessary connection between democratic government (generally understood in its liberal electoral form) and the achievement of human rights. Popular government may even work against human rights, as when a majority chooses through the electoral process to suppress a minority. But some form of political participation is more clearly justified in human rights discourse, and with both an inherent and instrumental purpose: A right to political participation in the decisions that affect people the most takes those people seriously as choosing human beings; and it makes the trampling of other rights less likely, by opening the process up to protest.

The proposition that governance policies represent a human rights agenda has come under withering criticism in recent years.

Among the most cogent critiques is that of Peter Uvin, who suggests that these policies are little more than a rhetorical repackaging of measures primarily intended to reinforce liberal economic policies; they do not, he suggests, do anything to truly change structures of power (Uvin 2004, 87–88). However, Hugo Slim has written that there is power even in rhetoric; the fact that the Bank must use these justifications is itself, he suggests, a form of progress (Slim 2002, 4). Gudmundur Alfredsson, conversely, has written that "with states carrying the primary responsibility for the national implementation of human rights, it is suggested that democracy and good governance in practice will contribute to respect for the human rights standards" (Alfredsson 2002, 26). Improvements in citizen voice, access to justice, and accountable government have a connection to respect for both positive and negative rights, although it is by no means inevitable that improving governance will improve rights conditions—they help but are not enough. Mac Darrow has written that anticorruption initiatives also have substantial human rights implications and that this connection has been made explicitly by Bank staff and researchers (Darrow 2003, 189–90).

Perhaps the most serious critique of the Bank's notion of good governance might be that it remains largely unimplemented; as the next section discusses, only the anticorruption component has been given real emphasis and resources. Though the Bank has, on occasion, explicitly made the connection between rights and good governance, it should not be surprising that its definition of governance remains focused on what Hans-Otto Sano refers to as the "technical aspect" rather than the "legal aspect" of governance—improving outcomes, not improving procedures (Sano 2002, 7). Nor is it surprising, within the context of this study, that the Bank has had so much difficulty effectively designing and implementing a human rights agenda that focuses on political rather than social and economic rights. These are, of course, the rights most at odds with the Bank's mission, culture, and legal status. It seems a mistake, however, to say that the governance agenda is merely a rhetorical exercise or damage control; there is a genuine, if not entirely successful, effort under way to incorporate political rights into Bank lending. But as these efforts stray further and further from the core mission of the institution, they also become less cohesive and effective.

## Implementation

Considering the wide range of activities generally grouped under the idea of a more people-oriented or rights-oriented approach within the World Bank, it would be impossible to thoroughly examine all the various activities termed "implementation" of these new standards. The main question here is, What explains the success or failure of the Bank to effectively implement a rights-based set of policies within its operations?

To address this question, this section considers two separate issues. First, it is important to look at the organizational changes that have been implemented within the Bank to allow it to address human rights issues more effectively. The Bank is an enormous organization, and effective change requires organizational reform as one step in overcoming bureaucratic inertia. The second issue is to see how rights are actually built into lending practices; in other words, how they are translated into actions by the organization. What does the talk of protecting the vulnerable, or empowering communities, mean in terms of actual programming? The consideration of these issues here, it is important to note, ends with the end of the Wolfensohn presidency, because Paul Wolfowitz has not yet made clear his intentions in the area of human rights; at the time of this writing, the policy was "business as usual" with no clear signal as to whether the implementation of these policies will be helped or hindered by the change in leadership.

### Structural Reform and Human Rights

More so than either WHO or UNICEF, the World Bank has undertaken some basic structural reforms to better align its activities with its revised policies and goals. Any large organization trying to change its way of doing business will likely need to revise its structure to better integrate new policies; because the Bank is larger than either WHO or UNICEF, these changes will have to be more numerous and wide-reaching. A number of key changes are addressed here.

## THE INSPECTION PANEL

In terms of internal reforms, the creation of the World Bank Inspection Panel has the most significant implications here—Fox and Brown refer to it as part of a "wave of reform" in the early 1990s, as the Bank tried to cope with the costs of structural adjustment and with other human-rights-related issues (Fox and Brown 1998a, 9). The panel was created in 1993 largely as a result of high-profile human rights problems and issues of environmental degradation. In particular, it was designed to address the concerns of the Wapenhans Report (World Bank 1992a), an internal Bank study that found organizational biases favoring increased lending volume rather than a focus on project quality and adherence to ethical guidelines; this was an important impetus for the Bank's management to consider new institutional mechanisms for improving project quality and oversight (Umaña 1998, 1).

Along with this general critique, the Bank was severely criticized in the early 1990s for its dam- and canal-building project in India's Narmada Valley, which raised severe concerns about both the dam and canal's environmental impact and the large number of people who were being displaced from their homes with inadequate governmental assistance (Schlemmer-Schulte 1999, 6; Umaña 1998, 1). The Inspection Panel was first proposed by the Bank's management, although with considerable pressure from both NGO groups and the U.S. Congress (Dunkerton 1995, 446), which itself had been convinced that the World Bank was not paying sufficient attention to the human rights implications of its projects. The Bank's board of directors established the panel in 1993.

The Inspection Panel is made up of three members, chosen by the World Bank board (using a weighted voting procedure). They are expected to have substantial knowledge of the Bank's operations but not to have recently worked for it. The panel is empowered to hear complaints from individuals in countries regarding Bank-funded projects (including both the IBRD and IDA lending windows of the World Bank Group); this is a substantial fact in and of itself, for it is the first international body of its type to accept

petitions from civil society groups rather than only from governments. The panel acts, in essence, as an arm of the Bank's board;
once the panel has determined that a review is warranted in response to a petitioner's request, it reports its findings to the board,
and the Bank's management is given an opportunity to address
and, if necessary, redress the problems.

This, at any rate, is how the process is supposed to work. In
practice, the initial part of the process, when the Inspection Panel
determines if a review is warranted, has become a highly complex
affair in its own right (Bradlow 1999, 8). Initially, the management of the Bank would present its own investigation, including a
remedial plan of action, to the board *along with* the panel's initial
findings. This led to serious problems, because it appeared that the
Bank's management was intervening in an investigation before it
had even gotten under way (Bradlow 1999, 8). A 1999 reform effort attempted to resolve some of these problems, establishing the
panel's independence and preventing management from interfering before an investigation has been completed (Clark 2003, 17).
This reform effort also tried to prevent board members from interfering with the process for political reasons, or out of fear of interference with state sovereignty (Clark 2003, 18). The 1999 reform,
however, failed to include the panel in supervising the remediation
of Bank errors, perpetuating a "key weakness" in "achieving real
change on the ground in particular projects" (Clark 2002, 219).

It is important to note that the Inspection Panel is not designed to determine if Bank projects are in compliance with international law or other human rights standards. The panel's
only mandate is to investigate whether a project is following
the Bank's own guidelines, for example, on forced relocation or
the protection of indigenous cultures. To the extent that the relevant codes of conduct reflect an interest in the rights of those
affected, of course, the panel can be seen as an instrument of human rights protection. But it is not specifically so or, at any rate,
not explicitly designed with this in mind, a condition made necessary by the Bank's rhetorical hands-off policy toward human
rights. Technically, it is more in the nature of "a logical extension
of the rights of employees of international organizations to redress
. . . to the provision of similar rights to specific categories of the
general public" (Bissell 1997, 741).

However, it is obvious, if not explicitly stated, that many of those sufficiently harmed by Bank projects to seek such redress will insist that their human rights are being violated; this will be limited, but not eliminated, by the need to find a corresponding regulation within Bank guidelines. The first appeal to the Inspection Panel concerned the Arun III hydroelectric dam project in Nepal. The appeal said, among other things, that the project had not considered more suitable alternatives, that it was environmentally irresponsible, and that there were not sufficient provisions for the resettlement of displaced populations (Umaña 1998, 7). Although Bank management tried first to block the inspection process, and then to modify the project so as to bring it into alignment with Bank policies (thus fixing the problems before the panel had made a determination), these efforts did not prevent the panel from issuing a report condemning the project, in essence questioning the ability of the Bank to implement its own safeguard policies (Bissell 2003, 37). Ultimately, the panel's activities, and a sustained effort by NGOs and civil society groups, led James Wolfensohn, who had only recently become the Bank's president, to cancel the project. His decision never actually referenced any human rights issues, but it did mention both the economic effects on Nepal and the questions about the Bank's ability to adhere to its own policies (Bissell 2003, 38).

Most subsequent appeals have also centered on large infrastructure projects. Examples include the Jamuna Bridge project in Bangladesh, where an NGO claimed that the effects on the surrounding populations had not been considered, and the Yacyreta Hydroelectric project in Paraguay, which also would have resulted in large-scale flooding (Umaña 1998, 742–73). These projects were accused only of violating Bank standards; as one legal analysis notes, "the implementation of the Bank's policy standards does not result in substantive rights that individuals in borrowing countries may claim against the Bank, nor does the Inspection Panel represent a legal remedy mechanism"; yet the same study says the panel "complement[s] and reinforce[s] the World Bank's role as a transformer of human rights ideals into realities" (Schlemmer-Schulte 1999, 16).

Most important, however, is the mere fact of the panel's ability to hear appeals from affected groups directly, rather than requiring the intervention of states. The panel, writes Daniel Bradlow, is "the first forum in which private parties can seek to hold international organizations directly accountable. . . . Given the broad scope of the Bank's operations, the Panel has the potential to influence the evolution of international human rights, environmental, and administrative law" (Bradlow 1996a, 248). The effectiveness of this process in the long term is not entirely clear; as a number of analysts have noted, some safeguard policies have been rewritten in ways that make projects "panel proof," meaning that the policies are so vague that it is very difficult to make a case that they have been violated (Darrow 2003, 198–99). It also appears that the role of the Inspection Panel may be diluted by the Bank's gradual implementation of a "country systems" policy (discussed in the conclusion of this chapter), which is intended to move more responsibility for guaranteeing safeguard policies from the Bank to borrower countries. Even so, the Inspection Panel remains a significant effort to give voice to nonstate actors and to increase the Bank's accountability for human rights matters affected by its programming.

## MANAGEMENT CHANGES AND THE STRATEGIC COMPACT
The greatest impediment to successful adaptation at the World Bank, particularly where a social agenda is concerned, has been the culture of the organization itself. Though there has been substantial rhetorical commitment to change, and some genuine efforts to implement new policies, the process of integrating this commitment and turning it into real outcomes has had mixed results. Early efforts to create a more socially responsible and responsive Bank were of very limited success; to a large extent, this is because these efforts had trouble getting beyond a mere rhetorical commitment and were therefore easily ignored by staff accustomed to "business as usual." Changes occurred as the idea of a more socially responsible Bank took hold among more staff, particularly during the presidency of James Wolfensohn, beginning in 1995. Wolfensohn brought with him both an interest in more socially responsive and responsible development and a willingness to implement wide-ranging management reform to accomplish his goals. The successes and failures of these reforms say a great deal about the difficulty of implementing major changes in large international agencies or any large organization.

The first real step toward implementation was the process of revising the Bank's basic operating guidelines. Well before Wolfensohn became president, a variety of progressive policies had been written into the Bank's operational directives. The earliest policy on forced resettlement, Operational Manual Statement 2.33, was adopted in 1980, providing guidelines on how to protect the rights of those displaced by Bank-funded projects, and Operational Manual Statement 2.34 of 1982, on the rights of tribal peoples (Davis 2004, 3). The adoption of the earliest statement on the role of women in development, in 1984, was described above. Simply placing these concerns within the Bank's official operational manual, however, proved ineffective in many ways. Standards were often ignored or poorly implemented; Bank staff, as noted by the Wapenhans Report on project effectiveness, were poorly supervised and had few incentives to implement projects properly. The creation of the Inspection Panel was the most visible response to the repeated accusations that the Bank was not following its own policy guidelines in the social development arena.

In terms of efforts to turn new ideas about social development and governance into actual outcomes, the main effort was President Wolfensohn's launch of the Strategic Compact in April 1997. The Strategic Compact was a "renewal" plan for the Bank, designed to revamp the Bank's operations and strategies on a number of fronts. The "pillars" of the compact included "refueling current business activity," by which was meant an improvement of the Bank's business activities through decentralization and a more results-oriented focus, among other components; a reframing of the organization's basic identity as a "Knowledge Bank" able to lead development through its "comparative advantage" in intellectual capital; and "retooling the development agenda" to focus on previously neglected areas such as social development, governance, and the environment (World Bank 1997).

The effort to revise the development agenda (technically, the second component of the Strategic Compact) directly approached the problem of making staff take more seriously the social component of development. The Social Development Task Group (1997) issued a report in May 1997 that laid out the case for and components of increased activity in social development. Part of the Strategic Compact's management reform process included the creation of a thematic "network" for Environmentally and Socially Sustainable Development (ESSD), which included social development issues. "The formation of the Social Development Network," according to a Bank study, "did not occur without a struggle and would not have happened at all were it not for the strong voice and support of Ismail Serageldin, Vice President for Environmentally Sustainable Development" (Davis 2004, 15).

Serageldin's and Wolfensohn's determination to make social development a key issue within the Bank overcame resistance from entrenched interests, and Serageldin's early support explains why social development was placed with the ESSD framework. As was the case with UNICEF, the location of responsibility over new issues—in UNICEF's case, moving responsibility for the rights agenda out of the public relations office and into that of the Program Division—can critically affect the chances of a new set of programs. It is not enough simply to declare a new set of policies; the institutional setting must be carefully considered. In June 2006, President Wolfowitz announced a plan to merge ESSD with those units that oversee infrastructure and energy projects, ostensibly to bring increased environmental and sustainability standards closer to major projects. It is not clear whether this move will have the desired effect or whether it will actually undermine the effectiveness of socially and environmentally sustainable development. The Bank continues to struggle with the most effective way of implementing new policies, and this struggle continues to hinder successful organizational change.

## Social Development and Women in Development

In the World Bank, gender issues are addressed within the Poverty Reduction and Economic Management (PREM) network. Gender issues have their own Gender Sector Board (GSB) within the network, which is tasked with "knowledge management, regular monitoring and reporting on the status of policy implementation, and building capacity" (World Bank 2001b, 22). There is also a Gender and Development Group, which "acts as [the GSB's] secretariat" (World Bank 2001b, 23). There are regional representatives to help with the integration of gender issues into Bank lending, although the precise arrangements vary from region to region.

Gender issues are expected to be written into each country's Poverty Reduction Strategy Paper (PRSP), and a key aspect of Bank strategy toward gender is the mainstreaming of gender equality into the PRSPs (and all other aspects of Bank operations) (Bryn et al. 2005, 96).

In practice, the Bank's own OED consistently gave the Bank mediocre grades, at best, on its efforts to actually implement a far-reaching gender strategy. Success at creating an effective gender strategy can be considered in two ways: Has the Bank successfully integrated gender concerns into its lending operations? And have these policies effectively promoted gender equity, improved the lives of women, and aided development overall? Both dimensions of effectiveness have been carefully studied, both within and outside the Bank.

In the first category, the OED report and other studies consistently point to the gap between rhetoric and action in terms of gender mainstreaming, that is, making gender analysis and programming part of regular Bank programming. As early as 1994 the Bank found that careful staff attention to gender issues and effective supervision, as well as real effective commitment (rather than just rhetorical or short-term efforts) from borrower countries was crucial to successful mainstreaming (Murphy 1997, 14). A later study confirmed that the majority of projects studied by the OED showed attention to gender goals but that only nine of twenty-seven "benefited from good attention to gender issues" and only seven "fully achieved their gender objectives." Of the rest, "the remaining 14 projects paid only superficial attention to gender" (Murphy 1997, 24). The conclusion, in line with the earlier study, was that gender issues were being considered by Bank staff because they were now part of the general operational mandate, but that only when there was adequate supervision were they taken seriously by staff rather than considered merely a matter of show.

Subsequent studies of Bank gender policy continue to emphasize the importance of bureaucratic and managerial factors in adequate gender policy implementation. The situation had apparently improved somewhat by the time of 2002's OED study of gender issues, "The Gender Dimension of Bank Assistance: An Evaluation of Results." "Overall," the study notes, "the treatment of gender in [country assistance strategies] has improved significantly over the evaluation period." Conversely, integration of gender issues in analytical work was found to be weak, and the "relevance" of Bank gender analysis to practical programming was found to be "modest" (World Bank 2002a, 5–6). Another study reached much the same conclusion:

> Gender has become more visible within the Bank in the last few years, and the initiatives have emerged at the central and Regional levels that could affect operations. Despite these developments, however, gender considerations have not been systematically integrated into Bank assistance with any speed. Gender policies are not fully understood, and instructions to staff are unclear. The responsibilities for integrating gender are not well established, nor are there any processes to monitor quality at entry or during implementation. Staff do not systematically receive training and technical support on matters of gender. The resources have not been sufficiently allocated to jumpstart the process of policy implementation. The systems that monitor how well gender policy is implemented and its effectiveness are weak. (World Bank 2005b, 37)

The same study blames, among other issues, poor monitoring, weakly worded operational guidelines, and little or no consensus on the content of Bank strategy (World Bank 2002a, 37).

As with the Bank's own reports, outside studies of Bank gender strategy also focus on the lack of commitment and focus at the organizational level. An analysis by the Heinrich Böll Foundation determined that there appears to be a commitment at the higher levels of the Bank to gender issues but that this has failed to translate into acceptable program outcomes. The study notes the increased number of gender experts within the Bank and considers them to be "of high quality . . . sophisticated conveyors of the value derived from addressing gender issues in Bank activities" (Zuckerman and Qing 2003, 10). Yet, the study notes, the message does not seem to be reaching non-gender-expert staff. Echoing the Bank's own study, they suggest that staff are aware of the Bank policy but prefer to follow their usual patterns of behavior, paying only slight attention to gender issues (Zuckerman and Qing 2003, 21). An examination of how gender is integrated into PRSPs—as noted above, a key Bank strategy to mainstream gender—finds that "attention to gender is shockingly limited. . . . Gender issues appear in a piecemeal and fragmented fashion—being addressed very little or not at all in the policy sections of the documents" (Whitehead 2003, 14).

Both internal and external analyses of the Bank's gender policies, then, consistently praise the Bank's *intentions* while faulting its *implementation* of gender-based policies. Though there have been good-faith efforts to integrate gender at key phases of the lending process (e.g., the preparation of PRSPs and Country Assistance Strategies), these have failed to work their way through the entire bureaucracy. The conclusion of a 2001 study by the OED was that, despite the rising profile of gender, "gender policies are not fully understood and instructions to staff are not clear. Responsibilities for gender integration are not well established, and there are no processes to monitor quality at entry or during implementation. Training and technical support are not systematically available to staff" (World Bank 2001b, 31). Thus the problem is not actually formulating a policy, nor is it commitment at the top—the issue, in other words, is not that the Bank as an institution has not made a commitment but rather the difficulty of changing an organizational culture. Much of this has to do with the notion of "mission creep": the idea that the Bank has added too many new priorities to its core mission of project lending (Einhorn 2001). Unconvinced that gender is a key priority for them, and overburdened with other tasks and priorities, staff members have been unable to fully accept and implement this new set of guidelines. The OED considered closer supervision and greater commitment of resources to be vital if the gender policy is to be adequately implemented in the future.

The same sense of mission creep, it must be noted, has slowed the implementation of the larger social development agenda. "Overstretched and underloved" is how one study of Bank change (including social development implementation) describes the organization, borrowing from an earlier analysis (Weaver and Leiteritz 2005, 371). The study goes on to discuss the resistance to change by Bank staff, and it blames the "tenacity of organizational culture" for this resistance. As with the gender policy, an OED study in 2005 found that Bank staff were generally well aware of the nature and basic ideas of social development. "A large majority of task managers (93 percent) said that the nature of their work routinely required attention to social development themes. Country directors rated the importance of social development quite high" (World Bank 2005d, 42). The study noted in one of its strongest statements that "to be quite succinct, the Bank needs to do more than it has to date to convince both its own staff and its borrowers of the potential of social development. Even though the majority of staff strongly support the Bank's social development aims, an important minority . . . do not, and consequently are less likely to design projects that take social development into account" (World Bank 2005d, 42). The study goes on to mention the importance of cultural factors in an organization dominated by economists: "[You] have to demonstrate win–wins to economists and country directors, reduce transaction costs, and learn to communicate in Bank jargon," it notes, quoting an anonymous task manager (World Bank 2005d, 42). Michelle Miller-Adams reaches the same conclusion regarding the "participation" feature of social development, laying the blame for slow implementation on cultural factors and noting the "privileged position of economists within the organization" (Miller-Adams 1999, 94).

By no means is organizational culture the only constraint on the implementation of social development policies. Along with resistance to the notion of social development by professionals with economic training and those well inculcated with the Bank's prevailing ideology, a number of other impediments were brought up in OED studies and confirmed in interview research. One of the most common is the sense that social development staff were taking an overly negative approach to selling their services—that social development was more about telling staff what they could not do (e.g., regarding the protection of indigenous cultures) than what they could do (World Bank 2004b, 18). A shortage of staff with the necessary skills has also been cited as an impediment (World Bank 2004b, 19). In another parallel with the gender experience, it has been noted that "there is a lack of clarity about what social development is about and when to use its different instruments" (World Bank 2005d, 39). It is also true that cultural or organization factors cover a very wide array of issues, ranging from the resistance of staff with specific training (e.g., economists who feel unable to carry out social analyses), to personal incentives to favor quick approval of loans over careful analysis, to the cultural norms of the country from which specific staff come from (e.g., staff members who resist greater gender equality because of their own upbringing in a patriarchal society).

One example of how a rights-based development paradigm could work for the World Bank, and a case often pointed to by Bank staff, is the Kecamatan Development Project (KDP) in rural Indonesia. This project, started in 1998, is pointed to by a number of social development staff as a model of how they would like to see future projects incorporate social development themes. KDP is characterized as a "programmatic project," in that it seeks at least as much to restructure local institutions and processes as to "deliver tangible physical evidence" of development (Edstrom 2002, 2). The primary innovation of KDP is in its attempt to bypass state control of development and to maximize local control, transparency, and capacity. The project itself is highly decentralized, relying on *kecamatans*, or local government agencies, to make all key decisions about what projects to fund and how they are to be implemented. The working of the *kecamatans* was designed to maximize transparency and citizen participation, in a structured manner.

Although it is too early to comment decisively on the success or failure of KDP, it has become a model used by social development staff for other projects. KDP is intended, first of all, to increase project performance by going around a corrupt and inefficient government development system and instead to directly involve local people in the decisions that directly affect them. In this way, it is perceived as being rights based in that it seeks to empower local people and provide them with meaningful voice, through a community process, in development decision making. It is designed to support "participation" rights, and more generally to provide some meaningful democratic decision making at the local level. KDP has a heavy emphasis on local control over natural resources and group decision making on their exploitation, in the name of the welfare of the community. As an antipoverty program that is designed to benefit the poorest people in rural Indonesia, it also fits well with the Bank's contention that its commitment to reducing poverty is a key component in guaranteeing such positive rights as that of education, nutrition, and a healthy environment.

On the whole, however, the social development framework remains somewhat opportunistic, and it is not a directed effort to implement a rights-based approach to development. The Social Development Department now considers talk of a rights-based approach to be acceptable (as opposed to being a taboo subject) and has commissioned reports on how this would look. There has also been extensive contact between Bank social development experts and some national governments—in particular, the Nordic states—to discuss the importance and meaning of rights within the World Bank context. This was evident, for example, in the preparation of the 2006 annual *World Development Report*, whose theme, "Equity and Development," drew directly on work being done by the Social Development Department and supported through consultations with these progressive member states. Perhaps the most suggestive development in this area was the creation of an official "Social Analysis and Human Rights" team within the Social Development Department. The team was short-lived, done in by the lack of direct human rights work available to the Bank. Its creation and demise are both suggestive of where social development finds itself at this time.

The content of international human rights law encompasses far more than the concepts of empowerment and community voice in development. Yet the Bank can make a legitimate case that in KDP, there are the basics of a rights-based approach. Such an approach does not depend on the protection or implementation of a wide range of human rights standards; rather, it has more to do with "the *process* by which development aims are achieved, . . . [which] can build on, strengthen, neglect, or undermine local capacities, local networks, local knowledge and ways of generating it" (Uvin 2004, 123; emphasis in original). The primary problem remains, of course, the actual replication of the KDP project, and its acceptance by the staff of the World Bank at large.

### Governance and Human Rights

As with the social development agenda, governance issues are implemented in World Bank lending first through their place in one of the Bank's networks—in this case, the PREM network. This network includes staff in Washington, at the Bank's headquarters, who set policy direction and produce guiding documents, as well as staff in each region and in particular countries, who provide technical expertise in their field to country staff. The Public Sector Group is divided into thematic divisions covering administrative and civil service reform, anticorruption, decentralization, legal institutions, and public finance. Together, they are intended, as the group's website puts it, to "focus more of [the Bank's] efforts on building efficient and accountable public sector institutions—rather than simply providing discrete policy advice" (World Bank 2007). The Public Sector Group is also responsible for conducting training for Bank staff on governance-related issues and for making sure that these issues are generally well integrated in Bank operations.

The general notion of governance reform—that is, a focus on the institutional context of development—is now reasonably accepted as part of how the Bank does business and how Bank staff think when designing a country strategy or specific loans. Much like children's rights in the UNICEF case, the notion of governance languished somewhat until there was a clear signal from the top of the organization that this was to be a priority. In the Bank's case, this signal was James Wolfensohn's 1996 speech at the annual World Bank–IMF joint annual meeting, in which he spoke of the "cancer of corruption" that was holding back the developing world. Although talk of governance reform predated that speech by several years, after 1996 there was a real effort to fully integrate public-sector reform into Bank operations. Corruption in particular has remained the primary focus of the Bank within the public-sector area, but the other program areas have also grown in prominence.

Not unlike the other new issues covered in this chapter, the implementation of a governance agenda has required an infusion of people into the Bank with new skills. Once again, the early efforts to make governance an important priority were hampered by a lack of staff with the right training and education and by resistance from the more technocratic staff and trained economists. Interviews with current staff, as well as internal studies, bring up the recurring theme of resistance from older staff to governance concepts, and a lack of skill even by those tasked with carrying out these programs (World Bank 2002c, 50). There has been some influx of new staff with the necessary background, but they continue to speak of themselves as being somewhat marginalized, and with limited common language with regard to older or more traditional Bank staff. Still, a lack of qualified staff seems a common refrain, albeit one difficult to quantify.

A 2002 OED study expressed general satisfaction with the progress of the governance agenda, and interviews with Bank staff suggest that the program has been steadily if slowly gaining acceptance. The OED study found that discussion of "governance and corruption" issues was universally present in Country Assistance Strategies in the most recent years studied (fiscal 2001), and that discussion of "institutions and other accountability mechanisms" had risen to 79 percent of Country Assistance Strategies (World Bank 2002c, 3). The report concludes—and interviews with various Bank staff seem to confirm—that governance issues are now taken seriously by Bank staff and are considered an important component of the Bank's overall strategy. As with many other issues discussed in the current study, many of the components of the governance agenda met initial resistance from Bank staff with more traditional economic training, but this resistance, though hardly ended, has somewhat lessened.[1] The overall impression one gets is that this is particularly true in Latin America and Eastern Europe, and less so in Africa, with Asia being somewhat in the middle. Various cultural factors are cited to explain the regional variations.

The Bank's governance strategy, as it is implemented, still is not referred to or defended as a human rights approach to development. Rights are not *officially* invoked either in the loan agreements or in the main strategy documents being produced by the Public Sector Unit. In essence, whether one views the governance program as the implementation of a human rights program or not depends on how much legitimacy there is to the argument that these activities have a real effect on rights promotion. It is difficult to ascertain how much truth there is to this assertion, given the vagueness of the terms involved and the paucity of statistics or other data that might shed light on the answer. Certainly improvements in the administration of justice in developing countries can only have a positive effect on the rights of individuals living within that country, and a review of Bank-funded legal reform programs shows that these reforms are not limited to the commercial sector. Fighting corruption is less directly connected with rights-related issues, but there are certainly overlapping concerns. Small projects, such as a recent $40 million IDA loan to Tanzania for the Tanzanian Accountability, Transparency, and Integrity Project, have tied anticorruption strategies to the larger goal of making government accountable to its citizens, increasing access to information, and reforming justice systems. The Public Sector group has also experimented with training government officials in ethics and responsibility, with the expectation that this will have spillover effects beyond the purely economic.

None of this is to suggest that there is anything like a real human rights program being implemented within the Bank's governance sector. Projects have, by necessity, focused on the technical side of governance issues, and the connection to a larger political agenda remains largely aspirational. Decentralization, for example, though a significant Bank priority, has largely remained in the most technical areas of fiscal and administrative reform. The Bank has initiated programs to decentralize "revenue-raising and spending authority" and the way "civil servants . . . influence their distribution across space and their own accountability" (Kaiser 2006, 317–18). It has already been noted that legal reform programs have focused largely on creating the necessary conditions to enable commercial transactions, although these conditions often overlap with the broader need to administer justice for the larger population. Anticorruption efforts remain the centerpiece of the governance agenda, again with their tangential effect on larger issues such as accountability and transparency.

An internally circulated document—actually a PowerPoint presentation—within PREM and the Public Sector Group (and obtained by the author) has raised the possibility of treating human rights, development, and security as three parts of a larger, holistic approach to development, connected to the governance agenda. What will actually become of this proposed shift in emphasis is not at this time clear, and even were it to be made more explicit, it would likely (judging from experience) take a very long time to be integrated into operational efforts. It is also likely to depend on a shift in the Bank's interpretation of its Articles of

Agreement. The outcome of this shift—at least in the short term—is not likely to have a substantial effect on Bank policies. It is, however, at least suggestive of how staff at various levels of the institution are agitating for change.

## Conclusions

Given the large number of World Bank activities that invoke human rights in some form, it is difficult to generalize about how the Bank is approaching the issue of rights or rights-based approaches to development. Uncertainty, at the time of writing, about the policies of the new Bank president, Paul Wolfowitz, adds to a sense of caution. A few things, however, stand out.

Clearly, the World Bank has no single, coherent policy on the integration of human rights issues into its lending operations. This does not mean that there is no commitment to the concept. Highly placed managers and some executive directors have periodically committed the Bank to consider and promote human rights, and apparently they have done so in good faith (rather than merely spouting rhetoric designed to placate critics). Any number of issues have conspired to leave the notion in disarray, ranging from the Bank's own legal limitations, to the resistance of some member states, to resistance by staff, to a lack of commitment by senior managers. This does not, from a normative standpoint, excuse the failure of the institution to grapple with this problem in a more structured way or to make effective reforms. It does, however, help explain why so many positive ideas have yielded relatively few positive results.

Along with this disarray, there are some clear countervailing tendencies at the Bank away from the effective implementation of a rights-based policy. The most prominent of these is a decision (mentioned above, in regard to the Inspection Panel) to move toward a "country system" of safeguard implementation. The general idea is to rely on a borrower country's systems rather than the Bank for the oversight of projects, when the Bank "consider[s] a borrower country's environmental and social safeguard systems to be equivalent to the Bank's" (World Bank 2005c, iv). The Bank presents this new policy as a way of improving efficiency (by streamlining the process of project design and implementation) and increasing country "buy-in" and ownership of development projects. Although the actual results of this new policy are not yet known, a number of NGOs and other Bank watchers have expressed concern that this is intended to weaken Bank social policies (e.g., Wilks 2003). It is connected, more generally, with an decrease in IBRD lending to middle-income countries and a perceived need to cut costs and refocus on infrastructure lending. The Bank, naturally, is careful to present this not as a backing away from safeguard policies but, on the contrary, as a way of increasing state commitment to such policies.

Despite this lack of a coherent or effective policy on rights, it is noteworthy that the language of rights has been used in such a variety of different areas. It seems useful here to recall the Bank's own distinction between those rights areas where it considers itself following a "do no harm" principle—primarily in the area of safeguards policy—and those areas where it is actually trying to promote certain rights. Where certain safeguards are concerned, such as indigenous peoples and those subject to forcible relocation, the Bank has implemented a policy that explicitly mentions the rights of those affected (albeit carefully defined). In other areas the Bank is more circumspect, although not entirely so—the WID policy clearly seeks to promote the rights of women, in a very specific legal sense, with the Convention on the Elimination of All Forms of Discrimination Against Women providing legal guidance. In other areas of rights promotion, such as governance and social development, the Bank is still more circumspect, although the language of rights seems to weave itself into this policy as well.

Unlike the other two cases presented in this volume—and this point will be taken up at greater length in chapter 5—the World Bank's initial interest in human rights issues was more a result of external than internal factors. The regular and continuing criticism of the Bank's neoliberal development paradigm, the high-profile failure of structural adjustment programs, and the various public relations disasters that have attended some large development projects—all have pushed the Bank to begin considering its moral position. The language of human rights, the most widely accepted international body of normative standards, presented an obvious place to turn. It's clear that these ideas were fed into the Bank far more than they were developed by internal advocates.

However, there is no clear narrative to suggest that any single powerful state, or coalition of states, was pushing for action in this area. Though the United States has been generally supportive, particularly on some governance matters, it has not been at the vanguard, and it has occasionally been very cautious about such reforms. Instead a variety of different factors were pushing Bank staff to begin developing their own ideas about where the institution needed to go. The obvious failure of the Bank to develop a coherent policy was also largely based on internal factors; though some states have resisted the Bank's talk about human rights, no single set of opponents has been able to force the issue. And James Wolfensohn, when he was Bank president, was clearly determined to go his own way with such policies. If meaningful institutional reform has been difficult to achieve, this is due largely to the internal factors just mentioned—staff resistance, internal culture, and the like. Wolfensohn's own management style also had something to do with it—staff repeatedly complained that he imposed so many different new priorities on them that they were unable or unwilling to carry them all out.

It is certainly a valid critique of the World Bank to complain that its talk of implementing human rights protections and safeguards, or pursuing a rights-based approach, masks the larger problem of its sometimes deleterious effect on the well-being of people in developing countries. However, this argument is not exactly relevant to the larger issue of human rights within the Bank. It is entirely consistent to think that the Bank is concerned with human rights yet is pursuing a wrong-headed and counterproductive economic ideology. It is perhaps more relevant to the current argument to say that those policies being grouped under the rights banner by the Bank are less about human rights than simply about trying to be a better international citizen. The connection between the Bank's legal reform programs, or enhanced citizen input in development projects, and human rights in a strictly legal sense may be rather tenuous. These policies may well be simply good development practice, with the Bank rather conveniently pointing to them as promoting rights. Still, there seems to be more going on here than a mere rhetorical exercise. Interviews with Bank staff at every level confirm that they take these concepts seriously, even if they are not always able to implement them as they would like.

The more valid critique is that the Bank has contained rights-based issues in areas tangential to its main operations and continues to keep the bulk of its lending in areas that do not consider social welfare or human rights. There is no single or official human rights policy within the World Bank, and the obvious rights-based language of some sectors continues to coexist as a "junior partner" with more traditional forms of lending. In a sense, the language of rights has been oddly diffused throughout the World Bank, becoming a regular part of the discourse on development without becoming a solid factor in decision making. In some areas—notably gender and protection policies—the concept of rights as central to development has become fairly solidly established. In other areas, it has had little or no effect, and in still others it is not even present.

Yet the fact that change has been incomplete should not blind analysts to the reality that there has been change and that the World Bank has been considering these issues. It has done this in a way uniquely its own, both for better and for worse. In its manner of doing so, it has shown some fairly close similarities to the other organizations being studied here. What is most important, perhaps, from the perspective of the scholar of international relations, is the extent to which the Bank's successes and failures have been uniquely its own rather than imposed from outside.

## Chapter Four

# The World Health Organization:
# A Case of Incomplete Development

Progress by the World Health Organization (WHO) toward an integrated human rights strategy is difficult to characterize. WHO's interest in human rights (beyond a purely rhetorical one) is today more than a decade old. An expanded concept of rights found an early, powerful voice in Jonathan Mann, the first director of WHO's Global Programme on AIDS (GPA). The notion that an effective response to the HIV/AIDS pandemic required a political as well as a medical response fairly quickly became accepted by Mann and a circle of others inside WHO or connected with it. And this notion received sustained advocacy from the late 1980s until Mann's resignation from WHO (in 1990) and the separation of the GPA from WHO (in 1996, when its functions were transferred to the Joint United Nations Programme on HIV/AIDS, or UNAIDS).

Mann and his colleagues argued that protecting the rights of those who carried HIV, or who were members of vulnerable groups, was a vital public health priority. His argument that integrating a rights-based perspective into WHO's work would help the organization pursue its mandate was therefore at least as direct as that made in the other two organizations under discussion. This makes it more surprising that in the ensuing decade, WHO has clearly had the least success defining a clear human rights agenda.

Despite the faltering progress toward an effective human rights policy, WHO has consistently spoken of rights as being central to its operations and mandate. It has placed human rights experts in high-level positions, created an office with responsibility over rights issues, and produced numerous policy papers on the topic. Although subsequent directors general of WHO have been more cautious, at least one director-general, Gro Harlem Brundtland, was fairly direct in her statements concerning rights. She was also willing to use human rights as a way of prodding member states into taking the steps she deemed desirable, even while her commitment to internal reform was less than total. The concept of human rights has become part of WHO's official agenda and seems likely to remain, even if the meaning of that concept in this particular context remains vague.

As with the other agencies under review, the pressure at WHO to adopt the language of human rights and to incorporate rights into programming has come largely from environmental factors: from new challenges to programming (largely but not entirely HIV/AIDS related), from civil society (particularly nongovernmental organizations, or NGOs), and from the UN secretary-general. In the case of HIV/AIDS, WHO was able to avoid a great deal of outside pressure simply by getting rid of primary responsibility over that issue area, through the creation of UNAIDS: WHO took the area with the greatest pressure for change and allowed it to be spun off. Though then–WHO director-general Hiroshi Nakajima had misgivings about losing authority over the era's greatest global public health issue, by all accounts he was also aware of the social implications of this disease and not entirely sorry to be rid of the need to respond to them. HIV/AIDS, and the social change that came to be seen as central to controlling its spread, has never fit well with the technical orientation of WHO, just as the social side of development has been a challenge to the traditional orientation of the World Bank. But with the departure of Mann—after he feuded with Nakajima—WHO lost an internal true believer in a position of authority to champion the human rights cause. Without these two key elements—consistent environmental pressure and an internal champion—the rights agenda was left to flounder at WHO. Efforts at being more independent in the rights area have been defeated by a combination of resistance from states parties and bureaucratic inertia within the organization. Change has come much more slowly to WHO, which feels more tightly constrained than either the United Nations Children's Fund (UNICEF) or the World Bank: constrained in that its mission leaves it with less leeway for invention, and constrained in the competency of its staff—mainly doctors and public health professionals—to bring in policy ideas outside their area of expertise.

## Adoption

The origins of WHO lie in the original International Sanitary Conference of 1851 and a series of subsequent conferences. These conferences were aimed primarily at the international control of contagious diseases and were largely the result of the rapid spread of cholera and similar diseases brought on by new transportation technologies (World Health Organization 1958, 4). As scientific knowledge and an understanding of the nature of disease increased, so did the effort to create a formal multilateral health organization (Dubin 1995, 57). In 1907 the inaugural meeting of the Office International d'Hygiene Publique (OIHP) was held in Paris, with the function of both assisting states in combating diseases and in collecting and spreading knowledge of the nature of disease and the best way to ensure public health. This was an important shift from the emphasis of the earlier conferences, which had mainly been about protecting the Western countries from diseases originating abroad, through quarantines and similar actions. Thus the international effort to improve public health and control disease gradually took a more scientific, expert-led approach, as science gradually came to a more modern understanding of the nature and control of disease.

With the signing of the Treaty of Versailles and the creation of the League of Nations, an international League Health Organization was also recommended. The perceived need for international cooperation in the health arena was only heightened by the influenza pandemic of 1918–19 and a 1919 typhus epidemic in Russia and Poland, which itself affected over 2 million people (Siddiqi 1995, 19). Already in 1920, the League of Nations Council was considering the creation of an international health organization to supercede the OIHP, soon after the Treaty of Versailles came into force. Both the scale of the postwar health crises and the desire to see the League of Nations as an important international coordinating body fueled the desire to see a larger, more comprehensive body created than the old OIHP (World Health Organization 1958, 22–23). A temporary health committee was set up by the League in 1922, with the intention that it would lead to such a comprehensive international health agency.

The creation of a permanent League of Nations health organization was complicated from the beginning by the United States, in a bureaucratic battle that would presage similar conflicts later in the life of WHO. It was originally assumed by the League that the new health organization would take over the tasks being performed by the OIHP and absorb that organization into the larger body being created. However, the United States opposed this move, because it was not itself a member of the League; thus, if the OIHP become part of the League though absorption into the new health agency, the United States would either have to withdraw altogether or enter into a relationship with the League.

This early effort at international health cooperation had already come into contact with the realities of power politics and national preferences, to its own detriment. As Siddiqi points out, the U.S. position only reinforced the prejudices of those within the OIHP: "[The U.S.] veto reinforced the chauvinisms of those OIHP officials who did not wish to be subordinated to the League" (Siddiqi 1995, 20). The OIHP then rejected several overtures from the League for amalgamation between 1920 and 1926, for reasons that have been described as "unclear" but seem to have had as much to do with organizational as international politics (Siddiqi 1995, 20). Thus, throughout the interwar years, two parallel international health organizations coexisted with limited cooperation, with the older organization sticking largely to its traditional role while the newer one sought to expand the scope of international health cooperation (World Health Organization 1958, 28–31).

This state of affairs lasted roughly until the outbreak of World War II and the end of the League of Nations system. WHO's own account of the genesis of international health cooperation states that the lesson of these years is that "the will to effective international collaboration in questions of public health preceded by many years the existence of the scientific knowledge needed to make such collaboration effective" (World Health Organization 1958, 37). It was during the years before and after World War II that the scientific knowledge garnered at the beginning of the twentieth century "came to fruition"; there was now finally sufficient knowledge of the causes and treatment of disease to begin a really effective international public health effort. The approach to international public health by international organizations therefore expanded beyond questions of quarantine and the sharing of knowledge about outbreaks of disease: The new WHO began with an early focus on disease research and prevention as well as a broad mandate in such areas as maternal and child health, nutrition, and environmental sanitation, where new scientific progress suggested the possibility of real solutions to age-old problems (Allen 1950).

If the new WHO was to have a distinctly technical and scientific cast, this went in tandem with a much broader and more "human" conception of what was meant by "health" in the WHO Charter. WHO was founded in 1946 as a specialized agency of the UN, to coordinate international efforts in the health field. Its creation was quick and relatively smooth, with a general consensus that such an organization was necessary. No history of WHO fails to mention the unusually broad mandate incorporated into WHO's Constitution; this document describes the purpose of the organization to be the "attainment by all peoples of the highest possible level of health," and it defines health as "a state of complete physical, mental and social well-being and not merely the absence of disease or infirmity" (WHO Constitution, preamble). This broad definition departs in two respects from traditional notions of international health. First, it moves away from the older idea of health as an "absence of disease" and implies a more positive definition of health as a state of overall well-being. Second, it is notable in that it goes beyond a scientific notion of health and includes mental and social factors as well. As one contemporary observer puts it, "This mandate implies a broader program than that usually contained in the philosophy of the orthodox epidemiologist, sanitarian or public health officer" (Ascher 1952, 27).

This expanded definition of health would be referred to often as WHO evolved; it leaves a broad range for understanding how human rights fits it into its operational mandate. Yet despite the latitude built into the WHO Constitution in this area, the initial efforts of the organization were almost entirely technical. These included traditional sorts of disease prevention measures and assistance—originally focused on a "big six" of malaria, venereal disease, tuberculosis, maternal and child health, environmental sanitation, and nutrition (Ascher 1952, 29) but later expanded to include other issues—and various forms of program assistance to member states in areas such as training and coordination in the health sectors

(Mingst 1990, 208). WHO was from the beginning seen as an organization for medical personnel, for doctors and those with expertise in public health. Its focus was and remains scientific, and its expertise is in areas of medical rather than social policy.

The notion of a human right to health was not entirely absent from international discourse before the 1980s. The preamble of the WHO Constitution, after expressing its broad notion of what health means, goes on to say the following: "The enjoyment of the highest attainable standard of health is one of the fundamental rights of every human being without distinction of race, religion, political belief, economic or social condition." As Brigit Toebes has shown in her exhaustive work on the legal status of a right to health, this text was toned down from an earlier draft that did not include any reference to the highest attainable standard but did include further statements presenting a rather idealistic view of the importance of health in international affairs (Toebes 1999, 28–33). Similarly, although health standards are mentioned in Article 25 of the Universal Declaration of Human Rights (UDHR), they are combined with other important issues and the final text is "very broad and vague" (Toebes 1999, 40). The right to health is also mentioned in the International Covenant on Economic, Social, and Cultural Rights, as well as in the Convention on the Elimination of All Forms of Discrimination Against Women and in other documents. Mostly it is done in similarly expansive terms.

According to Daniel Tarantola, "Until [the 1990s], public health and human rights were often considered as two distinct, almost antagonistic sets of principles and practices" (Tarantola 2000, 1). Tarantola's work captures a key contradiction of the rights–health link: Though the concept of a "right to health" has existed at least since the founding of WHO and drafting of the UDHR, it has existed in tension with other basic and important concepts within the field of public health. As one study notes, in some situations, "human rights protect the rights of individuals, and public health protects the collective good. . . . Thus, the two compete" (Gostin and Lazzarini 1997, 43). Some ostensibly reasonable, and even vital, public health measures—such as testing, surveillance, and even quarantine when necessary—may seem to be in direct opposition to certain civil liberties and human rights. Mandatory testing may infringe on privacy rights; quarantine stands in obvious tension with the basic right to liberty. Given these conflicts, it is not surprising that public health officials have been wary of bringing human rights language into the field of public health, however much they agree with the idea of human rights in theory.

One early and important development toward a right to health approach within WHO was the launch, in 1979, of WHO's "Health for All" strategy. The program "represent[ed] a departure from the disease-specific, hospital-based, technological orientation characterizing traditional public health programs" (Taylor 1992, 314), and it instead brought a social agenda and a larger, political awareness to the subject of international cooperation on public health. The Alma-Ata Declaration, which launched the Health for All Program, includes many of the same themes that would characterize more specific references to health as a human rights: the need to address inequalities of health care access (Article II); community participation in health care decisions (Article IV), the need for an integrated social approach rather than a focus merely on technical health care provision (Article VII[4]), and greater government–civil society cooperation in health care policy (Article VIII), among other points. The Health for All statement included the goal of "an acceptable level of health for all the people of the world by the year 2000" (Article X). The strategy also contained references to obviously political issues such as the "New International Economic Order." Health for All remains a central WHO strategy, reaffirmed most recently in 1995. It added a social dimension to WHO's view of its own mission, tempering its particular concern with the scientific aspects of public health with a larger view of development and even international distributive justice.

Health for All, with its emphasis on distributional issues and community participation, was not in itself a declaration of a human rights approach to public health, but it did contain many themes that would later be important. It certainly did lay the groundwork for a more activist policy by placing new emphasis on the social context of public health, on the politics of health care provision, and on the empowerment of individuals as key to their own long-term well-being. Mann, for example, noted its importance in shaping the future of WHO: "The countries know WHO," he said in reference to the activities related to Health for All; "we built upon that trust" (Taylor 1992, 322). Mann is the significant figure in the early development of a human rights approach within WHO, through his position as the first director of the GPA.

Thus both the Health for All initiative and, later, issues of women's rights and reproductive health prepared the way for the much more explicit interest in human rights that came from the AIDS pandemic (Tarantola 2000, 2). These at least prepared the ground at WHO for a wider appreciation of the challenge of international public health, beyond the merely scientific and technical: they had a long-term and important effect on the bureaucratic culture of WHO and the way it perceived its mission. Mann had already developed an outstanding record as an AIDS researcher and activist, and he had worked in Zaire as director of a project studying, among other issues, heterosexual and mother-to-child transmission of AIDS, before joining WHO (Wojcik 1998, 129). At WHO, he was hand selected to be the first director of the GPA (initially called the Special Programme on AIDS) and, as such, led WHO's initial reaction to the pandemic. WHO had in fact been slow to recognize the worldwide importance of AIDS; in the early 1980s, WHO had seen AIDS as being primarily a problem afflicting developed countries and therefore one better left to national action in countries that were well able to afford their own research and treatment (Gordenker et al. 1995, 37).

It was the onset of the AIDS/HIV crisis of the 1980s that first elevated human rights from a largely rhetorical exercise within WHO to an issue requiring serious consideration; and Mann, WHO's first GPA director, was central in this development. He would refer to three "periods of HIV prevention efforts": a first one of "uncertainty and urgency," which focused public information campaigns to prevent the spread of the virus; a second period, from about 1985 to 1988, focused on risk reduction and in particular on reducing the incidence of risky behavior; and a third period, after 1988, adding a "societal dimension" to the risk-reduction campaign (Mann 1999, 217–18). It was during this second period, according to Mann, that WHO became aware of the need to consider the human rights side of the AIDS pandemic.

The extreme, sometimes panicked responses to the spreading AIDS pandemic were the basis for Mann's concern and the concern of many other AIDS activists. Gostin and Lazzarini lay out the human rights challenges presented by AIDS:

mandatory screening of homosexuals, sex workers, injection drug users, foreigners, or other perceived "risk groups"; prohibition of HIV-infected persons from certain professions; isolation, detention, compulsory treatment, or medical examination of persons with HIV infection; limitations on international travel by requiring HIV testing for entry into certain countries; classification of HIV/AIDS as a special or dangerous disease requiring differential treatment by medical personnel; and the requirement that AIDS be listed on death certificates. Criminal sanctions for homosexuality, prostitution, and injection drug use have contributed to stigmatization. (Gostin and Lazzarini 1997, 75)

Largely through Mann's activism within WHO and his leadership of the GPA, the issue of rights, and the violation of the rights of those who were HIV positive or in high-risk groups, became part of WHO's agenda in the late 1980s. In 1988, the World Health Assembly, the governing body of WHO, adopted a resolution "urg[ing] Member States . . . to protect the human rights and dignity of HIV-infected people and people with AIDS, and of members of population groups, and to avoid discriminatory action against and stigmatization of them in the provision of services, employment and travel" (World Health Assembly 1988, 1). In a speech later the same year, Mann built on this resolution, arguing that there was "a strong and clear public health rationale for this emphasis on protecting the human rights and dignity of HIV-infected persons" (Mann 1988, 2).

Mann felt WHO and the international community in general needed to clearly oppose the discrimination, and even the repression, experienced by many people who were HIV positive around the world. But it is important to note that his original concern was for the public health implications of such discrimination, not for the human rights aspect per se. His argument, in other words, was distinctly the one from effectiveness, similar to those used by UNICEF and the World Bank: that discrimination and other human rights abuses toward those infected with the HIV virus were hampering public health efforts. The 1992 Global AIDS Strategy document, published after Mann's departure but building on his influential ideas, clearly lays out the public health rationale. It specifically blamed ignorance, a lack of available information on HIV's spread and its prevention, and societal taboos for hampering prevention efforts; and it stated that these problems are "aggravated by the continued stigmatization of HIV-infected persons. . . . As a result, there is still insufficient high-level political support for the prevention and control efforts needed" (World Health Organization 1992, 9). The failure to address the rights of those with HIV, it argued, was counterproductive in the fight against its spread. Discrimination prevented those who needed help from seeking it, interfered with public information programs, and generally drove the problem "underground" when what was needed was open and frank discussion. All this undermined the main thrust of the anti-AIDS strategy of this time, which was a combination of risk reduction with a consideration of the societal context within which AIDS continued to spread (Mann 1999, 218).

The 1992 document included a further expansion of the idea of human rights as being important in the fight against AIDS. The notion of a "societal context," as the GPA and others were beginning to conceive of it, went beyond the specific question of discrimination and instead included all the social factors that allowed AIDS to spread as quickly as it did. These included "the subordinate social and economic status of women," certain social practices (e.g., prostitution or drug use) that facilitated the spread of the disease, the reluctance within many societies to discuss sexual or health matters openly, and a host of other issues that had not traditionally been part of the public health discourse. Thus the discourse within the GPA and WHO was expanding from a focus on the rights of people with AIDS to a view of human rights *in general* as being part of the larger effort to control the spread of AIDS. This included tying the rights agenda of the AIDS control effort to the larger universe of international human rights instruments: the Convention on the Elimination of All Forms of Discrimination Against Women (CEDAW), the Convention on the Rights of the Child (CRC), and the UDHR, among others (Mann 1999, 223). This represented a substantial expansion of the human rights agenda within WHO, albeit one confined for the time being to the question of HIV transmission. Nevertheless, the argument developed within the GPA that states have preexisting human rights obligations, which they must observe if they are to have a successful approach to the AIDS pandemic.

It is important to note here that the connection between HIV/ AIDS responses and human rights was not an idea exclusive to WHO by any means; this was also something widely recognized and developed outside WHO, and particularly in civil society and AIDS NGOs. By the late 1980s, the political rights of those with HIV were a central focus of many NGOs within the United States and in Europe, and these ideas were becoming more a part of the international agenda. In 1990–91, international NGOs, incensed by what they perceived as discriminatory visa regulations in the United States that restricted the travel rights of HIV-positive people, forced the Sixth International Conference on AIDS to move its meeting from San Francisco to Paris. The pressures felt by Mann and WHO were intense, and they led to considerable division within WHO on the appropriate response (Gordenker et al. 1995, 118–25).

Mann left the GPA in 1990, largely because of his feud with the incoming WHO director-general, Hiroshi Nakajima. Mann had enjoyed a very close relationship with Halfdan Mahler, the director-general when he was hired, and Mahler had also by all accounts agreed with Mann regarding the need to consider a rights agenda in WHO's approach to AIDS. But Mann experienced personal problems with Nakajima essentially from the moment of Nakajima's hiring, in 1988. These problems were based partially on Nakajima's perception of AIDS as a minor problem compared with established killers such as Malaria (Gellman 2000), but also, according to eyewitnesses, because of Nakajima's resentment of Mann's personal style, and of his high profile within the international AIDS community. An early, significant event occurred in 1988 just before the first World AIDS Day summit, when Mann discovered that Nakajima was preparing to give a speech mentioning "the need for balance between the rights of AIDS patients and the interests of society at large" (Gellman 2000, 9). Mann perceived these words as a backing-away from a rights-based approach, and he pressured Nakajima to remove them; but their relationship never improved, and Mann left WHO in 2000, to Nakajima's evident relief.

Much of the rhetoric of human rights continued under Nakajima's directorship: yet the actual policy was in abeyance between Mann's departure in 1990 and 1996, when the GPA was "spun off" from WHO to create UNAIDS. WHO concentrated on the technical aspects of HIV/AIDS and did little in the rights field. By the mid-1990s, the GPA was being criticized for its failure to adequately coordinate the efforts of the various UN bodies involved in the response to AIDS (Jonsson 1996, 68); it was also true that many UN agencies simply resented the idea that one agency, WHO, through the GPA, had been given so much authority over what was becoming a highly visible global issue. It ultimately became necessary to move responsibility for HIV/AIDS issues outside WHO to UN-AIDS—a move that Nakajima publicly opposed, but, according to more than one insider, he secretly welcomed, because it rid WHO of a series of issues he felt unprepared to take on. Ultimately, however, this meant that WHO had rid itself both of the issue that had led it to face the reality of human rights issues in its work and of most of the last true believers who might have worked from the inside to change its organizational culture.

Meanwhile, Mann continued to teach at Harvard University, where he had taken a position in the School of Public Health, and he worked with a number of other scholars on health and human rights. Though WHO paid scant attention to the social aspects of the AIDS crisis—and, by extension, to the rights–health link in general—this became a primary aspect of NGOs' response to the AIDS pandemic. Mann and others working with him came to understand both the ethical *and* the public health aspects of a human rights approach to AIDS. He and his colleagues began to advocate for the right to health more generally, as did many others in the public health community outside WHO and Harvard. These two aspects of human rights in international public health—both the "argument from effectiveness" and the moral argument—became inseparable in writing on the topic of human rights in public health during the 1990s.

There were, then, strong external factors working on WHO (and on UNAIDS, after its creation in 1996). However, there was not any strong pressure *within* WHO to adopt a more rights-oriented approach, and Mann's relationship with Nakajima had made it clear what direction the organization was going in on that score. There also was not strong support for any such approach from member states, whose attitude in this period might most charitably be considered benign neglect toward the realities of international AIDS control (Gellman 2000). Given the circumstances, it would not have been surprising if WHO had entirely disavowed any interest in discussing human rights issues, and in fact this might have seemed the most logical course of action to many within the organization. It was and remains staffed primarily by doctors and others with similar scientific training, who are happy to leave the "fuzzy" social issues to others. However, there was a fairly substantial change of direction on the issue of human rights when Gro Harlem Brundtland became director-general of WHO in July 1998. Brundtland, the former prime minister of Norway as well as a trained physician, signaled this change almost immediately, with a speech in Paris marking the fiftieth anniversary of the UDHR.

Brundtland's motivation for doing so had a great deal to do with her background, for she had always shown a great interest in social issues. Clearly, the support of Scandinavian countries for her election was significant; they had consistently supported international human rights issues in other venues, and it was expected that she would continue to get their support as she brought that agenda to WHO. Also, it appears, there was a simple desire to distinguish her leadership from that of Nakajima, and to signal to staff that things at WHO would change.[1] Though it was evident during the debate over whether to keep Nakajima on for another term of office that the United States was not happy with his leadership (Crossette 1997), there is no reason to suppose that Brundtland's support for human rights was the primary factor in her hiring. It was understood that she had interests in this direction, but they were never made explicit as a condition for hiring her.

From an organizational perspective, it is significant that WHO appeared uncomfortable from the beginning with HIV/AIDS, a disease that did not fit within its primary organizational mandate. Mann's dismissal, Nakajima's uncomfortable relationship with the GPA, and the eventual creation of UNAIDS all served to keep at arm's length the primary issue motivating those who wanted to link health and human rights. Having been deprived of Mann, its "insider" champion on human rights, WHO was forced to look outside when the need to address this issue became more pressing. Director-General Brundtland herself had to come in from outside, and she also needed to turn to others for assistance. Daniel Tarantola, a colleague of Mann at Harvard, had been hired as a policy adviser within the office of the director-general, and he became an important resource on human rights issues.

Not surprisingly, perhaps, those charged with creating a health and human rights policy met, in the words of one participant, "all kinds of resistance" in implementing an organization-wide human rights agenda.[2] Those suspicious of a human rights agenda argued that such a strategy would require a basic rethinking of important public health strategies—such as the quarantining of infected people, restrictions on movement, and testing—that had been highlighted in the context of HIV/AIDS. They also worried—in a close parallel to the experience of UNICEF and the World Bank—that a human rights strategy would hamper the ability of WHO to cooperate with states, by bringing into its work a politically charged issue. In an organization based on highly technical and ostensibly "neutral" scientific issues, this was seen not as progress but as a dangerous step. Later in her tenure, Brundtland established a health and human rights office in the WHO Strategy Unit to serve as a focal point for efforts in the human rights field, giving them more institutional presence.

This resistance from below might have been more easily overcome had there been countervailing support from the highest levels, and the advent of Brundtland in 1998 might have provided an opportunity for that. However, by late 1999, Director-General Brundtland "step[ped] back" from her promotion of a human rights strategy—most notably, bowing to outside pressure, she held up a draft strategy that had been prepared within WHO with the intention of educating governments on their human rights obligations in the field of health.[3] This became a full retreat in 2000, when opposition became more noticeable from states parties as well as from staff.

The precipitating event here is the publication of the 2000 *World Health Report*, which tried to rank health care systems internationally in new ways, looking not only at performance versus gross domestic product (as WHO had done) but also at performance compared with "what the experts estimate to be the upper limit of what can be done with the level of resources available in that country" (World Health Organization 2000b). The study also quantified and compared health care achievements among similar countries on such measures as "responsiveness of health systems" and "fairness of financial contribution to health systems." As the deliberations of the WHO executive board show, the response to this initiative from a number of badly ranked countries was decidedly negative. The members of the board took action; they noted that they were "aware of the technical difficulties and political sensitivities associated with comparing the performance of national health systems" and instructed the director-general to consult with them before any further such exercises were undertaken (WHO Executive Board 2001, 2). Aggrieved states also sent letters directly to the director-general expressing their displeasure, particularly over the fact that the information they had provided to WHO had been made public in a way that they found embarrassing.[4]

Although Brundtland continued to speak of human rights issues until the end of her tenure at WHO, it was clear that she would not push for a comprehensive rights-based program. The result was instead a more haphazard process that was far less effective and coordinated than those of the other organizations under study.

## Definition

When Gro Harlem Brundtland began to seriously consider the place of human rights within WHO and its mandate, her approach was not entirely without precedent; and though little had been done within WHO to consider the place of human rights in health planning, there was an established and growing body of literature outside the organization. The idea of integrating a rights-based approach into WHO presents very substantial challenges, which might not be immediately apparent. The WHO Constitution, beginning as it does by defining health as "a state of complete physical, mental and social well-being," is generally taken in as the starting point for a right to health policy.

Yet the very scope of this mandate can make it difficult to know what a human rights approach would mean for WHO: Given that health itself is a human right according to the WHO Constitution, and that health includes social, psychological, and physical factors, what does a rights approach add to what WHO is already doing? The UN special rapporteur on the right to health, Paul Hunt, puts it this way: "Because there is overlap between human rights targets and socio-economic progress, there is likely to be a resemblance between human rights indicators and the standard indicators of

socio-economic progress" (Hunt 2003, 2). In other words, working to promote health in developing countries, and implementing
their right to health, will often look quite similar. Hunt suggests
that the difference will often lie in the intent (development vs.
rights promotion) and, more saliently, in the desire to hold the
duty bearer (usually governments) to account. The breadth of the
WHO Constitution affords it considerable latitude, if it wants to
use it, in determining what is or is not a rights issue, and what is
or is not within its mandate. Much as with the World Bank, there is
the potential to simply take old policies and redefine them as rights
protection. It is important, therefore, to be careful in distinguishing real institutional change from mere rhetoric.

WHO begins with the basic claim that health, in its broadest
definition, is a human right. That is, health is a key component
of human dignity and something to which all are entitled—or at
least, of which no one may be deliberately deprived—by virtue of
their status as human beings. In a 1998 speech, Director-General
Brundtland specifically connected WHO to the most general notion of health as a general right of all people: "It is no coincidence
that the idea to establish a world health organization emerged from
the same process that identified the universal value of human
rights. WHO's mandate is also universal" (Brundtland 1998). She
included reducing the "burden of disease" and increasing access to
health services as basic to human rights and to the mission not just
of WHO but the UN in general. Her speech made reference to the
goal of the "highest attainable" level of health for all citizens and
placed this foremost among WHO's goals. The notion of a right to
the highest attainable level is, of course, a recognition that health
for citizens per se cannot properly be considered a right, because
different societies will be able to afford different levels of health
care provision (and because no person can be guaranteed health,
no matter what resources are available).

Significantly, however, this very broad notion that health itself
is a right to be promoted (although it can never, of course, be guaranteed) does not play a prominent part in subsequent WHO thinking on human rights. As Virginia Leary has put it, "On first hearing
it, the phrase 'right to health' strikes many as strange. . . . Superfi-
cially, the 'right to health' seems to presume that government or international organizations or individuals must guarantee a person's

good health. This interpretation is obviously absurd" (Leary 1994, 25). There is a substantial divergence between the right to health, on the one hand, which is in practice both vague and unattainable as a universal goal; and a "'human rights approach' to health," which seeks specific interventions consonant with WHO's mission. Although, as will be discussed below, WHO has not entirely stopped discussing health itself as a right, what WHO really has in mind when it talks of human rights is a rights-based approach to health care. This includes both positing the provision of health care as a right in itself (to the extent that a society's resources allow) and determining how health, health care, and human rights interact. Violations of basic rights (e.g., the right not to be tortured, or discriminated against on the basis of race) might have adverse health consequences; health care itself might be improved by attention to matters of discrimination or political participation. Again, the limitations on how health can actually be provided, or guaranteed, as a right make health a very specific sort of right, one that has to be spoken of very carefully. So the right that is actually being spoken of is not the right to be healthy, nor even the right to a particular level of health care, but something more complex.

Recall that that connection between rights and health was brought to the foreground within WHO by the HIV/AIDS crisis, and that the earliest formulation of this argument was the argument from effectiveness. It is worth fleshing that argument out here, because it plays a central role in defining the rights–health link. Advocates for the rights of those with HIV/AIDS argued that mandatory testing of those perceived to have a high risk of acquiring HIV/AIDS—thereby likely discriminating against high-risk groups or those already infected or violating their rights in other ways (e.g., by arresting or quarantining them)—was counterproductive in the fight against the disease. To Mann, the challenge of HIV/AIDS and human rights were inextricably linked: "The modern movement of human rights," he wrote in a seminal article (after leaving WHO), "born in the aftermath of the Holocaust in Europe and born of the deep aspiration to prevent the recurrence of government sponsored violence, provides AIDS prevention with a coherent conceptual framework" (Mann 1999, 222). The violation of human rights contributed to the spread of HIV/AIDS, he argued, and therefore protecting basic human rights would benefit public health efforts. After the creation of UNAIDS, primary responsibility over the AIDS issue moved to the UNAIDS offices across the street from WHO. The guidelines titled *HIV/AIDS and Human Rights* (United Nations 2001), published jointly by UNAIDS and the Office of the High Commissioner for Human Rights, generally follow the same ideas, with greater detail on the actual legal implementation of rights protection.

The rights being enumerated—political participation (through community involvement in HIV/AIDS programming), due process (to reform criminal law so that HIV/AIDS sufferers or vulnerable groups are not targeted), gender equity, and the like—are part of general international human rights law and are referred to as such in the guidelines. The actual aim was not to define new sets of rights but rather to discern the specific ways in which human rights law has an impact on public health. In other words, it was clear to Mann and others that there was no need to invent new rights concepts. The need was only to fully enforce those that existed. Therefore, one could take the not very politically controversial course of simply demanding that states live up to their existing obligations where HIV/AIDS sufferers were concerned. Of course, the basic right to not be discriminated against (on the basis of health status, race, membership in a high-risk group or category, etc.) is not in itself usually a key component of health care or an overall right to health; it is left to WHO, UNAIDS, and others to make the connection between rights and health. But by speaking of these, WHO is not creating new categories of rights or stretching the boundaries of already existing rights, such as the broadly understood one to the highest attainable level of health. Rather, it is expanding its basic mandate into new areas of rights promotion, with the understanding that these areas are vital for promoting the broader goal of universal health.

The challenge of a mature health and human rights policy for WHO has been to develop, from the initial HIV/AIDS concerns, a broader framework for connecting health and rights. Gruskin and Tarantola, in a comprehensive article on health and human rights, explain two different ways that this argument can lead to improved public health programs: "The first [approach] focuses consideration on the ways in which health policies, programs and practices can promote or violate rights in the ways they are designed or implemented. . . . The second approach examines how violations or lack of attention to human rights can have serious health consequences" (Gruskin and Tarantola 2002, 330; see also World Health Organization 2000a, 2).

Both these approaches are visible in the way WHO has developed rights-based programming. WHO seems to be on firmer ground when it emphasizes the second set of issues, the health consequences of rights violations, and it has focused its own discussion on these, which it can most effectively argue directly pertain to its mandate. It can also claim that it is interested mainly in promoting health and only in considering rights as they have an impact on effective health promotion. It is here that one sees substantial overlap between the concerns of WHO and those of the other specialized agencies under consideration: questions of gender, minority status, poverty, and vulnerability, as well as other issues such as homophobia and traditional practices.

As WHO has developed the notion that public health programs need to consider human rights issues to boost their effectiveness, it has considered the ways that public health initiatives might reinforce existing social programs. Seeking to understand how human rights are applicable to health issues, WHO staff with responsibility over rights issues have paid substantial attention to how other UN agencies—most notably UNICEF—have defined and interpreted human rights. In interviews, staff members mention UNICEF in particular as a "role model" for WHO. It is not surprising, therefore, that many of the same issues arise in WHO program documents. Although this issue is distinct from the original "argument from effectiveness" that rights violations (discrimination, mandatory testing, etc.) have public health repercussions, it makes its own similar argument: namely, that tailoring public health projects to consider the violation of rights will help provide services by highlighting disparities among groups, underlying political issues that contribute to poor outcomes, and other structural factors that inhibit good health care provision.

Discrimination in particular remains a key issue. "Vulnerable and marginalized groups in society," a key WHO report notes, "tend to bear an undue proportion of health problems. Overt or implicit discrimination violates a fundamental human rights principle and often lies at the root of poor health status" (World Health

Organization 2002b, 13). One area of concern for WHO is gender discrimination, as it has been for other UN agencies. Although the unequal status of women has been a concern of WHO for some time (World Health Organization 1998), gender discrimination only received focused attention from WHO as a human rights issue in the mid-1990s. This was driven partially by HIV/AIDS, which required a focus on vulnerable groups such as women, along with intravenous drug users, prostitutes, and homosexuals (World Health Organization 1995); and partially by a growing interest in gender issues in other parts of the UN body (World Health Assembly 1992). It is important that the CEDAW also gives specific legal guidance concerning the rights of women and that it is generally mentioned as a key document on health and human rights.

Gender is now one of the best-developed and most complex human rights ideas within WHO. To some extent, this is because of the guidance given by the CEDAW, and also because of the general prominence given to gender issues within the UN system. Here a rights approach deals with the way that a particular type of rights violation—discrimination against women and other forms of gender inequality—has public health repercussions, specifically affecting the health of women and their children. WHO has taken a political attitude toward gender equality, advocating, for example, legal changes concerning marriage laws, access to family planning, prevention of violence against women, and other social problems that endanger women and their children (World Health Organization 2002a). The connection between health and human rights, therefore, involves removing gender discrimination not only in the delivery of health care but also in the structure of society in general, to the extent that that structure has serious health consequences.

In the context of gender, reproductive health is one area where there has been activity on human rights within WHO. In interviews, staff members working on reproductive health issues have tied their own concern for human rights issues to the women's movement of the 1980s and in particular to issues related to contraception. Research into contraceptive measures, and generally helping women take greater control over their reproductive choices, led to the first concern over empowering women in this area, and to connections between WHO and the NGO community working on women's health. By the 1990s, and particularly after the 1994 International Conference on Population and Development in Cairo (World Health Organization 2001b, 3), a unit within WHO's Reproductive Health Department was connecting women's rights generally with improved health outcomes in pregnancy and childbirth. Much of this early work was being done quietly, with neither great opposition nor great support from Director-General Nakajima, although that would change somewhat later when Brundtland took over that position.

Here, as with gender in general, the rights-based approach is defined as seeking legal and cultural obstacles that jeopardize women's health, particularly in the context of pregnancy and childbirth. Realizing rights in this context means removing the obstacles to adequate maternal health care. These obstacles include the various ways in which legal systems complicate health care delivery, for example, "laws that entrench women in roles subservient to their brothers and husbands," such as laws that require women and adolescent girls to get permission from parents or husbands before obtaining needed health care services (Cook and Dickens 2001, 14–15). They also include the larger problem of women's access to adequate information about their own health and their health care options. Other ways in which women are discriminated against, such as having limited education options or poor access to vital health information, contribute to maternal health risks and violate women's rights. A central study carefully delineates the various elements of key human rights documents—including the UDHR, CRC, and CEDAW—that cover women's rights to control their own reproductive choices and to have access to the care they need during pregnancy, childbirth, and motherhood, including the right to education, to "special protection" during pregnancy, and to enter freely into marriage, among many other points, as well as more general rights against discrimination (Cook and Dickens 2001, 21–65).

Along with gender, other forms of discrimination in health care delivery have been examined by WHO and accepted as part of the human rights approach. The rights of indigenous peoples have been explicitly recognized by the World Health Assembly (1994), and WHO is in the process of developing a "global framework" of activities to benefit indigenous peoples worldwide. In 2002, the World Health Assembly passed a resolution that

urges Member States: (1) to recognize and protect the right of indigenous people to enjoyment of the highest attainable standard of health,
as mentioned in the WHO Constitution, within overall national development policies; (2) to make adequate provisions for indigenous health
needs in their national health systems, including through improved
collection and reporting of statistics and health data; (3) to respect,
preserve and maintain traditional healing practices and remedies,
consistent with nationally and internationally accepted standards, and
to seek to ensure that indigenous people retain this traditional knowledge and its benefits." (World Health Assembly 2001, 1–2)

More generally, WHO has acknowledged the importance of racial discrimination, poverty, and other manifestations of inequality
as barriers to providing people with adequate health care (World
Health Organization 2001c). Of course, these issues need not necessarily be considered as rights issues; they can be thought of as
merely practical barriers to health promotion. However, WHO has
specifically tied the elimination of discrimination and other barriers to a rights-oriented approach: "The principle of Health for All,
and of equal access to health services for all, is . . . as central to hu-
mankind's development, and the securing of basic human rights,
as economic or any other type of social development" (Brundtland
1998).

This clarifies the extent to which the promotion of an expansive
rights-based approach to health is clearly distinct from the earlier
HIV/AIDS-focused priority of preventing specific discrimination
based on health status. Still, the two ideas do share the basic belief that a respect for the abstract notion of human rights will lead
to more effective delivery of health care, in this case by making
sure that services are delivered to underserved populations. It is
important to note that in some cases, as WHO sees it, the connection may be indirect between protecting or implementing a right
to health, on the one hand, and actual public health outcomes,
on the other. The elimination of systematic inequalities—by making certain that underserved populations are taken care of—may
not add to the total amount of health care being provided to the
larger population. Rather than lowering the incidence of a particular condition or increasing spending on health care, attention to
rectifying discrimination in health care might simply mean that

resources are more fairly distributed among certain identifiable groups. Where resources are limited and insufficient, making sure that a fair share reaches some marginalized group (say, street children) may in fact mean taking some resources away from other uses.

Thus, political issues such as equity and empowerment (particularly of women and indigenous peoples) play an important role in WHO's thinking about the meaning of a right to health: It entails not just increasing the provision of health care but also making its distribution more just. In a sense, when WHO speaks of its responsibilities to protect and promote human rights, it is not just saying that it has a responsibility for health issues as a human rights area; rather, it is arguing that other important human rights issues—gender equity, child welfare, and the like—can and should inform the way that public health is envisioned and pursued. Much of this is based on already-issued human rights documents, and WHO has been careful to tie its activities to the existing concerns of the UN Commission on Human Rights (Economic and Social Council 2003). Those WHO staff involved in addressing the rights strategy regularly state their conviction that the integration of these "outside" human rights norms will make public health programs not only more just but also more effective and that the effective promotion of health requires attention to underserved populations, discrimination, and other social issues. As true as this likely is, it remains a fairly revolutionary idea within WHO and has met vocal resistance—primarily from those who feel that such an overtly political agenda for WHO's programs would weaken its ability to work cooperatively with states, and also from a minority who simply feel that such political goals are no business of WHO, which is supposed to focus on technical matters of health.[5] The policy implications of this divide will be discussed at length below.

All this has fit generally into the notion of considering how human rights violations, broadly understood, lead to poor health performance. The other side of the distinction made above, recall, is the understanding of how health policies and programs promote or violate rights in the way they are implemented. The distinction between these two categories, though useful, is not always entirely clear; for example, in the case of gender discrimination, one might say that a public health program that ignores discrimination against women (and thus ignores women's rights) has serious public health consequences in increased morbidity and mortality among women, and one might equally well say that such a program violated women's rights "in the way it is implemented" and thus fits the first branch of Gruskin and Tarantola's dichotomy. Thus the argument from effectiveness can and sometimes does cover a wide variety of health care reforms, if WHO chooses to use it that way.

Not surprisingly, much work within WHO on rights-based programming has been careful to focus on *specific legal rights* and the implementation of public health initiatives, rather than referring to a more expansive set of presumed rights determined by WHO staff. In the case of WHO, there is not much made of the simple moral imperative to consider and protect human rights. More so than UNICEF and even the World Bank, WHO is at pains to maintain that the argument from effectiveness is the driving force in considering rights. In the case of HIV/AIDS and other communicable diseases (tuberculosis is the other primary example), the actual connection is more clear than, say, protecting the rights of indigenous peoples and the advancement of national development goals; but the logic, and the bureaucratic imperative, are the same.

Although there is clearly a desire among some WHO staff to protect those whose rights might be violated, WHO is not a human rights enforcement body; to raise the issue of rights, it is helpful to link it to effective programming. Nevertheless, as a UN agency, WHO is bound to follow the directives of the General Assembly, including its human rights treaty law. Though some WHO staff members express a desire to play a positive role in promoting rights (e.g., by actively combating discriminatory practices in host countries), others are more circumspect when it comes to these sorts of decisions, fearing they will jeopardize working relationships with government partners. Thus, though there is concern within WHO regarding obvious cases where rights have been violated in the name of public health—most notably, the imprisonment of those with HIV/AIDS—there is little in official documents making the simple moral argument against such actions. The next section shows that such issues *do* concern some WHO staff members, particularly the "true believers," but are downplayed or ignored in official documents.

Finally, there is at least a rhetorical commitment from the top of the organization to what might be called the more general notion of the right to health, that is, the strict interpretation of health (or at least the prerequisites of health, such as adequate nutrition and basic health care) as a human right in and of itself. WHO's Nutrition Department, for example, has enumerated a vision for the future where "everyone without distinction of age, sex or race has the right to nutritionally adequate and safe food and to be free from hunger and malnutrition" but has admitted the difficulty of translating such "lofty goals" and apply them to actual operations (United Nations Standing Committee on Nutrition 2000, 4.3). WHO has taken a position on "water for health" as a human right in and of itself, and it has used the general idea of a "right to water" to support its "Healthy Environments for Children Initiative," with the implication that water and health are both rights in and of themselves (World Health Organization 2002c).

A prominent area where an actual right to health has appeared in WHO's thinking is in the issue of essential drug provision, particularly where AIDS-fighting antiretroviral drugs are concerned. WHO has taken an active role in formulating international policy on patent rights concerning expensive pharmaceuticals such as antiretroviral drugs. The question has largely centered on the Agreement on Trade-Related Intellectual Property Rights (TRIPS) of the World Trade Organization—in particular, the extent to which developing countries must respect the patent rights of foreign pharmaceutical firms. In essence, the TRIPS agreement limits the ability of foreign firms to make low-cost copies of patented drugs, which often means (according to critics) that millions in the developing world do not have access to affordable medicines. WHO has gone so far as to insist that "access to essential drugs is part of the human right to health" (World Health Organization 2001a, 5), although this statement was carefully balanced by reinforcing the need to protect patent rights and encourage innovation in drug research. As WHO's director-general, Brundtland had used morally laden terms to discuss the issue. She referred to the lack of affordable drugs in the developing world as "tragic" and an "outrage" and is reported to have raised the issue as a human rights one in her discussions with WHO member states and with pharmaceutical firms. WHO has had to walk a fine line in discussing any human right to essential drugs and especially to antiretroviral medicines, but it has raised the issue in those terms, and discussions with WHO staff members make it clear that many see the issue this way.

Generally speaking, however, the notion that health itself is a human right is quite poorly developed in the WHO literature and remains a largely rhetorical exercise. It has also, not surprisingly, been the most difficult right to translate into effective policy prescriptions, despite being enshrined in the WHO Charter. Yet the right to health is not really the most politically sensitive issue facing WHO—the problem of public health issues that violate individual human rights is the issue with the most potential to create host-state opposition—and, as the case of UNICEF demonstrated, a general notion that states have rights obligations to protect certain groups can be very politically useful to an international organization. The fact that WHO has failed to exploit this issue as completely as UNICEF is indicative of the larger resistance within WHO when the rights issue is raised.

The overall picture of the development of human rights thinking within WHO is one of relatively slow and halting progress. Like the other institutions under study, WHO has paid most attention to those rights specifically linked to its mission; and also like those others, it has devoted a fairly large portion of its effort to determining how its existing operations fulfill certain rights goals. Where WHO differs is that it has been even less aggressive than the World Bank in finding novel ways to connect the moral side of rights; that is, those things that are good in and of themselves, regardless of their direct connection to the organization's mission. Rather than pursuing a directed approach to determining the relevance of human rights to its mission, WHO has made a number of halting efforts to see how rights have an impact on its existing programs. The ineffectiveness of these efforts is even more apparent when one examines the organizational and programmatic changes that have accompanied them. Resistance within WHO has been as effective at limiting the implementation of a rights agenda as resistance from outside. Although Brundtland's efforts did meet resistance from some member states, as has been shown above, it was not so great that there were not ways around it; the other cases under study here show the limited direct effects of such resistance. Other, cultural factors have been at least as important.

## Implementation

How has the emerging interest within WHO regarding human rights issues led to concrete programmatic changes? The most obvious and important changes within WHO have been structural ones: The new interest in a rights-based approach has led to the creation of new job descriptions and several new offices. Organizations often both signal their interest in new issues and attempt to institutionalize those interests through the creation of new offices that can form a focal point for those issues. It is necessary to create advocates for new priorities within the organization, if the existing organizational culture is to be effectively changed. What is surprising, perhaps, is the relative ineffectiveness of these changes. Though WHO has certainly signaled its interest in human rights outwardly, its internal commitment has been weak, and this has been reflected in the institutional steps it has taken. Those charged with pursuing human rights standards have expressed frustration with this process, and it is also evident that WHO staff members have not received clear indications that the organization's top management is committed to change. Their frustration at the slow pace of organizational change says a great deal about the underdeveloped state of rights thinking in WHO.

Rather than being able to present a clear picture of efforts at institutional reform—successful or not—a description of WHO's activities in the field of human rights is necessarily episodic and, at times, quite disjointed. This very lack of a clear narrative of progress says a great deal about the difficulties WHO has had in formulating a workable human rights policy that will be accepted by its staff members. The resistance that has come from within the organization, caused largely by the "evidence-based," scientific culture of the WHO staff, is similar to what has been seen in the other two organizations under study. Staff have also worried about how a rights-based approach will affect relations with member states. The rights agenda has also raised the sort of staff resistance one inevitably sees when any organizational culture is challenged by radical new ideas. The lack of internal support has interacted with, and magnified, the external opposition to an extensive rights-based policy faced by Brundtland. Although both UNICEF and the World Bank have faced similar internal as well as external opposition, in the case of WHO, this opposition has been more effective at frustrating a concerted policy of rights promotion.

If the key intellectual moment retarding the early development of a WHO health and human rights agenda was Mann's departure from the GPA, then the key organizational one was the removal of responsibility over HIV/AIDS issues from WHO, when UNAIDS was created in 1996. The primary reason for this decision, as documented by Christer Jonsson (1996), was an opinion among AIDS experts that WHO was unable to coordinate the sort of worldwide, interorganizational response needed to combat AIDS effectively. It was hoped that a separate organization built on a specific mandate to coordinate among UN agencies would be better able to organize such response; the GPA, conversely, had been seen as being both too beholden to WHO and too ad hoc to effectively coordinate the broad range of activities it needed to oversee. But Nakajima's dislike of the HIV/AIDS issue and his battle with Mann also played a part. The effect of this decision was to remove from WHO the one issue that most directly connected it with human rights promotion. Though Peter Piot, the first director of UNAIDS, demonstrated a strong commitment to continuing a rights-based approach to HIV/AIDS treatment and prevention, WHO had lost this galvanizing issue area. Recall that Director-General Nakajima, who was in charge at the time of the creation of UNAIDS, was not entirely sorry to see authority over AIDS issues go, precisely because of the myriad social issues they entailed.

To a large extent, it is now clear, the reaction from member states to the effort described above to rank their health performance in the 2000 *World Health Report* made it unlikely that WHO would pursue an aggressive rights policy. How, it was asked, could WHO push for the transparency needed in a human rights strategy when states were unwilling even to have their basic health data used by WHO?[6] The common fear of specialized agencies that their ability to function would be weakened by politicizing ostensibly technical policy areas appeared to have been borne out by experience. At the same time, however, other factors continued to mitigate in favor of greater emphasis on human rights from both inside and outside WHO, most notably Kofi Annan's decision to make it a key component of his vision for the future of the United Nations that all specialized agencies make clear how they can contribute to the promotion of human rights. This call struck a chord with those within WHO already mobilized to pursue a human rights strategy by Brundtland's earlier decisions in this area, and who now perceived that they had a mandate to continue actions in this field. UNAIDS continued to work on rights issues, and NGOs also advocated a rights approach, particularly for HIV/AIDS. Though UNAIDS of course continued to be the main focus of this effort, WHO was also criticized over issues such as access to affordable antiretroviral medicines in the developing world.

The organizational response to these various pressures, from both within and outside WHO, has been a fragmentation of responsibility for human rights issues. Organizationally, this ambiguity is best seen in the retention of a senior human rights adviser within the director-general's office (the same as served under Brundtland) combined with the transfer of operational oversight (or "focus point," in WHO parlance) for human rights to a new, oddly defined Office for Ethics, Trade, Human Rights, and Law. The effects of this change remain unclear even to those within the organization, who remain uncertain whether it means greater autonomy or diminished authority (or both) for the human rights issue area. The change did introduce a certain amount of confusion and uncertainty, which did nothing to help the rights issue gain traction in the organizational culture. Though there still remains a dedicated (if small) set of staff at the high reaches of WHO with a mandate to pursue human rights issues, their perceived power and authority is small and their status, uncertain as it is, does little to advance their work.

Brundtland's departure from WHO slowed progress to a crawl; it became clear to the staff that her successor, Lee Jong-Wook, had his priorities elsewhere. By the time of Lee's death in 2006, the full-time professional staff of the human rights office had dropped from four to two (with one support staff person). Of course it is now impossible to know directly, but Lee's lack of interest in human rights issues seemed to have several sources. For one thing, it was clear from the beginning to many staff that Lee was going to emphasize traditional medical interventions over more socially oriented policies and that his training and background made radical change unlikely. He was simply not inclined by temperament toward new, "unscientific" policies at WHO. It was also communicated to human rights staff that the time was "not ripe," according to one knowledgeable participant, for a greater emphasis on human rights issues.[7] Some member states, including the United States, had made it clear that they are not convinced that there is a right to health or that such a right, however defined, should be a centerpiece of WHO's efforts. Although some staff, particularly in the human rights office but elsewhere as well, have expressed an interest in trying to resist this outside pressure, little can be done with no support from the top.

Perhaps nothing sums up WHO's human rights implementation experience as well as the creation of a task force to look at rights issues within the organization. With the blessing of top WHO management, this task force was created during 2004 and 2005 to look at cross-cutting human rights strategies and move the WHO effort forward. One of its key tasks was to develop arguments in favor of a rights-based approach: to do the "homework" (as one participant put it) of finding arguments for the technical benefits of such an approach, in order to help sway the more technically oriented staff, and to justify a rights-based approach to member states, among others.[8] In this sense, it was as much a political as a technical endeavor. By 2006, however, the task force had essentially ceased to function, after its chair retired and no one stepped forward to fill the gap. The failure of the task force to produce substantial results was another indication of the lack of support from the highest reaches of WHO for a rights-based initiative, even as WHO was still paying lip service to human rights standards.

What has developed instead is an approach to programming best described as "opportunistic" by several WHO personnel. The level of commitment to a rights-based approach varies widely among program areas, with the Human Rights Department helping those who show an interest while gently prodding those who do not. Thus a core of true believers has been developed—much as in the World Bank—to push the issue, even as they feel resistance from skeptics. There are no clear links between those programs that have shown an interest; though rights-oriented personnel are clearly aware of who else has a similar interest, and no clear pattern has emerged as to which departments have and have not initiated rights-based programming. The decision seems based more on personal factors—the opinion of program managers, the availability of qualified personnel, the persuasiveness of the Human Rights Department—than on anything intrinsic to certain program areas.

One example of this opportunistic approach has been the development of rights-based programming in the Child and Adolescent Health and Development Department (CAH). Child health has been particularly fertile ground because it is able to directly reference an outside human rights document, the Convention on the Rights of the Child. And the interest of CAH in a rights-based approach largely stems from the CRC, and in particular from the perception (paralleling that of UNICEF) that the CRC would be a useful document to support existing programs. In this case, that program was the Integrated Management of Childhood Illness (IMCI) approach to health, shared by WHO and UNICEF and forming the backbone of WHO's child health initiatives. CAH, in consultation with UNICEF, perceived Article 24 of the CRC (dealing with the right to health) as being directly applicable to the IMCI approach to child health, which advocates, according to WHO's website, "an integrated approach to child health that focuses on the well-being of the whole child." It was left to CAH to bring on its own child rights adviser and to develop (again, often in collaboration with UNICEF and other outside advisers, such as the François-Xavier Bagnoud Center for Health and Human Rights at Harvard) a departmental approach to human rights.

Given this interest, however, the actual work of CAH in this area has been careful and circumspect; for the most part, it has remained in the realm of education and advocacy rather than actual programming. In collaboration with UNICEF and other partners, CAH has developed a rights-based health training package and presented workshops in a number of countries, at which the general idea has been to use the concept of children's rights to develop a framework for the IMCI's holistic approach. The goal of CAH is to broaden the way states perceive child health and development away from disease prevention, and the CRC is seen as a platform for this expansion. As with other parts of WHO, discussed in turn below, it considers promoting the rights of children (as defined in the CRC and elsewhere) that are essential to improving child health.

CAH has also expressed an interest in addressing other rights-based issues, particularly the question of nondiscrimination; there are plans to begin systematically gathering and disaggregating indicators of child health along such lines as gender, ethnicity, and family income, to address the issue of equal access to health care (a rights violation often masked by a reliance on indicators that include averages for entire populations). In another area more specifically directed toward CRC promotion, CAH has seen considerable value in helping countries implement recommendations made by the CRC; this has been described as a "platform" or "entry point" for future rights-based programming.[9] In Romania, a course on deinstitutionalizing children was prompted by a recommendation under the CRC; workshops in Cameroon and Gambia were also prompted by this strategy. CAH has developed what it refers to as a "generic" training package "to facilitate the integration of 'rights-based thinking' into all aspects of child and adolescent health and development" (World Health Organization 2006a).

Yet even here, there remains a substantial amount of caution in using the CRC for further programming activities. Members of CAH report that they downplay references to rights-based activities in reports to the World Health Assembly and other oversight bodies; one example brought up in an interview was the removal of references to family planning from reports, in deference to the sensitivities of the American government.[10] As with other parts of WHO, CAH personnel report that they struggle with the evidence-based culture and feel that this is an important hindrance to progress. Finally, the true believers in CAH question the commitment of higher levels of management and consequently find the rights-based approach in a tenuous position.

Gender and reproductive rights is another area where some serious efforts have been under way to incorporate human rights issues into actual programming. The political side of this has been noted above; on the issues of gender and women's health, it has been accepted, for example, that specific political changes are needed to fully ensure women's rights in the health field, such as seeking legal changes regarding marriage, control over property, and the general status of women within society and the health care system. Along with advocating for legal change, WHO has begun a training initiative on addressing the social aspects of safe pregnancy. As with the other institutions under study, the general notion that the rights of women must be protected has become a standard and institutionalized part of WHO programming. It is notable that a Women's Health and Development Programme predates Brundtland's speech on health and human rights and has been operating since 1996 through a Gender Working Group to develop a more strategic approach to women's rights. Brundtland did reaffirm the central role of gender in WHO operations and the "promot[ion] of equality between women and men" (World Health Organization 2002a, 2), and this policy did not change during the tenure of Lee Jong-Wook. Gender equality and the promotion of the rights of women therefore has been and remains an important feature of WHO programming, albeit one that, as late as 2002, still required the creation of a "senior level Task Force" to "ensure . . . [the] overall coherence" of the agenda (World Health Organization 2002a, 1).

The relation between the overall gender policy and WHO's work in reproductive health has already been noted, as has the (relatively) long-standing interest in the Reproductive Health and Research Department (RHR) toward rights-based programming. As with CAH, the RHR has been active in determining how rights-based approaches might fit in with the overall direction of the department's programming, and it has produced substantial research in this area. To a not insignificant degree, implementation in this area has been aided by the fact that there exists within the RHR a separate body, the Special Programme of Research, Development, and Research Training in Human Reproduction (HRP), which has taken the lead in reproductive health rights. The HRP actually has a legally independent status within WHO and its own funding sources, which have given it greater freedom to innovate and to discuss rights matters (e.g., the HRP has been active in developing guidelines for safe abortion practices, with a freedom from U.S. political pressure that it would not have without its semi-autonomous status.[11]) The HRP began to show its interest in rights by thinking in terms of how contraceptive choices affect women's lives and their control over their reproductive health and future, and from there it began thinking more specifically about women's empowerment and voice. The overall policy, as already described, is to see safe motherhood as being affected by women's rights as well as by technical interventions: Women who are educated, who are free to make choices about their future, who are protected from abusive practices such as genital mutilation, and who are protected by the law will have better health outcomes than those who do not.

To implement a rights-based approach, the HRP (with the RHR) has been studying how to move beyond a strictly medical model of reproductive health to one encompassing all societal and legal factors. One focus of this has been to create a tool for working with national governments on a comprehensive, rights-oriented strategy for maternal health. The notion is to use human rights concepts—including rights to education, expression, and political participation, among others—to identify all the changes needed for the social and legal structure within a country to improve women's health. Framing the issue as one of human rights, the RHR argues, allows WHO to identify those who are accountable for implementing needed reforms and empowers women to demand these changes. One example of this was a program in Mozambique, carried out in 2001, which aimed at "reviewing and improving the legal, policy and regulatory aspects of the operational [health] plan from a human rights perspective" (World Health Organization 2006b). This means including questions of women's equality, education, and freedom to choose, among many other factors, in creating a nationwide policy on safe pregnancy, as opposed to looking strictly at medical interventions. This means, of course, involving WHO (much as was seen with UNICEF) in the promotion of legal reform, and it opens the door to a much greater political role than WHO has traditionally played; although the RHR points out that this is done entirely with the consent of the country (or countries) involved.

In addition to this new, more political and holistic approach, the RHR is using the rights concept and women's empowerment to inform other aspects of its work. One notable aspect of this, again paralleling UNICEF's approach, has been to increase WHO's cooperation with the main human rights treaty–monitoring bodies, particularly those monitoring the CRC and CEDAW. Like UNICEF, the RHR has worked with the monitoring bodies and with states to help craft concluding observations on state submissions to the monitoring bodies and then to assist states in following up on recommendations. The RHR has also developed rights-based training programs for states, to help educate personnel in all health-related fields about reproductive rights and their impact on women's health. This training program has been used in over a dozen countries and is still being refined.

The relatively direct link between "health as a human right" and access to affordable drugs was noted above; and WHO's Drug Action Program, within the Essential Drugs and Medicines Department, has hired several experts on human rights issues. As with other departments, this decision has been driven by department staff rather than being mandated from above. Access to essential medicines has been put into a larger context of human rights, and in particular a right to adequate health care. Similarly, WHO's HIV/AIDS Department has been trying to move itself back to the center of the HIV/AIDS struggle, and to reinvolve WHO in the human rights side of the issue. Despite these moves, WHO's HIV/AIDS Department (as opposed to UNAIDS) has not made rights a centerpiece of its efforts—a recent publication by the department contains only a single reference to human rights, in the last paragraph of the document (World Health Organization 2003, 7).

In contrast to UNAIDS, which puts the issue of rights at the forefront of its activities, WHO's HIV/AIDS Department is almost entirely focused on medical issues such as drug treatment, prevention, and data gathering. For several years, the department had only a single staff person serving as a human rights focal point—an attorney with experience in the legal side of HIV/AIDS issues. The goal of the department, however, is now to reintegrate rights issues, addressing such matters as stigma and discrimination against those infected or in high-risk groups; involvement in legal change for the benefit of sex workers, young girls, homosexuals, and other groups; and pushing for access to treatment as a right. Perhaps more important, WHO has involved itself, albeit very carefully, in China and elsewhere, where there have been reports of activists and people living with HIV/AIDS being detained and arrested.[12] This willingness of WHO to take on a highly political issue, and one only tangentially related to its core mission, is an important step for WHO—and is recognized as such by those involved.

This process, however, has been painfully slow, and rights remain largely peripheral to the work of the HIV/AIDS Department, while UNAIDS continues to take the lead in promoting rights-based approaches to HIV/AIDS prevention and treatment.

There is, therefore, a fair amount of action within WHO regarding rights-based approaches to health. Of particular importance, the image that emerges is one of single efforts by various departments, rather than an organization-wide concerted effort, and staff members often express their frustration with this situation. There is a palpable sense that rights-based programming is hindered by a lack of coordination—and a pervasive notion that this comes from a lack of commitment by the majority of WHO staff, including those at the top. There is no central commitment to a set of values and ideas, as there is at UNICEF; nor is there an institutionalized effort to integrate rights ideas into operations, as there is, for example, at the World Bank, with its policies on indigenous peoples and its cross-cutting strategies such as social development and governance reform.

These differences in themselves might not be such an interesting finding—many UN agencies do not have rights policies—were it not for the *rhetorical* support from WHO for a rights-based approach. Although WHO has declared itself to be in favor of putting the right to health at the center of its operations, and although it has a health and human rights focal point under a deputy director-general, this has not translated into a concerted effort by WHO to present a comprehensive or even effective policy. WHO staff within the true believer category consistently express frustration with the difficulties they have convincing most staff of the usefulness of rights-based approaches, and of the lack of support they feel they get from the higher echelons of WHO. The Health and Human Rights Office has made the development of indicators a top priority; the ability to show the public health benefits of a human rights approach with scientific rigor is considered a key element if the organization is expected to embrace human rights in a consistent way. Yet there appears to be a long way to go.

Among those committed to human rights programming, there is also a strong sense that outside allies are vital to success—that to change the corporate culture of the organization, it is necessary to link WHO's human rights efforts to those of other agencies and to the general UN mandate in the rights area. There is also a desire to link health outcomes to various human rights documents, to reinforce the idea that there is a UN mandate to pursue rights standards. CAH sees cooperation with UNICEF as vital to promoting human rights, and as serving a variety of purposes. These include helping to define child rights in a health context, providing evidence of the efficacy of the rights-based approach, and convincing staff that rights-based approaches are the new standard to which all UN specialized agencies will be expected to adhere. Perhaps most important, there is the example of UNAIDS, and a sense among the true believers at WHO that this issue "got away" from WHO, to WHO's detriment. In a reverse of the depiction by Gordenker and his colleagues (1995) of the GPA as a "linking pin" bringing together various actors in the effort against HIV/AIDS, elements within WHO now look outward, viewing lack of progress on human rights (in the HIV/AIDS field and elsewhere) as creating a gap in the global health effort. Thus there is a desire to use outside allies as part of an effort at internal transformation, with the hope that those outside WHO will provide both leverage and legitimacy to their efforts.

## Conclusions

WHO's interest in integrating human rights standards has come primarily from two sources. The first source is the growth of HIV/AIDS as perhaps the critical global health issue, and the clear human rights implications of that pandemic. The second is the more general movement among international agencies to consider the impact of human rights standards on their work. Significantly, the first of these factors is the more important. Though WHO has taken note of the UN secretary-general's interest in human rights, in fact the global HIV/AIDS crisis has had the more powerful impact on the attitudes of WHO personnel. In this particular case, the UN secretary-general and the example of other agencies appear to have had less effect on WHO's overall direction than the way its mission has interacted with the world around it. As a part of international civil society, it interacts regularly with its environment; and as a bureaucracy with organizational needs and priorities, it must remain cognizant of the context within which it works. The words of the secretary-general are certainly important; but the lesson WHO learned when it lost control over the largest public health issue of the era is not something to be ignored easily.

Although WHO is a relatively large organization, with an annual budget somewhat above $2 billion, it is comparable in size to UNICEF but dwarfed by the World Bank, which annually lends more than $10 billion and reports total assets and liabilities in the range of $200 billion. Chapter 1 speculated that large, complex organizations with large budgets and sprawling responsibilities would exhibit more independence than smaller organizations; this certainly appears to be the case when WHO is compared with the World Bank, but it works less well when UNICEF is considered. Certainly, the level of oversight with which WHO has had to contend—exemplified by complaints over the 2000 *World Health Report* and subsequent efforts by the executive board to stifle similar efforts—is not insubstantial, and it shows the ability of states to reign in their creations when they feel it is necessary. Staff often reign themselves in, too, for they remain cognizant of what states want; in interviews, many WHO staff members said they or their colleagues were reluctant even to raise rights issues for fear of drawing resistance from states parties, and questions such as the treatment of people in China who are HIV positive were cited as rights issues that simply were too potentially controversial even to approach. There is a sense that these sorts of decisions are noticed.

The nature of the issues involved also appears to militate against a wide-ranging change by WHO. Though WHO is a highly technical organization staffed by doctors and others with advanced scientific training, for those with the proper background, its mission is quite straightforward. Unlike the World Bank, which has had to contend with (and occasionally has been on the forefront of) changes in the very definition of international development, WHO's notion of what constitutes public health—and an appropriate response to it—has been relatively stable. This is by itself a difficult factor to gauge, because WHO's very resistance to changing the definition of its work is what is at issue; one cannot really cite that stability as both cause and effect. Nevertheless, given that the organization resides in an environment where there also have not been substantial changes (except with regard to HIV/AIDS, an issue over which it lost control), it seems likely that the nature of its operations has militated against a higher level of independence. UNICEF, conversely, charged with a more amorphous mission (child welfare, however understood), has had a greater ability to redefine its operations and has evolved as the concept of development has evolved.

The most striking lesson of the current state of human rights within WHO might be the clear need for leadership at the top of the organization to bring about effective change. Both UNICEF and the World Bank benefited from commitment at the top of their hierarchy, with the work of James Grant, Carol Bellamy, and James Wolfensohn. These leaders and their immediate staffs became convinced that a rights agenda would further an organizational interest (in UNICEF's case, greater political leverage; in the World Bank's case, less resistance from civil society) and worked to convince others in the organization of their views. They faced resistance from outside the organization as well as inside but were able to overcome that resistance, because of the factors mentioned above: organizational size, the complexity of the issues, and the agreement of the major donors (particularly the United States). In the end, however, it seems that personal qualities are at least as important as organizational ones when radical change is contemplated. WHO had the opportunity to effect radical change when Jonathan Mann was at the GPA, but it lost that opportunity with his departure.

## Chapter Five

# What Do Intergovernmental Organizations Want?

If international organizations are more than simply arms of their member states, and if they are capable of independent and purposeful action, what can they do with their independence? Chapter 1 showed that a substantial body of work has developed, drawing on principal–agent theory and the sociology of organizations, to argue that intergovernmental organizations (IGOs) can and often do slip the bonds of their creators and act on their own volition, at least within certain parameters. It is not the intention of this work to suggest that they do this more often than not; IGOs are hardly rogue elephants loosed to wreak havoc on the international savannah. All IGOs are created by states to pursue a certain function that gives them their claim to resources and legitimacy. Fulfilling this function will always be the primary motivation for IGO activities. At the same time, IGOs learn, they adapt, they take on new functions (for the most part related to older ones), and they change their form and rhetoric.

The first part of this chapter briefly summarizes some of the major themes from the case studies that make up chapters 2 through 4. It shows that in each case, the process of adopting, defining, and even implementing human rights norms (to the extent that they are implemented) has followed very similar patterns. Despite these similarities, the actual policy outcomes—that is, in the level of commitment to a human rights agenda—have been considerably different. How can these differences be explained? Three models of IGO change and adaptation will be discussed. Though each model provides some important insight into the change process, each by itself is not sufficient to explain why all three IGOs tried to adopt human rights standards into their operations, and also why the degree of adoption was so markedly different in different cases. This chapter argues that the power of principled ideas—the belief among IGO staff that some things are simply right to do—is important in understanding how the IGOs have changed. The persuasiveness of change agents within organizations is a key variable in explaining IGO change that is not covered by theories that focus on environmental factors and other exogenous forces.

## Adoption, Definition, Implementation

As with chapters 2 through 4, this section divides the process of creating rights-based policies into adoption, definition, and implementation. It highlights the similarities (and differences) of the processes in the various organizations.

### Adoption

It is surely significant that each organization discussed here was founded with a healthy dose of idealism. Each one had at least a rhetorical connection to the concept of human rights before rights became an important programming issue. This idealism, built into the culture of each organization, helps explain their receptiveness to human rights ideas. The fact that the one organization with the most direct reference to rights in its charter—the World Health Organization (WHO)—has been the least successful at adopting a more explicit rights-oriented policy highlights the obvious point that simply having such language in a founding document does not translate directly into substantive policy interest.

That being said, it is certainly also relevant that all these organizations are charged with pursuing essentially humanitarian tasks. It is difficult, for example, to imagine a significant rights-based policy for the International Telephone and Telegraph Union, or the Law of the Sea Convention (although it would not be impossible, given a sufficiently broad definition of rights). But the United Nations Children's Fund (UNICEF), the World Bank, and WHO were predisposed to adopt new ideas concerning rights and to find such ideas are relevant.

In all three cases under study, the initial idea that a human rights agenda might serve the interests of the organization was championed by a single person or a small group of people within the organization. In UNICEF, this was a very small group at the Geneva office working on the early drafts of the Convention on the Rights of the Child (CRC). In the World Bank, the early impetus was from the Social Development Task Group. And in WHO, the direct antecedent is the work of Jonathan Mann and a few others both inside and outside the organization. This is not to say that these people were working in a vacuum; each was taking ideas from outside the organization and acting at least as much as a conduit as they were an idea creator.

There is a substantial literature on how ideas on development or economic policy can become part of the general policy environment and sway policymakers (Hall 2003; Biersteker 1992). But the notion of using human rights as a programming tool did not enter any of these organizations via osmosis; in none of the three examples did ideas simply become part of the general development debate and slowly convince organization staff (or, for that matter, member states) that they were the best way to proceed. Rather, they were picked up by some "champions" on the staff and developed internally.

There was also little or no consensus among the organizations examined here that implementing a rights-based programming agenda was the best way to achieve their existing goals. The closest to such a consensus was the case of HIV/AIDS, where Jonathan Mann was part of an emerging (although by no means universal) view that the spread of HIV could not be controlled without reference to social and even political considerations. In the case of the World Bank, though the notion of "development with a human face" was certainly an important part of the discourse in the early 1990s, it was seen as (and remains) largely an "add-on" to a more traditional neoliberal development model, not an alternative to it (Henderson 1996, 122), and was not by itself a rights-oriented concept. Nor was there anything like a consensus at UNICEF that rights-based programming was the best way to pursue the organization's mandate throughout the late 1980s and into the 1990s. Indeed, it was not even clear to those who first pushed for a policy centered on the CRC that it would improve UNICEF's effectiveness: The real policy implications of the CRC were not thought through until much later.

There also appears to be little evidence that new human rights policies were the result of pressure from states or civil society. UNICEF, for example, was already pursuing an extremely successful set of policies as part of the child survival revolution and was under no particular pressure to change its ways. Indeed, James Grant was initially reluctant to get involved in the CRC exactly because he was afraid to depart from his already-successful policy, and he was convinced to change his position by the argument that the CRC would *build on* this success. (Note, too, that the United States and other Western nations had initially opposed the very idea of the CRC, considering it a Cold War propaganda effort.) The World Bank, conversely, came under the most sustained pressure for reform. WHO had somewhat less pressure to change, and that was concentrated in a single issue area, that of HIV/AIDS (and much later, on the issue of intellectual property rights and essential medicines).

This is not to say that outside pressure on agencies is not a factor in their reform efforts. At the World Bank and WHO, where critics have been the most insistent, it's clear that they have had an effect. The important lesson to be taken away, however, is that the mere presence of new ideas and an international civil society pushing for those ideas—even effective, well-considered new ideas—is in itself neither sufficient nor necessary to explain all IGO adaptation.

Once the ideas had some purchase within the organizations, it was necessary for the early true believers in each organization to convince their leaders that these new ideas were worth adopting. In no case was this easy. Pressure to change came from relatively small cadres of people within each body. These cadres then turned their attention to convincing upper management—and especially the top officer—of the worth of their ideas. The true believers were first driven to make the "argument from effectiveness." Their strategy was to argue that a rights-based programming policy would advance the institution's core mission. In some instances this was rather a stretch, but the argument was made regardless. This was coupled with the more ethical argument, that advancing human rights was simply the "right thing to do"; but the "argument from effectiveness" was always the primary argument put forward to the organization, even if it was not always the main motivation of the true believers. In some cases, those who argued for a rights-based approach felt that the organization where they worked was actually acting in a way that ignored important moral issues (as those in WHO have argued that the rights of people with HIV/AIDS must be respected on simple moral grounds). In other cases, there was a sense that an organization was following an essentially flawed development model (e.g., UNICEF staff convinced that child welfare was about more than life expectancy or literacy rates). But it seems clear that the moral argument was always an important motivation for those who pushed these issues, albeit coupled with other more practical considerations.

In all three cases, there was initial success at convincing the top level of the organization of the worth of the new ideas being expounded. Ultimately, the personality and preferences of the top leader cannot be ignored. Jim Grant was an innovator by nature and was receptive to the notion of the CRC as a rhetorical tool; his successor, Carol Bellamy, had a well-known interest in human rights promotion and in social issues in general, rather than a single focus on the technical side of UNICEF's work. At the World Bank, James Wolfensohn also came to the organization having already indicated his interest in reform in this direction. At WHO, the fortunes of the notion of a "right to health" rose and fell with the change of leadership: Mann found a close ally in Halfdan Mahler, and lost this support (and his job) when Mahler left. Hiroshi Nakajima was less receptive, and he actively moved to get rid of rights issues; his successor, Gro Harlem Brundtland, took up the issue again and tried to move it forward, with limited success.

The experience of WHO and Brundtland's relation to the executive board is certainly instructive. It is the only one of the three cases where determined opposition from member states against a human rights agenda had the effect of really derailing efforts. The opposition was clear and communicated to WHO in an unmistakable fashion. It represented a vivid demonstration of how states can control their creations when they choose to do so. It is not certain, however, that the rights-based policy in WHO failed to take hold because it presented a greater threat to state interests than one in, say, the World Bank—or that the activities of WHO were less complex (and therefore easier to oversee on a regular basis) than those of UNICEF. The World Bank has certainly seen opposition from states to its governance and social development activities in particular, but it has found ways to continue developing these ideas in any case and has maintained an interest in them. What seems more likely in the WHO case is that following the departure of Jonathan Mann and, later, the spinning-off of the Global Program on AIDS, WHO had divested itself of its most insistent advocates for reform. Brundtland hired her own staff to advise on human rights, but this staff was small and separated from the day-to-day operations of WHO. Without a clear mandate at the top for change, and without a grassroots effort to support adaptation, WHO was less likely than the other two agencies to sustain an interest in rights after the initial opposition from states was made clear.

### Definition

The process of defining a human rights agenda was very different for UNICEF than for WHO or the World Bank. UNICEF had a single foundational document that had been largely drafted by outside parties—the CRC—on which to base its early efforts at definition. WHO and the World Bank, conversely, had less guidance; though they could and did look to other rights documents as well as other sources, they largely had to consider on their own which rights were applicable, and what they would mean in the specific context. In many cases, of course, this led to a definition of "human rights" that had little to do with the content of international law—often, it meant more of an ethical or people-centered policy attached to the term "rights."

The actual process of defining human rights in each case was generally a messy and highly decentralized process. Even after decisions were made at the top of the organization to embrace the rights concept, there was little formal infrastructure created around the new priority. Without clear guidance, individuals at lower levels often tried in an ad hoc way to see what rights or related concepts would mean for their own programming. In the case of UNICEF, resident representatives in various countries took the lead in determining what the CRC would mean for their own operations. Not infrequently, they chose simply to develop human rights policies by themselves, rather than to wait for directives from headquarters in New York. The work of the Innocenti Centre in Florence added to this sense of far-flung efforts rather than centralized planning. The process was somewhat more organized at the World Bank, where the social development group took the lead in the main area of effort; but even they were, by and large, pulling together various strands that had been determined elsewhere (women in development, indigenous people, social safety nets) rather than creating policy from a central office.

Furthermore, the definition of rights at the World Bank also came to include governance and anticorruption efforts, which were separate from this main effort. At WHO, despite the creation of a rights focal point under the director-general in Geneva, the process quickly fragmented, with certain departments (Child and Adolescent Health, Essential Medicines, Reproductive Health) developing their own policies rather than taking the lead from the senior levels of management.

Member state preferences did make themselves felt at the definition stage. National sensitivities were often in the minds of those charged with interpreting human rights standards, even when they desired to go beyond what they believed states would readily allow. For example, UNICEF carefully avoided issues regarding family planning, as well as various other issues that would annoy the United States in particular; WHO has been very cautious regarding HIV/AIDS and human rights; and the World Bank deemphasized those aspects of the governance agenda that were most likely to be seen as overtly political. This is not surprising, and it certainly demonstrates that the kind of adaptation under study here results from a complex interplay of organizational needs and external constraints. What is more interesting, and surprising, is how often organizations and their staffs found themselves testing the limits of their freedoms, and the willingness of IGO staff to push for their agenda even when they knew it would not be popular with states.

It was the lower-level staff members of IGOs that most often wanted to push the limits of what member states would allow. There is a regular pattern of those near the top preferring a careful, nonconfrontational definition of what a human rights policy would mean, while others in field offices or lower on the chain of command pushed for a broader interpretation. Those at the top of the organization, in other words, were more aware of the need to be pragmatic, while those in the field or in programmatic departments had more of a tendency to want to take a more principled stand. This general pattern appears to be more true in the case of UNICEF and WHO than the World Bank, but elements of it can also be seen there. Interviews suggest that staff at IGOs often struggled to accommodate their own preferences for a stronger line on rights with what they knew would be allowed by states. At the same time, they were also struggling to convince their own peers, many of whom, due to their training and backgrounds, were uninterested in what a rights-based agenda had to offer. Of particular importance, their efforts were not without result; ideas do travel up as well as down in IGOs.

Given the salience of the argument from effectiveness and its importance in legitimizing rights-based programming, it is understandable that IGOs put substantial emphasis on how this programming would increase the influence and effectiveness of their organization. UNICEF almost immediately began asking itself how the CRC could be used to expand its scope of operations (or to justify ongoing expansion) into new issue areas, such as children in especially difficult circumstances. WHO, similarly, looked (rather cautiously) to rights to expand its work in the HIV/AIDS field, to leverage aid for underserved or discriminated-against populations, or to have extra leverage to use against both industrial and developing countries on political matters.

The case of the World Bank, however, is something of an outlier. The primary thrust of its human rights programming was in the areas of protection and social development (including gender). None of these policies really represented a substantial opportunity for the organization to accrete greater influence or resources. What they did, however, was to help answer those who were calling for major changes in the Bank, or even its elimination, and to give it ammunition to use against its critics. Some aspects of the governance agenda and other issues did in fact foresee an increase in Bank operations and influence over domestic affairs, but this was not the central thrust of what the Bank meant when it began to discuss rights.

The overwhelming sense that comes from the interpretation process is of confusion between the practical and moral arguments for a rights-based approach to programming. Because the basic question of *why* adopt rights as a central feature of programming was never fully resolved—each organization had to consider both the moral and practical sides of the equation to convince the largest number of people of the ideas' value—the question of what rights to consider, and what they meant in a particular context, was never fully resolved either. It also was not unusual for each organization to look to what others were doing to guide its own interpretation. Generally, the interpretation process belies the notion of a large organization changing direction in a well-organized and controlled way. Instead, there was a general desire to do things differently and then a fairly disorganized effort to determine what this new way would be.

## Implementation

Internal obstacles to implementing a set of policies based on human rights principles are every bit as daunting to IGOs as external obstacles. Many of the most important external battles had already been fought by the time each agency considered what a human rights approach would mean in terms of actual policy changes. It is typical of change in large organizations that much of the most sustained resistance came from within the organization, where routine and training make staff wary of new ideas (Miller-Adams 1999, 31; Weaver and Leiteritz 2005, 16–18). Even after the decision had been made to try to integrate rights standards into programming, each organization had to deal with the difficult task of convincing staff at all levels to actually follow this decision. In all too many cases, there was actual resistance rather than simple passivity regarding the new programming requirements.

A key theme repeated throughout the study is the difficulty of convincing staff with technical training to consider more social factors in their work. Staff complain that their training is "scientific" or "evidence-based" and therefore that they are uninterested in what they see as a "moral" or "ethical" set of policies. This attitude pits the true believers directly against the majority of personnel within the organization. The fact that many of the most innovative ideas came from field offices did not change the fact that the much larger percentage of field staff were indifferent or hostile to the same concepts that the true believers were adopting. Top officials seemed regularly surprised and frustrated by the level of resistance they encountered, even after they made their policy preferences clear.

IGOs are not unaware of how difficult it is to control what is happening in various corners of a far-flung and diverse institution—far from it. Management reform was often seen as necessary to control the implementation process and to signal commitment to recalcitrant staff. The degree of signaling and integration varies. For example, Grant's initial effort to create a structural home for the CRC within UNICEF was the half-measure of moving responsibility for the CRC to the External Relations Department, commensurate with his belief that the CRC was mainly a propaganda tool: Carol Bellamy later raised the profile of the CRC within the organization, moved responsibility to the programmatic side, and also took firmer control over activities in field offices. Similarly, at WHO, organizational changes such as creating a human rights coordinator within the Office of the Director-General was an important step in raising the issue of rights within WHO, albeit again a half-measure that sent mixed signals to staff. At the World Bank, Wolfensohn saw the need for more assertive organizational steps than had been taken, placing the creation of a Social Development Network at the heart of a wide-ranging institutional reform effort.

The actual process of turning human rights standards into policy changes has had mixed results. Even at UNICEF, which has been the most enthusiastic about the notion of human rights, the implementation of the CRC has mostly been in areas that are themselves new to the organization, such as protecting children caught up in the criminal justice system. There has been more incremental progress determining what a rights-based program would look like in the traditional areas that make up the bulk of its operations, such as health and nutrition, sanitation, and education. The World Bank has made noticeable changes, but they remain tangential to what would be considered a real turn toward protecting and promoting international human rights norms. And WHO has made less progress still. The failure to consistently and significantly turn rights-based programming into real changes in activities seems to be almost overdetermined; among various causes are the resistance from technically oriented staff to new social development ideas, the fear of politicizing development cooperation, resistance from member states in specific policy areas, and general organizational inertia.

In other words, organizations that say they will support human rights programming do, for the most part, actually follow through on that pledge—it cannot be said that these are purely exercises in public relations—but the connection between words and deeds is not a simple or direct one. It is instructive to see just how little appreciation there was early on in each IGO of what a rights-based policy would actually mean in terms of on-the-ground programming; it can seem, at times, that there was little connection or communication between various parts of each organization. This is as true for UNICEF, with its considerable commitment, as for WHO with its half-hearted effort. The implementation stage once again shows the necessity of viewing IGOs as more complex than mere unitary actors behaving in rational ways. In extreme examples, in fact, units within each organization have acted in ways actively opposed to the official rights policy set in headquarters. This substantially complicates the question of how one can say that an organization *did* one thing or another, when it might actually be a programmatic division of the organization acting with minimal direction from the headquarters staff. Any theory of IGO agency that does not consider the way policies chosen by an IGO might not be followed by its personnel is not fully considering the issue of how IGOs choose their own policies.

## Understanding IGO Change

Given the differences in outcomes among the three organizations under study, there are surprising similarities in their efforts to change. In each case human rights ideas were picked up by small groups of individuals within the organization, who then developed them and pressed them on upper management. There was experimentation by field staff and others in remote parts of the organization with limited guidance from headquarters. There was resistance by technically oriented staff who resented or mistrusted more "fuzzy" development ideas. And there was limited support for change from member states—but also limited resistance, usually centered on specific policies that threatened their interests rather than on the concept as a whole. Many of the same bureaucratic dynamics played themselves out in each case, and often with the same results. How, then, can one explain the differences in actual policy outcomes? Three ways of looking at IGO adaptation will be briefly considered for their usefulness and insight before introducing a different explanatory element, that of the power of principled ideas.

### State Control

The most obvious place to look first for an explanation of IGO change in the area of human rights programming is in the interests of member states. This might mean the interests of all states taken together, the interests of only the most powerful and influential states, or the interests of the most active and engaged states (i.e., those that find it worth the time of their government agencies' staffs to maintain constant and active oversight). It assumes that some single state or coalition of states has the ability to shape IGO activities to fit their goals and preferences. This is, in other words, the realist position that international organizations are tools of state policies and operate at their sufferance (Martin and Simmons 1998, 746).

A key element of this study's methodology has been to attempt to control for state preferences by looking at a single issue area across several different organizations. It appears from what was said above that there is not a strong correlation between state preferences and IGO rights adaptation. Indeed, the most successful adapter—UNICEF—received less support from its member states than did the World Bank, which has been pushed by the United States in particular to consider good governance issues in its lending policies, and by others to incorporate social development and "adjustment with a human face." WHO, the least successful adapter, did in fact run up against state resistance, which caused it to retreat from a broader rights strategy. But this opposition was no greater than what UNICEF faced from the United States over issues pertaining to sovereignty, criminal justice norms applied to minors, and a handful of other issues (Renteln 1997). UNICEF was able to sidestep such issues, as was the World Bank when developing countries made clear their objection to some aspects of the original governance agenda without abandoning their overall commitment to reform.

Briefly put, none of the organizations came under strong state pressure to reform; most pressure was against reform. It is possible to speculate that state preferences were not really consistent across these issue areas. But here again, the variation—for example, the relatively greater pressure on the World Bank, the lesser pressure overall on UNICEF—does not seem to correlate with outcomes. There remains little evidence that states had substantially different interests or expectations from each agency in this particular issue area.

## Principal–Agent Theory and Public Choice

A public choice approach provides another way of looking at organizational change and independence in IGOs. The assumption here is that bureaucracies are staffed by individuals acting as agents, who pursue their own interests, to the extent that they can, while also serving the interests of their principals. It takes for granted the realist view of self-interested states forming organizations to solve collective problems, but it includes an understanding of the complexities of organizational dynamics and, in particular, of the self-interested nature of secretariat staff. States create public institutions to provide certain services, but they find it difficult in certain situations to control their creations. The bureaucrats who staff these organizations will have their own interests and agendas, which may not be the same as that of states. In a simplistic model, bureaucrats desire to maximize their budgets (Mueller 1989, 250); in more complex models, they may see other ways to best advance their own careers and utility, such as increasing the overall influence of the bureaucracy itself (Wintrobe 1997, 433–35). Agents exploit asymmetries of information to find room for independent actions in their own interests.

A public choice approach is important but not sufficient to explain both the desire of IGOs to take on principled ideas as a central programming idea and the variation in outcomes observed across organizations. Regarding the former, there is no question that the desire of bureaucracies to increase budgets, influence, staff, and other trappings of power and resources does explain part of the observed interest in human rights. It is, in fact, a powerful explanatory variable and needs to be considered carefully. UNICEF staff, for example, were motivated by their desire to increase the organization's power and influence in first taking up the cause of the CRC. Memoranda from involved staff make it clear that the early believers in a human rights approach felt that the CRC would give UNICEF increased leverage when dealing with host states. Grant, after his conversion to the CRC cause, seems to have had this as his primary motivation; his decision to place the main responsibility for the CRC in the Public Affairs Office only highlights his belief that this was largely an instrument of influence rather than a central programming idea. Some of the same reasoning appears in the statements of both the World Bank and WHO; the Bank seems to have turned to rights language more defensively (to shield itself from criticism) than as a positive instrument of influence, but the logic is the same, in that it is intended to help the organization retain influence, increase resources, and insulate itself from criticism. Staff within WHO, as with UNICEF, also hope that casting their programs in the language of human rights will give them more power and influence over host states.

Still, this line of reasoning has serious shortcomings. For one thing, in each case there were at least as many people arguing that an emphasis on rights would *weaken* the organization as strengthen it; it fails to suggest why one view prevailed over another. Also, human rights language and standards have existed almost from the creation of the United Nations; an emphasis on power and influence does not explain the onset of an interest in rights by IGOs when it did occur in the late 1980s and early 1990s, rather than at some other time, even if it does help explain why they did show an interest in adopting such ideas once they were presented. The World Bank was certainly criticized by outside forces for its human rights record, which certainly gave it some incentive to change at the time that it did (when criticisms of structural adjustment in particular were on the rise), but this is much less the case in the other two examples.

This approach also does not provide a convincing reason for the variation one sees across organizations in their interest in rights-based programming. WHO and UNICEF are similar enough to suggest that they ought to approach human rights in the same manner. Each, for example, ought to have found the same rhetorical power in rights; it is hard to see why the World Bank was a more successful adopter than WHO, because it has substantial financial power and must rely less on its (admittedly still considerable) powers of persuasion. The Bank did want to insulate itself from criticism and head off future attacks, but the language of human rights was only one way to do this, and if it was perceived as an effective way to leverage institutional clout (or to preserve what clout existed), then why not pursue a more substantial embrace of rights language than it actually did?

## Learning and Adaptation

A third approach to understanding change in IGOs is to focus on the process of learning and adaptation. Ernst Haas distinguishes between adaptation by international organizations (which he further breaks down into two forms), and learning by international organizations (Haas 1990, 128). Learning occurs when international organizations, and their member states, determine that mere adaptation is no longer sufficient to deal with new problems, situations, environments, and so on. Learning is an effort to "manage interdependence" and depends on coalitions of member states coming together to seek new solutions to persistent problems. In trying to manage interdependence or, more generally, to pursue organizational goals, IGOs "are . . . permeable and open to influence by all member governments, as well as nongovernmental organizations," although their "particular organizational characteristics may encourage or discourage" the adoption of new ideas and solutions (Kardam 1993, 1774).

Epistemic communities can take advantage of the situation to build coalitions and persuade relevant parties regarding new solutions to current problems. They can form within a single IGO or among several with overlapping interests; and they may take advantage of uncertainty or a situation of turbulence to push for commonly shared ideas about solutions to the problems of interdependence. These communities can be "triggers for learning" (Haas 1990, 45), although they often have to fight against organizational inertia as well as entrenched political interests: "Epistemic communities are relevant for decision makers because

they may convene new patterns of reasoning to decision makers and encourage them to pursue new paths of policy making.
. . . Epistemic communities play an evolutionary role as a source
of policy innovations" (Reinalda 2001, 23–24). Work on learning
in IGOs often focuses on the resistance of bureaucracies to innovation, and in this, epistemic communities can play an important but still limited role in convincing staff to consider new ideas
and ways of doing things. Their effectiveness will depend in part
on their persuasiveness—the extent to which they can convince
not just states but also their coworkers within IGOs (Bartkowski
2003, 11).

Organizational learning is certainly a factor in each of the cases
presented in this book. In each example, an IGO had by the 1980s
found itself dealing with a wide variety of issues that had not been
foreseen when the organization was first created. Each agency
had tremendously expanded its scope of operations in the decades
since the end of World War II, and it had been engaged in a constant process of expansion and adaptation. For the most part, this
process had taken the form of what Haas refers to as "incremental growth," the sort of growth that does not threaten or question
the core assumptions of the organization in question. Tasks were
added to the mission of each organization and were dealt with in
much the same way as had the older missions. At some point, however, it was inevitable that each would come against a new task that
would force it to rethink the way it does business and to reconsider
some basic assumptions.

This process of learning was particularly noticeable at the World
Bank, which, like the International Monetary Fund (IMF), found
its traditional way of doing business increasingly attacked as both
ineffective and unethical. The debt crisis and structural adjustment
accelerated this sense, as did a variety of public relations disasters
surrounding forced relocation and other abuses. At WHO, HIV/
AIDS and the resurgence of tuberculosis required a substantial
rethinking of the health care mission, in light of ongoing health
crises with social as well as medical causes and implications. Epistemic communities formed within each organization to push for
new ways of doing business and to introduce new assumptions
about "causal pathways"—the best way to reduce poverty in the one
case, the best way to solve health crises in the other. Much the same

phenomenon is present at UNICEF as well, particularly the growth of the organization's mission and the creation of communities of experts dedicated to pushing for a new way of doing business. New ideas were created in response to the challenges facing UNICEF, were developed by a core of experts, and were then "sold" to upper management as an improved operational paradigm.

What makes UNICEF different, however, is the rather jarring fact that the child survival revolution had already made UNICEF extremely successful at pursuing its agenda. It is true that the new focus on children in especially difficult circumstances required new thinking, but this was a relatively minor element in the UNICEF operational mandate when it began (and remains so today), and it generated no great sense of failure or turbulence when it was introduced. In other words, the organization with the least need to learn from its mistakes was the one that most fully embraced change and adaptation. This change process followed the general outline of organizational learning as described by Haas and others, as did that of the World Bank; and WHO, while ultimately unsuccessful, went some ways in the same direction. But the ultimate cause of this change remains underdetermined.

Looking at more general environmental factors as a source of new ideas for IGOs, as opposed to their own incremental growth or to the failure of "business as usual," is more helpful but still incomplete. Studies have demonstrated how IGOs learn from environmental factors, particularly from NGOs (Fox and Brown 1998b; Weiss and Gordenker 1996; Willetts 1996), but also from general international environment and technological change (Ness and Brechin 1988, 249–50). Environmental factors are relevant in the present case: Change within the World Bank was helped along by the charges leveled at it by NGOs and other critics; WHO was influenced by academics and by HIV/AIDS activists; and all three were picking up ideas from other UN agencies, from NGOs, and from various other sources regarding the need to mainstream human rights standards into their operations. UNICEF would not have changed had it not been for the CRC and for the NGO community that had gathered in support of children's rights. There is clearly no way to understand the direction of change (or attempted change) in each organization without reference to the way they interact with their environment and learn from the ideas that surround them. Like states, IGOs engage with other actors and redefine their identity and interests based on that interaction. The ideas under study were not simply imposed by states, nor forced on them by the irrevocable logic of cause and effect, but were an important part of their environment. Each agency was part of much the same environment, but each reacted in very different ways to the forces working on it. How can this variation be explained?

## Power, Principle, and Leadership in IGOs

Each of the three models of organizational change presented above is useful and contributes to understanding change (or lack of change) within the IGOs studied here. Clearly, there are times when member state preferences are the main, and even the only, factor in IGO change; when the U.S. Treasury Department made its preferences known to the IMF during the Asian Financial Crisis of 1997–98, it was clear which way the IMF would go in terms of policy implementation (Blustein 2001). But not every issue before IGOs rises to this level of concern by member states. Clearly, too, bureaucratic imperatives—the desire to increase the resources and power of an organization—play an important part. Managers themselves are only human and respond to the same incentives as everyone else. Finally, organizational learning is an important source of new ideas, when epistemic communities can fill the gap left by the failure of previous ways of doing business.

The force of principled ideas, and the way they are both picked up and developed by IGO managers, is also an important variable and helps to explain the variation in outcomes. Chapter 1 proposed that the turn by international organizations toward human rights as an element of programming could be explained neither by state preferences (which varied from tacit support and outright hostility) nor by the self-interest of the organizations themselves. The element of principle, defined as "beliefs about right and wrong held by individuals," remains a key factor (Risse and Sikkink 1999, 7). Ideas (and the norms that can develop from principled ideas) can help shape the identities and therefore the interests of international organizations, just as they can shape the identities and interests of states. Despite their claim to act rationally and dispassionately, bureaucracies (including IGOs) are embedded in a cultural environment that shapes the interests and actions of those who work for them (Barnett and Finnemore 2004, 37). In each case here, ideas regarding human rights as a worthwhile goal to be pursued, and as something that deserves consideration by an international agency regardless of its core mission, helps explain why rights-based programming became a consideration for UNICEF, the World Bank, and WHO at roughly the same time. Although the outcomes were different, much the same dynamic is present in each case: a core group of staff members, motivated by principled ideas, determine that rights are a desirable programming element; they find others who share their interest in this field from a principles perspective; and they then press those ideas on upper management with a combination of principled and practical argument.

The power of principled ideas shows itself in the fact that human rights norms are rarely adopted (or even considered) at the behest of states. Nor are they driven by a determination that such ideas will best advance organizational interests. It does not seem likely that IGOs will adopt policies that actually weaken them. Yet it seems that these organizations have, where adaptation has been successful, chosen to "stand on principle" in a way that is not best calculated to advance their interests.

Proving this with a counterfactual argument—that is to say, by considering other policy options that would be more effective in advancing IGO interests, and showing why they were not adopted—is not easy, because it is hard to know what other policies were considered, other than "business as usual." Rights-based programming was never presented in these organizations as an alternative to some other wide-ranging change, and it is therefore impossible to see how various changes were compared. Yet even the comparison with business as usual is illuminating. In UNICEF, the early true believers certainly did suggest that an interest in the CRC and in a rights-based policy would enhance UNICEF's ability to fulfill its mission. The earliest argument in this vein was that the CRC could be used to convince states to increase their aid to children. Rather than simply asking states to improve services for children, UNICEF would be able to accuse states of violating their human rights obligations if they did not follow certain policies. There was an appeal to organizational interests in the early days in the CRC. But there was also considerable resistance to the CRC within UNICEF, based on the presumption that the CRC would actually *harm* UNICEF's interests by damaging its close working relationships with states. This was strengthened by UNICEF's notable success over the previous decade; there was a strong incentive not to upset what had been a successful set of policies and activities.

More important still, once Grant had accepted the CRC as a rhetorical tool, and had made it clear that he intends to leave it there, there is no clear institutional reason why the epistemic community made up of resident representatives, policy analysts at the Innocenti Center and elsewhere, and others within UNICEF began pushing for a wider-scale adoption of the CRC as a programming document. Grant had made it clear by the early 1990s that his interest in the CRC stopped at the advocacy level, yet staff determined to go ahead with a fuller implementation on their own and continued to lobby Grant for more action. It was this lobbying, encouraged by a belief that the CRC represented a real advance in child programming, that drove UNICEF's actions regarding the CRC, even when it meant actually opposing the decisions made by Grant and others at the top of UNICEF. Finally, Carol Bellamy's own personal interest in human rights and her belief that such an approach was effective in helping children worldwide provided further impetus for change within UNICEF.

The World Bank case is more complex. Much of what the Bank considers a human rights program can readily be explained with reference to basic theories of institutional learning. Anticorruption activities and other governance issues were a reaction to the failure of development policies in the 1980s; protection strategies regarding indigenous peoples, women, and other vulnerable groups were adopted in light of public relations disasters and pressure from outside groups to reform; other aspects of social development also stem largely from lessons learned during the early years of structural adjustment in the developing world, and the criticisms directed at the Bank and the IMF from outside the organizations. The incorporation of social development and other issues grouped under the "rights" category was intended to prevent a loss of power and legitimacy, by addressing the various attacks made on the Bank's existing policies, and more important to keep the Bank "relevant" to international development by showing it was able to learn from mistakes and change accordingly. As Miller-Adams shows, the case for a more human development–oriented program came from within the Bank's hierarchy and developed through a process that included both learning from failure of past projects and from interaction with NGOs and other intellectual movements in the 1990s (Miller-Adams 1999, 76–78). The World Bank case conforms most closely to the learning model proposed by Haas and others.

Conversely, many of the World Bank's reforms seem driven by more than a simple desire to head off criticism and restore its prestige as a leader in development. The process of adaptation at the Bank was strikingly similar to that at the other agencies, with the same small communities of true believers developing new ideas, and the same institutional and cultural barriers slowing down adoption of their ideas. At the very least, the example of the Bank's experience with rights demonstrates the importance of leadership at the top in the process of successful adaptation: Choosing between those ideas that led to real change (e.g., expanding institutional transparency) and those that did not (e.g., those aspects of the governance agenda that went beyond anticorruption efforts) was done mainly by Wolfensohn and not forced on the Bank by member states.

The experience of WHO cannot be understood without reference to the principles that motivated its staff and director. When the idea of human rights is first introduced as a major programming guideline by Mann, the motivation is mainly practical: when Mann was director of the Global Program on AIDS and began pushing for a rights-oriented approach to the disease, he was primarily arguing—and actually believed—that the main reason for such an approach was its effectiveness. When WHO agreed to allow the Global Programme on AIDS to spin off into the Joint United Nations Programme on HIV/AIDS (UNAIDS), it did so partly to avoid having to deal with social and moral issues outside its purview; yet the argument made for involvement in those issues was still primarily practical. By the late 1990s, however, the argument for a human rights approach to health had moved well beyond HIV/AIDS to encompass any number of issues concerning equity, access, and gender, among others, which have overtly political and moral rather than practical justifications. The "argument from effectiveness" was never entirely lost; indeed, the need to justify new policies by discussing their practical effects on outcomes was stronger at WHO than in any of the other organizations under discussion, and its limitations may explain in part WHO's failure to take bold steps toward a rights-based approach.

Neither Mann's departure nor the departure of the HIV/AIDS issue itself from WHO (with the creation of UNAIDS) fully eliminated interest in rights issues from WHO. Instead, ideas being largely created outside of WHO are finding an audience at various levels within the organization; despite Director-General Nakajima's overall disinterest regarding the inclusion of rights in WHO's agenda, small numbers of true believers continue to advocate for these issues—Brundtland did not need to begin from scratch when she took the helm of WHO in 1998. She ultimately moderated her interest in rights in the face of state opposition. It seems likely that she could have continued to develop rights ideas within WHO despite this opposition, which was after all aimed at a specific initiative rather than the rights agenda in general; although it is not possible to prove this proposition. Be that as it may, the true believers continue to work within WHO for change, with the tacit consent of upper management.

Generally speaking, the power of principled ideas in each of the three organizations worked in the same way. A small core group of agency staff begin to consider the importance of human rights ideals and the impact they might have on their organization. These ideas develop through interaction with NGOs, through other environmental factors, and also through a conviction that such ideas represent a more effective and ethically satisfying way to attack the issues addressed by their organization. They are not necessarily perceived as being good for the organization in terms of staff, budget, or influence, and they are sometimes seen as being potentially dangerous in those areas. Their value is at least as much moral as practical. The core group then works to convince others within the organization to adopt their ideas, and they typically look to other IGOs for ideas about what such ideas will mean in a practical sense. Eventually, an effort is made to convince the top levels of management of the worth of such ideas, combining both a moral and a practical argument (the argument from effectiveness).

Working from within, these core groups resemble epistemic communities in their devotion to a particular set of solutions to the problems facing their organization. They are not exactly the same as epistemic communities as defined by Haas, for example; he described epistemic communities as "professionals . . . who share a commitment to a common causal model and a common set of political values." The communities of professionals described here are not necessarily bound by a causal model. They do, however, share "a commitment to translate [their ideas] into public policy, in the conviction that human welfare will be enhanced as a result" (Haas 1990, 41). They might better be described as "principled communities," united less by a causal model than by a commitment to a particular view of what is an ethical and personally fulfilling course of action. They acted from a conviction that the ideas they were developing, and the policies that proceeded from those ideas, presented a normatively superior path for their organization, one that would objectively improve international welfare.

Variations in outcomes, then, can depend on the persuasiveness of these epistemic communities and their effect on the leadership of the organization. All three cases demonstrate the ability of norms to penetrate IGOs and to work against the prevailing culture of the organization, as well as the ability of that culture to push back against those norms. New norms are not automatically rejected because they meet resistance. It is possible for different sets of norms to coexist within a single organization, such as the uneasy relationship between the human development experts and the classical economists at the World Bank, a relationship that is on occasion openly hostile. Each side seeks the attention and loyalty of the executive head; and changes of leadership (from Nakajima to Brundtland; from Grant to Bellamy) can substantially change which set of ideas is ascendant. Executive heads can choose among competing voices, although they are not likely to silence either side entirely, because staff maintain their own views and occasionally push back against directives. Indeed, this happens in a variety of ways. If true believers can push the executive head to initiate change, others imbued with the old organizational culture can and do resist change even when top management has decided on it. Thus the process of change does not happen automatically once a decision has been made to accept new ideas. Instead, it continues through the definition and implementation stages, as a messy and difficult-to-control set of steps guided by bureaucratic imperatives and personal qualities.

The quality of leadership within organizations provides another important factor for understanding the variation in outcomes across the various cases under study. Leadership and the personal values of those within organizations has received some study in the context of IGOs (Bartkowski 2003; Kardam 1993) but remains understudied. It has attracted more attention in those works that deal with specific issues from a policymaker's perspective (Kraske 1996; Schechter 1988) or on the sources of specific initiatives (Ascher 1983) than in the general theoretical literature. With room to maneuver given by states to IGO directors, the quality of leadership and the commitment of leaders to the ideas being expounded by these communities of experts is a key factor in the success of organizational change. A leader can and should be seen as an important variable, intermediating between epistemic communities, pressures from member states, and actual organizational outcomes.

## Implications for the Study of International Organizations

That IGOs are more complex than the traditional view of them as simple extensions of governments is now a well-established proposition; and though the relative importance of this proposition is still contested, a number of different research projects are exploring the contours of IGO agency. These projects look at both the reasons why states might delegate authority to IGOs and how those IGOs use this authority to further their own ends. Understanding the bureaucratic nature of IGOs is extremely important for getting a sense of their capabilities and limitations. IGOs are, in many cases, large organizations with considerable institutional memory and substantial resources. They are staffed by professionals, many with their own preferences, biases, blindnesses, strengths, and limitations.

That bureaucracies should spring up around ongoing, routine international interactions seems an inevitable process. As sociologists have long noted, modernization and the growing complexity that comes with it exerts tremendous pressure toward the rationalization and routinization of oversight and control. The creation of bureaucracies is the primary way that modern society deals with this complexity. Market economics, Weber wrote, create particular pressure toward the creation of bureaucratic modes of control: "The extraordinary increase in the speed by which public announcements, as well as economic and political facts, are transmitted exerts a steady and sharp pressure in the direction of speeding up the tempo of administrative reaction towards various situations" (Weber 1946, 215).

States, it is true, are particularly reluctant to give up political control over international affairs to bureaucrats; but where interests and expectations converge, it is almost inevitable that formal institutions will emerge. "As rationalized institutional rules arise in given domains of work activity," according to Meyer and Rowan, "formal organizations form and expand by incorporating these rules as structural elements" (Meyer and Rowan 1991, 45). As Finnemore puts it, "International social life is highly organized. Social relationships in international life may be informal, but many, especially those that most directly affect states, are structured and channeled through bureaucracies" (Finnemore 1996, 3).

The creation of IGOs and their continued growth and expansion suggests an increasing need to focus on their design and activities. At one level, of course, IGOs are clearly agents in even the most positivist epistemology; an organization like the World Bank has a "mailbox," it sends out representatives who speak for it, it contracts for goods and services, and it spends and takes in money. At this level, neither its ontological status nor the epistemology appropriate to its study is problematic; to question whether they have agency might seem absurd. For most reflectivist theories of international relations, however, the focus is not on an organization's activities in the quotidian world but its effects on the way states and societies view themselves and their interests or respond to the challenges of power politics. Here the emphasis is not on agency as it is used in common parlance: the daily activities of people and organizations, the making of decisions, and the carrying out of programs of action. Rather, it is the role of organizations at the level of ideas: their ability to identify problems and conflicts within the international system, their role in shaping state behavior, and most particularly their capacity to alter the interests and identities of states by engaging in regular interactions with them at the level of national and international policy.

This is a peculiar notion of agency, more limited than commoner notions of what it means to act. Away from the rarified atmosphere of international relations theory, organizations such as UNICEF, the World Bank, WHO, and any number of others are spoken of as having acted in one way or another all the time. They are criticized constantly for having undertaken one or another objectionable act with little thought to the larger question of where agency actually lies. Kahler and Woods write of the United States' relationship with the IMF as exactly that: a *relationship* with its ups and downs, between two agents who face each other across a set of routinized interactions (Kahler 1990; Woods 2003). It seems obvious to those who actually work within these organizations that they have the ability to act independently, so long as they remember certain boundaries laid down by their charter and the desires of states. Given the highly organized, bureaucratic nature of many IGOs, with their multinational staffs of experts, expanding budgets, and delegated authority, it would be surprising if the two notions of agency described above—the common notion and more restricted one—were *not* in fact equally applicable to IGOs.

As open systems, IGOs interact regularly with their environment, drawing resources and ideas from it and affecting it through their own actions. Open organizations draw energy from their environment, interact with it, and are changed by it. In an open organization perspective, "the semiautonomy of the individual actor is stressed," as are "the reciprocal ties that bind and relate the organization with those elements that surround and penetrate it" (Scott 1992, 90–91). These individual actors take their cues from the environment in which they live, and their definition of rationality will be affected by that environment (Scott 1995, 47). Recall from chapter 1 that Berle and Means, in their groundbreaking work on the managers of public corporations, understood that managers bring their own preconceptions and beliefs to their jobs and will define their role in accordance with such ideas—and these ideas will be shaped by the society in which they live, and which overlaps with the uncertain boundaries of their organizational selves.

Ideas—including principled ideas—enter international organizations through a variety of different modes. They might be picked up by top management, smuggled in by low-ranking field personnel, or championed by states, among others. Their effect on the outcomes of that organization will depend on various factors discussed above: how well they help solve problems, whether they have moral power over staff, whether they comport with the wishes of powerful member states, whether they fit with the preconceived notions of existing staff members, and the like. The three cases examined in this book suggest that there is no simple model to indicate when a new idea, one that depends (at least) as much on a moral as on a practical argument, will gain traction. The personal decisions of top leaders within the organization might be the most important variable, but it is hardly the only one.

Nevertheless, the fact is that IGOs, no less than states, are affected by the intellectual environment in which they operate, and in return use their intellectual and material power to affect that environment. As UNICEF, for example, changed its operational model because of the power of the human rights norm, it in turn used its own influence to spread respect for children's rights to other countries and even to other organizations. More important, UNICEF and the other organizations studied here were not simply incorporating and developing ideas to meet specific material challenges; they were also developing and promulgating ideas based on their perception of right and wrong, a perception shaped by the organization's mission and culture at least as much as by a rational assessment of organizational needs.

To ask whether it is *desirable* that IGOs work in this way seems almost beside the point: It stems necessarily from several structural factors. Their size, the complexity of their mandate, the professionalization of their staff—all produce the ability for independence and make it inevitable that they will take such steps. Principal–agent analysis has continued to expand the understanding of where this independence comes from and what factors might allow it to expand or might allow states to reassert their authority. Still, IGOs play an important part in helping states to control and even "govern" globalization. But to see that IGOs act according to principled ideas, rather than simply the rational pursuit of a specific mandate, raises questions about the moral responsibilities of such organizations, and it is to this that the next chapter turns.

*Chapter Six*

# The Ethical Responsibilities of
# Intergovernmental Organizations

One goal of this work has been to explore the ability of intergovernmental organizations (IGOs), and by extension other types of highly organized international institutions, to independently set their goals and develop strategies. Most of what allows this ability stems from their bureaucratic nature: their size, the interests of individual staff members, the complexity of their operations, and the like. It seems likely that other organizations that share these traits will act with similar independence or will at least have the latent ability to do so. This suggests that the academic community needs to subject the activities of IGOs to continued scrutiny. For those directly involved in international politics, it will come as no surprise that IGOs have this ability for independent action (at least, when the interests of a handful of powerful states are not directly threatened), but the academic literature on this topic is still evolving.

Seeing IGOs as agents opens a new set of questions regarding their moral responsibilities. It seems appropriate that a study on the question of IGO agency—and particularly one focusing on their activities in the interpretation and implementation of principled ideas concerned with human rights—should at least briefly examine these questions. IGOs are actors on the world stage, working according to both their own bureaucratic logic and the whims of those who are hired by states to run them. Yet current thinking on ethics and international relations fails to appreciate the complexity of IGOs and their place in world politics. This is hardly surprising, because states have dominated international politics for as long as they have existed in some form, and moral thinking in international affairs has focused on their responsibilities. Still, the idea that organizations ostensibly set up by states to do their bidding may actually develop and carry out plans on their own raises obvious questions about their rights and responsibilities. Though this is not the place for a lengthy discussion of those responsibilities, a brief analysis will, it is believed, shed some further light on their nature as agents.

Two questions arise when one addresses the moral obligations of IGOs. First, if one assumes that IGOs are often forced to make decisions with ethical or value-laden implications, then what set of values ought to guide IGOs? What, in other words, would a moral policy look like for IGOs? Second, *should the international community want* IGOs to be making policy regarding ethics and values; and if there are problems here, then what limits should be put on their ability to do so? Although the moral responsibilities of states have been explored in some depth (e.g., Nardin and Mapel 1992), and the responsibilities of individuals have of course also been considered in the international context (Linklater 1982), IGOs have largely been neglected. What has been written has tended to be specific and situational—focusing on the failings of specific organizations in specific situations. Little attention has been paid to an overall theory of what these organizations *ought* to be doing.

The simple notion that IGOs ought to be cognizant of human rights standards, and seek to implement them in their work, is not overly controversial by itself; UN-affiliated agencies are by and large required to help pursue the goals of the UN Charter, which includes the progressive realization of human rights. One can certainly argue that IGOs, as bodies with a formal relationship to the UN system, are simply required to follow internationally recognized human rights norms; and as bodies bound by the UN Charter, they must incorporate these norms into their operations. This is a powerful and important argument. However, it is not sufficient, in and of itself, to explain how IGOs ought to be acting. For one thing, it ignores the fact, explicated at length in the previous chapters, that in implementing a rights-based agenda, IGOs have considerable leeway to define what human rights actually *are*; they are not just carrying out directions derived from international law but are also determining what constitutes human rights and how they are best implemented. This activity deserves scrutiny; it can be said that much of what IGOs take to be rights-based actions have only a tenuous connection to international treaty law. For another, it implies that the *only* way an IGO can depart from a policy of strict neutrality is when that departure is justified by human rights treaties; this would seem to be overly limiting, in terms of how IGOs can change their policies when those policies are determined to be unethical or ineffective.

This chapter first elaborates on the idea that there needs to be a moral theory of international organizations. One important element of such a theory is the problem of authority: Given that IGOs can and do adopt and promote value-laden agendas not envisioned by states when they created the IGO, what gives them the right to speak of values at all? First, an argument will be made that an appropriate, if limited, source of authority does exist for IGOs in the moral realm. It will then be suggested that human rights are an appropriate way to ground international action in a set of relatively unproblematic standards. Next, the problem of how to control IGOs—how to prevent them from going beyond their limited mandate—will be addressed. The overall argument is meant to suggest that current thinking about IGOs, both as agents and as moral entities, is flawed because of an unspoken assumption that IGOs are similar to government bureaucracies; instead, it is more useful to examine them as if they were private business enterprises or other forms of nongovernmental organizations (NGOs) and to borrow from research on business ethics to explain their limitations (Oestreich 2004). This metaphor was suggested in chapter 1 and will be further elaborated here.

## Do We Need a Moral Theory of International Institutions?

It has already been noted that most IGOs were created with a generous amount of idealism, which makes their interest in human rights and ethical programming not very surprising. What else should one expect from agencies dedicated to improving international health, to aiding children in emergency situations, to funding reconstruction and projects in the developing world? There is a constellation of agencies working for humanitarian causes or helping to overcome the problems of international cooperation in the pursuit of collective goods—all express the optimism of the internationalist movement of the post–World War II era. As IGOs adopt this moralistic tone—and, indeed, as civil society groups with value-based agendas push more and more for reform—it is important to understand both the advantages and disadvantages of IGOs as agents with an agenda that goes beyond the merely technical. Should anyone want this sort of independence to continue, and should they build on it? Or is there a way in which this is not a desirable development? Should the international community be pleased or concerned that some IGOs have decided to take more seriously the question of international values?

From the perspective of the realist school of international thought, the moral standing of IGOs is entirely unproblematic. This stems partially from the realist denial of the relevance of morality to international politics: In an anarchic world dominated by self-interest, why talk of morals at all? But it also comes, more concretely, from an assumption that IGOs are not capable of meaningful independent agency. The realist makes two interrelated assumptions about IGOs that deny their agency. The first is that IGOs are themselves merely tools of powerful states. They are set up to assist states in pursuing their interests, and they exist only at the sufferance of those states.

According to this line of thought, to understand, for example, the World Health Organization's (WHO's) policy regarding intellectual property rights and essential drugs, one needs to look to the interests of large Western-based pharmaceutical firms and the states that represent these interests. Powerful states with large pharmaceutical firms will have an interest in patent protection, and WHO will support this once those powerful states make their interests known. Rational states would not set up or fund organizations they could not control and use to pursue their own interests. WHO, then, is not a moral actor: the moral credit or blame falls on the states that dictate policy.

The realist's second claim is that *even if* IGOs do have some measure of independence from states, it is only because they are so peripheral to the interests of those states. Why not let WHO lobby for changed property rights, if its lobbying will be ineffectual? If IGOs have no ability to affect policy or outcomes, then their moral status is not important. This reflects the presumption that the international system was created by states and that states remain the only actors of importance in that system.

Rejecting the first of these claims has been the central feature of this study and requires no further discussion here. The second claim is more difficult to address, but it rests on a questionable definition of what it means to be important. If one is discussing matters of national power and survival in the starkest sense, then there is little avoiding the conclusion that IGOs are not important. At the level of issues just below that—regarding the possibility of long-term economic cooperation, of protecting the global commons, and even of helping states to define their own role internally and externally—the previous chapter and a number of other works suggest that IGOs do have the ability to make a significant difference within certain issue areas.

At the most basic human level, IGOs, and particularly the ones under discussion here, most certainly have an effect on the lives of millions. That effect deserves to be considered and evaluated. A World Bank anticorruption policy may have little bearing on the lives of people living in the industrial countries of Europe or North America, but it has a substantial impact on the lives of multitudes in those countries that borrow from the Bank and must implement (or resist) its policies. This much is self-evident. And it is also true that the ethical ramifications of these activities ought to concern those who live in the industrial nations as well. The wealthy nations of the world provided the impetus to set up these institutions, and their citizens ultimately provide the bulk of the money for them. Progress in the developing world will eventually have an impact on all nations. Therefore, even those states largely unaffected by IGO policy should be interested in how IGOs are doing their job in the less wealthy parts of the world.

Given, then, that IGOs are meaningful actors whose activities affect the lives of millions, it seems unproblematic to assert that they ought to act morally and to be able to adjust their policies as needed. Surely this is preferable to the alternative? In fact, things are not so simple. The vision of a technocratic bureaucracy, unfettered by democratic control and beholden only to its own staff, has been a matter of concern at least since Max Weber's work on the role of bureaucracy in making possible modern life. Weber and his contemporaries portrayed an ideal type of bureaucracy as a neutral, technocratic power helping to organize an increasingly complex political and economic system run in a "precise, soulless and machine-like way." Yet they immediately held this ideal "up to ridicule." In reality, "bureaucracy had an inherent tendency to exceed its instrumental function, and to become a separate force within society, capable of influencing the goals and character of that society" (Beetham 1974, 64, 65).

In the view of Weber and his contemporaries, bureaucracies inevitably take on their own interests, drawn both from the needs of the organizations themselves (e.g., for survival and resources) and from the interests and preferences of the social class that staffs them (in the case of Wilhelmine Germany, of the Prussian Junkers). Bureaucrats can and often do stifle the wishes of politicians, and they can act contrary to the needs of the people they are supposed to serve, not to mention in opposition to their democratically expressed wishes (Gruber 1987, 4). Therefore, it is not unproblematic to think of bureaucratic organizations making decisions based on ethical grounds, because the outcomes of those decisions will be both unpredictable and unaccountable. Human rights ought to be central to all UN agencies. But which rights? And how are they to be defined and implemented?

For those IGOs that are particularly powerful—notably, the financial institutions—there is the danger of violating sovereignty norms through the pursuit of an agenda that is not strictly morally neutral. If an IGO moves away from purely technical activities (however defined) and begins making decisions about political or social values, this can and often is perceived as a violation of national sovereignty. The World Bank's Articles of Agreement, as was shown in chapter 3, explicitly bar the Bank from using anything except economic judgment in making lending decisions, largely to avoid the appearance that it might violate national sovereignty and provoke a backlash from borrowers. The United Nations Children's Fund (UNICEF) promotes a vision of children's rights that is not indigenous to many of the countries where it operates; what limit does it face when it tries to push this agenda on countries that find it in opposition to their traditional norms? To show that UNICEF understands the difficulties of its situation, it is only necessary to note that UNICEF's documents on the Convention on the Rights of the Child (CRC) repeatedly raise the specter of sovereignty violations and advise staff on how to avoid such problems. Though UNICEF can, of course, argue that it is empowered to pursue the goals of the CRC through its connection to the United Nations, it also understands the limitations of that argument and uses it carefully.

Chapter 1 noted that only UNICEF is directly related to the UN, because it was created by a General Assembly resolution and reports to the Economic and Social Council. WHO and the World Bank, as specialized agencies, have a higher level of presumed independence. They are bound to respect the decisions of the Security Council but relate to the larger UN structure through specific agreements. Important work has been devoted to arguing that all members of the UN family are to be expected to help pursue the purposes of the UN Charter, including the promotion of human rights (Darrow 2003, 125). Conversely, both the Bank and WHO, as specialized agencies, have argued (or have had state representatives argue for them) that their independent status as specialized agencies means they are not required to work toward the implementation of human rights treaties, and that doing so would in fact violate their charters or involve them in issues not approved by the states to which they answer.

The relationship of IGOs with the UN, however defined, is certainly important, and it should form the basis of IGOs' rights-based programming. Yet it still is not clear how far IGOs should go before taking on extensive social agendas. Clearly, the United Nations itself is a very imperfect representative of any sort of democratic global will. Its problems in this sense are numerous: the General Assembly gives too much importance to small states over large ones, the Security Council gives too much power to the victors of World War II, and the practice of states-only representation means many societies are represented by nondemocratic and even repressive governments. To say that IGOs, at another remove from the already undemocratic UN secretariat, are somehow legitimately representative of a global consensus is a cause for concern, particularly when the standards being referred to are vague and open to interpretation.

More important, IGOs also suffer from a "democratic deficit" that calls into question their ability to speak authoritatively on moral matters (Nye 2001). Furthermore, most IGOs are simply not set up to handle rights issues; they have restrictive constitutions, lack mechanisms for effective implementation, and recruit the wrong type of staff, among other problems. The independence of IGOs, their influence over the lives of millions, and the dangers inherent in giving them excessive freedom in defining their own role all make it necessary to understand what their obligations, and limitations, might be.

## Authority and Responsibility

If IGOs are to help promote, and even enforce, human rights, they must understand their powers and limits to interpret, enforce, pressure, and generally act. This necessity stems from the problem of sovereignty; protecting human rights means both acting across borders to intervene in how a state treats its citizens and appealing to a moral standard that is not necessarily accepted in that context. How much authority does UNICEF or WHO, or any other IGO, have to promote, and more important to decisively interpret, human rights standards? How can it resist the wishes of a national government when that government objects to its actions?

Surely a key point of the previous chapters is that all IGOs face extreme difficulty in determining exactly what rights *mean* in the context of their own work. The international promotion of human rights through the official treaty bodies of the UN does claim such authority, through treaty law; yet IGOs lack such a specific source and must consider where else they might find one. Otherwise, IGOs' actions in this area will appear illegitimate, and questions will be raised about their accountability. The same might be said for IGOs' ability to *interpret* rights standards, as they have been doing. Unless the sources and nature of their authority can be determined, anything they do that departs from the strictest possible interpretation of their particular charter will be controversial and open to rejection by states parties.

A good example of the sort of problems that arise is the World Bank's role in structural adjustment. The Bank has often been criticized for interfering too much in the internal affairs of borrowers—for example, by setting conditions on loans that require substantial (and often painful) internal changes. At the most extreme, the Bank has been accused of actually taking over the governing of highly indebted countries. Conversely, it has been accused of not interfering enough in the internal affairs of countries—for example, not concerning itself sufficiently with environmental issues or with the undemocratic nature of borrower regimes (Head 2004). Some antiglobalization groups have made both accusations—a contradiction that can be resolved only by assuming that there are clear guidelines to show where the Bank should and should not exercise authority to make decisions on behalf of others. Other IGOs face similar problems, albeit to a lesser degree because they are less powerful than the financial institutions. Because these organizations are not specifically designed as rights-promoting agencies, they often find themselves facing these sorts of issues.

Authority is a key factor here, in two different senses of the term. First, if IGOs can and will take action in the field of human rights, under what authority can they act, and what are the limits of this authority? What gives a nonelected, nonindigenous organization the right to make such basic decisions for a state, and how extensive is that right? Second, in what sense are IGOs authorities on the matter of human rights—which is to say, how can one presume that they have the expertise to interpret the often vague standards of human rights norms in their concrete practice? If the international community needs to be wary of large, influential international bureaucracies with wide-ranging human rights powers yet wants IGOs to follow more ethical policies, what should be the scope and limits of those powers? In this sense, IGOs face the same limitations as corporations, which also are asked to act morally yet lack the authority of legitimate governments. Of course, corporations face further limitations; they must act in ways that are financially expedient, for one. Corporations also have the default utilitarian position, identified most famously by Milton Friedman, that they can best serve the public good simply by producing goods efficiently and fulfilling consumer wishes (Friedman 1970). Nevertheless, society demands that IGOs act ethically, just as it demands that corporations seek a social good beyond profit maximization.

One way to solve the problem of authority here is to appeal to what philosophers call "epistemic authority," that is, the authority conferred on those who possess particular types of training and expertise in highly technical fields. (This is not to be confused with "epistemic communities," a different concept, which is discussed above, especially in chapter 5.) Epistemic authority implies deference; it is the willingness of those without such expertise to accept the opinions of those they both believe to have greater knowledge and ability and also trust to use that knowledge and ability wisely. Epistemic authority fits quite well with the institutions' own self-image, for they like to see themselves at least as much as providers of expertise and knowledge as of specific services. The idea of epistemic authority also moves away from a simple notion of force and into more complex concepts of ideas and institutions. Discovering the nature and scope of the authority available to IGOs when they move into the field of human rights, or any other area not covered explicitly by their original mandate but with implications for national sovereignty, will help to determine their limits as well as their strengths in such fields.

Authority itself defies easy definition; although it is clearly related to both power and coercion, it certainly is not synonymous witheither of these concepts (Friedrich 1958, 29). Joseph Raz, like other philosophers, divides political authority from what he terms theoretical authority, "the authority of the experts" (Raz 1990b, 4). Theoretical authority is the ability to get others to willingly suspend their own judgment about a proper course of action in favor of the judgment of another. "A person is a de facto epistemic authority," according to De George, "if he is considered to be an authority by another or by others with respect to some field or area of knowledge" (De George 1985, 27). Epistemic authority is considerably better suited for IGOs than other types of authority because they cannot claim for themselves the executive authority of a government. Epistemic authority relies instead on the sort of technical expertise and dispassionate judgment that Weber, for example, characterizes as the realm of bureaucrats (in their ideal portrayal) rather than politicians (Weber 1947, 333–34). More to the point, given the presumption that IGOs are themselves driven as much by their own internal politics and personalities as by direction from states parties, epistemic authority appropriately places responsibilities on managers and other staff members as well as on the organization as a whole.

As the issues IGOs face become more complex as well as technically demanding—and as these issues become more central to the well-being of society in general—the difference between epistemic and political authority will tend to shrink. The work and interpretations of IGOs can and do come to represent a global agreement on how to address international development and other complex global matters. It is important not to misinterpret this point; without the other trappings of legitimate government (consent, representation, etc.), such authority is and should be limited. But this limitation is desirable in relation to the authority of international institutions. A technocratic elite with wide-ranging power but little accountability is as illegitimate and frightening internationally as it is domestically—perhaps more so (Gadamer 1981, 69–87). It is worth noting that in other areas where the concept of *epistemes* has become current in international relations theory—notably the epistemic community work by Peter Haas (1992b), research has focused on such areas as environmental protection and food aid, where a certain amount of moral authority is assumed to be a good thing. Little has been said about the creation of ideas that might be considered morally problematic, yet there is no reason to assume that this is not a real possibility. Finding a tightly constrained source of legitimacy is one way of limiting IGO action to desirable areas.

Finally, epistemic authority has the advantage of being highly limited in *scope* as well as in power, just as one accepts the authority of a doctor in matters of medical advice but does not defer to her opinion on legal matters (Raz 1990a, 119; De George 1985). Basing the authority of IGOs to pursue human rights goals on their presumed expertise automatically limits the application of rights language to areas where IGOs were originally set up to operate—and the international community has reason to be wary of efforts to expand that scope. To assert an epistemic authority regarding the interpretation and use of rights standards to guide IGOs reinforces the idea that IGOs ought to rely primarily on the argument from effectiveness when justifying their activities in the rights realm; in other words, rights-based programming ought to be limited to areas where such programming helps IGOs with their core mission and helps frame answers to problems with normative content, such as defining what social issues need to be addressed when improving child health and survival. Although IGOs need to use rights to guide them when values are at stake, they also need to recognize that there is no justification for a wide-ranging human rights policy beyond the scope of their work. But given the complexity of the issues involved and they way they become interconnected, this scope could be considerably wider than it might first appear.

## Moral Theory and International Institutions

IGOs, then, have a source of authority to draw on when making morally laden decisions. And it appears that they have no choice, in a sense, but to use that authority when making decisions regarding their own programming. This is both necessary and desirable. How, then, should this limited moral authority be put to use? What should we expect IGOs to do?

There is no single standard of moral rightness for evaluating the actions of international institutions. Clearly, the World Bank has been subjected to the most rigorous criticism and angriest vilification of the three institutions studied here. But even among the Bank's critics, there is substantial disagreement as to exactly what it does wrong. Either it interferes too much in the internal affairs of borrower countries, or not enough; it distorts markets, or it allows them to work too freely; it is a tool of power politics or corporate interests or local elites. Similar criticisms could certainly be leveled at the other institutions; if they have not been as much, it is because those institutions lack the World Bank's reach and influence. The fact remains that IGOs are not held to any consistent ethical standard.

Generally, ethical thought in international relations has consisted mainly of the application of particular schools of thought to specific cases that arise in the international realm. Thus Hugo Grotius, in *De Jure Belli ac Pacis*, appeals to a combination of natural law and biblical morality to suggest how states ought to behave when interests conflict; Immanuel Kant's plan for perpetual peace is ultimately founded on his categorical imperative and the tenets of right reason; and so forth. Opponents of particular viewpoints have denied either their relevance to the problem of international affairs (as Lassa Oppenheim says of Grotius; Bull 1966, 54) or their very claim to express moral truths (Carr 1939, 87). This reduces the issue to a question of what values one chooses to hold.

One way of exploring the difficulties of finding a consistent moral theory to apply to IGOs is to follow John Rawls's distinction between deontological and consequentialist moral theories. Rawls himself serves well as an example of an exponent of the former. "Justice," he writes, "is the first virtue of social institutions, as truth is of systems of thought" (Rawls 1971, 3). His modern, influential reformulation of contractarian liberalism has obvious affinities with the problem at hand. In *A Theory of Justice*, and even more so in *Political Liberalism*, he is concerned with the problem of establishing a just political order that is capable of satisfying people with widely divergent conceptions of the good—that is, he seeks a universalizable principle, but one grounded in the practical realities of a diverse society.

In Rawls's formulation of liberal principles, institutions embody and, when necessary, enforce the procedures that ensure a just distribution of rights and goods within a society. His emphasis on institutions, and the procedures surrounding them, would seem a good starting point for explaining the mechanisms of global governance, particularly those set up to provide assistance in the less wealthy parts of the world. For example, Charles Beitz (1979) has extended Rawlsean liberalism in this direction. But particularly in his essay "The Law of Peoples," Rawls clearly notes that his theory of justice is not meant to justify intervention in what he calls well-ordered hierarchical societies; nor is it the beginnings of a worldwide social contract beyond some basic rules of well-ordered interaction (Rawls 1993). Also, Rawls, in seeking a theory of justice that is capable of uniting diverse communities within a single political entity, has limited himself to a relatively narrow area of ethics, namely, to distributive justice. Neither *A Theory of Justice* nor *Political Liberalism* provides a comprehensive moral theory in the manner of utilitarianism or, for that matter, of more wide-ranging variants on liberalism. Rawlsean liberalism is incapable of generating the sort of specific policy prescriptions that would be necessary to explain the status of UN agencies.

As an alternative to Rawls's approach to ethics, a utilitarian theory might appear to need less stretching and fit well with the current activities of IGOs. The "argument from effectiveness" used to justify many of the new IGO programs studied here uses a form of utilitarian logic. Utilitarianism is "the moral theory that judges the goodness of outcomes—and therefore the rightness of actions insofar as they affect outcomes—by the degree to which they secure the greatest benefit to all concerned" (Hardin 1988, xv). No inherent feature of utilitarianism limits either the type of problem on which it is to be used or the institutions to which it can apply. When formulated as a cosmopolitan theory of ethics, it applies to all people and all organizations at all times. In terms of international development, a utilitarian philosophy for an IGO would mean an obligation to improve the quality of life of the people whom it serves. The presumption is that a utilitarian argument is apolitical and therefore not at odds with the neutrality of IGOs. However, an international calculation of utility is particularly troublesome; beyond a few primary goods such as food, shelter, and health care, utilitarianism's "felicific calculus" will differ substantially between societies. What most advances the quality of life in one country, or even one region, might not do so in another (Walzer 1983, 63–67). Even the committed utilitarian recognizes that situations arise where utilitarian calculation seems to violate our intuitive moral notions. Famously, utilitarian calculation leads to situations where a small number of people could be subjected to great injustice—deprived of rights, tortured, killed—to improve the welfare of a great number of others (Goodin 1995, 70–71). This is not likely to provide a neutral base for justifying IGO forays into value-laden areas.

Another possibility, after considering deontological and consequentialist morality, is to ask IGOs to act in a purely neutral manner—that they perform as merely technocratic institutions, carrying out their mandate as scientifically as possible. But is it even possible to imagine what such a policy would look like? One might, for example, argue that the "job of WHO is to cure disease," and that a morally neutral policy for WHO would involve a strict focus on the technical aspects of health promotion. But as was shown in chapter 3, the notion of what constitutes good health has changed over time, and no single definition can be privileged over any others. The World Bank, similarly, has been at the forefront of changing the definition of development, beginning with an emphasis on expanding gross domestic product and moving on to more people-centered antipoverty efforts under the name of "sustainable human development." UNICEF also has struggled with what it means to aid and protect children—with the question, for example, of whether it ought to concern itself with child labor as not just a human rights issue but also as a fundamental issue raised by the very notion of a mandate to help children worldwide.

It appears true, then, that an effort to create a morally neutral set of goals or strategies for IGOs is futile; the very definitions of "development," "health," or a variety of other goals are changing, contestable, and necessarily laden with moral language. Choosing among various development strategies, or public health initiatives, may call for moral judgments to be made; human rights further politicize these decisions, and they have a specific legal status that may not allow flexibility when it is called for. Organizations are not always free to interpret rights standards in ways that take into consideration local conditions. Developing countries also frequently allege that too much emphasis on the pursuit of human rights, particularly political rights, is counterproductive for them—that economic development must be a top priority, with political reform put off to a later date. Thus it is particularly important to justify IGOs' involvement in anything related (even rhetorically) to rights, because these organizations are supposed to be neutral international agencies that strictly avoid violating sovereignty. A human rights agenda in a technically oriented IGO might well heighten the perception that it is beholden to the ideas and interests of its largest donors.

Conversely, there are also good reasons for IGOs to look to human rights for guidance when making moral decisions. Their connection to the UN and the purposes of its Charter is the most important, but not the only, reason. Human rights represent the only set of moral principles that have both widespread validity and a firm set of documents to give them concrete meaning. The Universal Declaration of Human Rights is considered by many to have the status of customary international law, and the documents that build upon it and give it substance—on genocide, torture, the rights of women, and the like—provide a useful if not always entirely consistent guide to rights and their application. This does not mean, of course, that there are no controversies about the meaning of human rights standards, for indeed there are many; the disagreement regarding so-called third-generation rights, or group rights, is an obvious example. It is also true that some documents have contradictory or vague standards. Still, most of these problems can be avoided—as UNICEF has done when it comes to family planning issues—even if a few others are more difficult to overcome.

Focusing on the rights implications of development and humanitarian projects and activities seems, then, a practical way of holding IGOs responsible for their actions. Yet of more importance for this study, because IGOs will in fact act independently to make value-laden decisions and respond to outside critics, it seems desirable that they should do it this way rather than to select another vaguer or more controversial set of values. Promoting rights—rather than the less controversial idea of simply respecting rights—would be an inevitable and generally desirable result of using human rights as a moral basis for programming. And the authority for making controversial decisions regarding what rights actually mean in a specific context stems from the intellectual authority of the agencies involved, albeit within limits (to be discussed below). The decision by Kofi Annan as UN secretary-general to make rights implementation a mandatory part of the work of all UN agencies adds greater legitimacy to this—limited, to be sure, in light of the democratic deficit of the UN and its agencies but suggestive of an international consensus no larger moral system can claim.

## Accountability, Stakeholder Theory, and IGOs

IGOs, then, have a certain level of authority with which to act as independent agents and to make decisions as matters of moral value. Human rights, broadly understood, represent a moral compass to guide them when making decisions about how to choose among various value-laden choices. But how is their independence to be controlled and limited? The issue of the democratic deficit remains, and with it the danger of IGOs overstepping their authority in the field of human rights or more generally when pursuing principled ideas. Though many are concerned about the notion of IGOs as mere extensions of their most powerful members, doing their bidding without regard to the consequences, there is no reason to suppose that one should be less concerned by the notion of IGOs as being rogue organizations, redefining their mandate as they see fit. This may be an extreme characterization of their independence—there are certainly practical limits to their freedom—but the central fact remains that they are agents with considerable leeway, as well as a great deal of intellectual and financial power to use in pursuing their goals.

This concern over the freedom of action of IGOs in many ways mirrors a more common critique of the UN family in general and financial institutions in particular—that IGOs lack accountability to international society and act in favor of a few special interests rather than of those most directly affected by their actions. Interestingly, this trend in thinking about IGOs contrasts starkly with other research on the role of IGOs as "norm entrepreneurs" that create and disseminate new ideas with a positive effect on international society. Most works in this vein have focused on the creation of what might seem to be morally unproblematic or good ideas, such as nuclear nonuse and antislavery, as noted in chapter 1. Yet there is no reason to assume that the ideas created and spread by IGOs will always be good, and there are examples of more problematic ideas being propagated. For example, Biersteker (1992) has put the International Monetary Fund at the center of the "triumph" of a set of neoliberal economic ideas that he finds troubling, and Cox (1987) and Murphy (1994) have made observations about how hegemonic states, acting through international institutions, have helped shape international ideas in ways that serve particular interests rather than the common good. Though many are tempted to see IGO activity as a positive counterweight to self-interested states, it is not without its own dangers.

Barnett and Finnemore have pointed out that IGOs derive much of their legitimacy from their claim to impartiality, and to their role in pursuing goals that have been agreed upon by the international community as a whole (Barnett and Finnemore 2004, 166–69). As with other research, such as that by Woods (2001) and by Fox and Brown (1998b), their focus is on the problem of accountability; how, they ask, are IGOs (and mainly the financial institutions, which are at the heart of all these works) to be controlled and held to account for their activities? This is an important question, but it addresses only one side of the problem of IGO action. It is indeed important to examine how IGOs can be controlled and the best ways of providing oversight, transparency, and some measure of democracy. However, this implies that IGOs are to be thought of as either "rogue elephants" trampling on the rights of states and individuals through ill-conceived development activities or as tools captured by a narrow set of international interests that they serve, to the detriment of the international society that should be the true beneficiaries of their actions.

What the focus on accountability misses is the question of what the IGOs *ought to* be doing. It fails to ask where their comparative advantage lies in terms of other forms of international action, and what we ought to be asking IGOs to do. There are interests that will often conflict with one another—in the governments of wealthy states, in those of poorer or otherwise less powerful states, among NGOs, within scientific communities, and even in "international civil society" in general. IGOs certainly ought to be held accountable for their actions, but this is likely to be a more retrospective than prescriptive advantage; it will prevent bad actions but not necessarily encourage development in the right direction. To anyone who has studied IGOs and come to know something about the people who work for them, a persistent question is "Why do such well-meaning people end up so often following misguided or failed policies?" A moral theory of IGOs ought to lay out a positive direction rather than only bar undesirable ones. Focusing on accountability is certainly good, but it is also important to ask "Accountable to whom?" and "Accountable for what?"

If the source of their independence lies largely in their bureaucratic nature, then it seems likely that any effort to control that nature would want to begin in the same place. An effort to bring accountability and democracy to IGOs, and to control the worst aspects of their independence while maintaining the positive ones, can borrow from similar efforts to oversee the work of corporations in the private sector, to which IGOs bear more than a passing similarity. Recall, for example, that the earliest work on the separation of management from ownership was done in relation to corporations, as discussed in chapter 1. It is also worth noting that corporations, like IGOs, are called upon to make ethical decisions yet lack the authority to use their influence to impose a particular vision of ethical conduct (Friedman 1970). It is not enough to determine the parameters of ethical conduct; it is also necessary to pay attention to the organization itself and its structure. The actions of individuals are largely determined by the roles they play within an organization and by the situations in which they find themselves.

One useful approach to understanding how to integrate ethics into organizational behavior is to apply the concept of a "stakeholder." This is primarily a notion from business ethics. Stakeholder ethics is the dominant concept in the ethics of business, and the term stakeholder is often used by IGOs themselves, although with little consideration of its true meaning. A stakeholder is generally defined as any individual or group affected in a serious way—directly or indirectly—by the activities of an organization. The underlying concept is derived from a business's responsibility to look out for the interests of its stockholders; but, the theory continues, to act ethically, an organization must recognize that other persons and groups also have a serious interest in its activities (Carroll 1986, 73–74). Stakeholders include primary stakeholders, including stockholders, suppliers, customers, employees, and those with a contractual relationship; and secondary stakeholders, including environmental groups, consumer groups, and society at large (Carroll 1986, 76–77). The level of responsibility varies between primary and secondary stakeholders but exists for all. This is not to say, however, that every claim to be a stakeholder is legitimate, but it is up to managers to distinguish legitimate from illegitimate claims.

The stakeholder model emerges from a desire to understand how a corporation fits into modern society and, more important, "how . . . the corporation [can] respond proactively to the increased pressure for positive social change" that comes from society's changing attitude toward private business (Freeman 1984, 39). The same issue arises concerning large international bureaucracies. There is an explicitly practical emphasis of the stakeholder approach; it asks not just what an organization ought to do but also how it should do it. It ought to recognize its obligations, the theory argues, and should do so through a process that includes affected parties in the process of strategic management. Ultimately, the approach rests on the assumption that stakeholder management not only is compatible with effective operations but also often makes poor operations better. The stakeholder model "is useful in establishing the connections between the practice of stakeholder management and the resulting achievement of corporate performance goals" (Carroll 1986, 81). Carroll uses the example of the Nestlé Corporation and the controversy over infant formula sales. "Perhaps," he speculates, "if Nestlé had taken a stakeholder view before it got embroiled in this controversy, it would have saved itself years of grief and lost reputation" (Carroll 1986, 84). IGOs have reached the same conclusions when it comes to including local voices in development policymaking and implementation. One can only imagine that such disasters as the World Bank's involvement with the Narmada River Dam in India or the POLONOROESTE rural development project in Brazil could have been avoided in the same way.

In its most extensive formulation, a stakeholder theory can be analogous to a social contract theory, under which society and corporations enter into an agreement whereby the corporations provide needed goods in a socially responsible way (Donaldson 1989, 47–53). A stakeholder model does not hold IGOs to a single liberal, utilitarian, or any other moral model. Nor does it require them to do things beyond their ability, for example, to effect radical change in member states or to distribute funds they do not have. Rather than appealing to abstract and contestable ideas, it takes a practical and democratic approach to moral questions, one well suited to the international environment. Stakeholder theory *does* require that IGOs consider how their actions affect all concerned parties, not just those to which they have specific contractual obligations. If, for example, women form an identifiable group that has been particularly injured by economic policies advanced by international financial institutions or whose needs have been ignored by WHO-supported health programs, their interests need to be integrated into decision making. All those affected have a legitimate claim to have their interests weighed and their voices heard. Determining who might actually speak for a group such as these women is a difficult but not insurmountable challenge.

At its most general level, that of organizational goal setting, stakeholder management legitimates and indeed requires a welfare-oriented approach to organizational goals—even when competing priorities, such as growth or stability, seem equally legitimate. Stakeholder ethics does not prescribe any single set of goals that an IGO ought to adopt; but it does help to explain how IGOs should cooperate with civil society in the countries where they operate, and it delegitimizes a focus on purely utilitarian measurements of success. In particular, it insists that an organization cannot be held under the sway of a particular set of interests—whether the desires of powerful owners' coalitions or of professional staff groups with their own beliefs and agendas—and must instead be held accountable to society at large when it determines priorities. Stakeholder theory places the organization within the context of the goals of a particular society rather than holding it apart from them, but it does so without denying the essential nature of the organization. It thus provides practical guidance to an organization, without demanding that it undertake actions that are clearly outside its abilities.

The importance of legitimizing IGO policies by demonstrating their positive effect on individuals cannot be overestimated. A key example involves the World Bank. At its most extreme, the Bank has been likened to a religious organization in its pursuit of its preferred neoclassical economic prescriptions for countries with serious economic imbalances. This is the message of George and Sabelli's *Faith and Credit*; they compare the Bank to the medieval church, in that "it has a doctrine, a rigidly structured hierarchy preaching and imposing this doctrine and a quasi-religious mode of self-justification" (George and Sabelli 1994, 5). If the Bank acted immorally during the structural adjustment period, they imply, it was not because its policies failed; rather, it was because this religious fervor prevented it from learning from its failures. They describe World Bank thinking in this way:

> A hundred case studies showing that the earth is round, or that structural adjustment is an environmental catastrophe, a terrible ordeal for the poor and a social tragedy will not convince me, because I know that the earth is flat and that structural adjustment, given time, will bring about the "transition of an economy to a new, sustainable and poverty-reducing growth path," in the words of an authoritative Bank document. . . . Some truths are not disputable—they are just there, like Natural Law for the Church. (George and Sabelli 1994, 70)

Mihivc uses similar language. "The discourse of the World Bank's analysis and policy prescriptions for Africa closely resembles the discourse of fundamentalist theology" (Mihevc 1995, 27). He describes the Bank's approach to neoclassical economics as "self-confirming," supported through the same techniques that characterize fundamentalist theologies (p. 28).

A stakeholder approach would not insist that classical economics is flawed from a technical standpoint; what it would say, rather, is that classical economics cannot satisfy all the moral obligations imposed on a business enterprise. Organizations have wider obligations than can be explained through economic theory. Thus, where Stein and Nafziger, for example, note that in the Bank's classical economic orientation "an important component of structural adjustment . . . is a disciplined monetary and fiscal policy," which "can cause reductions in expenditures that are vital if there is to be a real focus on 'growth with poverty reduction'" (Stein and Nafziger 1991, 179), such distributive trade-offs would be more difficult to justify under a program of stakeholder accounting. Furthermore, Tripp notes how the Bank failed to understand in Tanzania that adjustment programs "have not incorporated policies that address the different ways in which . . . reforms have affected or ought to affect different sectors of society" (Tripp 1992); stakeholder theory recognizes the differentiated interests and roles of various members of society. It is also possible that the prevalent liberal economic ideas of the Bank's largest "stockholders"—the United States and the United Kingdom, in particular—would not have had the same sway over Bank managers if other stakeholders' voices had been heard (Moore 1995, 26).

At the operational level of an organization, two sorts of changes are mandated by taking a stakeholder approach. The first and more obvious change is the creation of organizational mechanisms for including the voices of previously excluded stakeholders. An orientation toward technocratic solutions and the hiring of experts who disdain the advice of nonprofessionals creates an institutional structure that is resistant to both change and criticism (Nelson 1995, 161). A typical stakeholder strategy entails the creation of a "stakeholder map," in which an organization graphically represents its relationships with various stakeholder groups (Freeman 1984, 54–55). This is only the first step in a stakeholder approach. It is also necessary, among other tasks, to assign relative weights to various groups with a legitimate claim to be stakeholders and, most important, to integrate stakeholder ideas into a strategic framework (Freeman 1984, 67).

A stakeholder approach must be seen as serving an instrumental as well as moral purpose, that is, as giving an organization an advantage as it pursues its goals. For example, it must make a convincing argument that health—properly defined and understood as more than service provision or improved mortality and morbidity statistics—is aided by a stakeholder approach. This fits well with WHO's own argument that a rights-oriented approach improves health outcomes. First, however, a stakeholder approach must change how an organization thinks about who its constituencies *are* and how they are best served, moving away from an emphasis on seeing governments as the only clients of importance.

More is required, however, than identifying or even listening to affected groups; for bureaucracies to act effectively on their responsibilities, the realities of bureaucratic processes must be addressed. Bureaucratic structures are often designed in such a way that new concerns are ignored by those whose decisions actually matter: "The nature of the organizational beast is that it doesn't like and doesn't reward bad news and can hardly tolerate innovation" (Freeman 1984, 67). IGOs recognize the need for rights issues to be mainstreamed, but until they receive the proper organizational support, this process will remain haphazard.

Ultimately, a moral theory of IGOs must also address the level of individuals working for them. The challenge of organizational ethics is to create an environment that encourages managers to act morally rather than (or in addition to) acting to advance personal interests. This is also the central challenge for all large organizations that respond to any number of incentives, including financial necessity, bureaucratic inertia, and political pressure.

A moral theory of the firm begins with the assertion that modern corporations, and also large international bureaucracies, have become "professionalized" and that the advent of professional management has loosened the control that owners once had over their activities. This is an important variable in explaining the independence of IGOs and other such organizations that answer to boards of directors. It is a mark of the professional, according to Ernest Greenwood, that she has mastered a coherent body of skills and theory not known by the general public (Greenwood 1983, 22). The expectation of such authority, however, carries with it considerable responsibility. "The professional is assumed to be sufficiently committed to some larger good than his own self interest, e.g., the welfare of clients and of the society itself, that the use of professional skills and knowledge will be oriented toward the benefit of these other parties and not just toward the professional's own benefit" (Camenisch 1983, 33). The responsibility of the professional, in other words, is to act not only for her own sake but also for the betterment of society, and in a way that recognizes the moral climate of that society rather than imposing an outside morality upon it. This responsibility arises precisely from the claim to epistemic authority, from the understanding that others will defer within the professional's area of expertise, because this deference also implies a contract with the professional that the outcome of the relationship will be mutually acceptable.

Ultimately it is people, not organizations, who act. The other changes recommended above are designed to enable individuals to act in ways that will ensure that the organization's decisions are ethical. The goal is to create an environment where good acts—not just acts that are good in themselves but also those that lead to correct organizational decisions—are encouraged. Stakeholder management—and the broader insight of the role of an organization's actors in pursuing socially responsible goals—is designed ultimately to act upon all levels of organizational activity.

Actually implementing a more stakeholder-oriented approach would not be easy, and no effort is made here to make it sound as if it would be. Some elements of such an approach have already been tried, and the term stakeholder is sometimes used within the UN and its agencies. For example, all UN agencies have been taking steps to incorporate NGO voices into their operations, and they sometimes do refer to NGOs as stakeholders. However, the difficulty of translating such voices into actual policy changes remain, as some of the preceding chapters have shown. The need for changes in hiring and promotion practices, to put in place individuals who perceive their role in wider terms than mere technical proficiency, has also been noted here and elsewhere. More important, however, there has been no concerted effort to create anything like a "stakeholder map"; rather, the norm seems to be to wait until a group complains about its voice being ignored and then to include it among those consulted in the future. In other words, IGOs need to begin thinking about who will be affected by projects before, not after, those projects are under way.

## Stakeholder Ethics and Human Rights

The concept that IGOs ought to be held accountable for their actions—that there should be some oversight to ensure that they are actually serving the people they claim to want to help—seems to have taken hold in international discourse (Fox and Brown 1998b). This chapter set out to address the issue of how to define such actions and, at the same time, to limit them. Human rights standards likely represent only a minimal set of obligations, a sort of baseline for decent government, and are therefore particularly appropriate standards for IGOs. If these organization have obligations, they will be fairly restrictive and limited to standards that have some international validity—standards very much like the current human rights regime.

In extending the analogy of IGOs to private-sector enterprises, an argument by Thomas Donaldson provides useful guidance. After establishing a modified version of stakeholder theory (in which organizations are part of an implicit social contract), he argues that "rights . . . constitute minimal and bedrock moral considerations for multinational corporations," and that while different entities have different responsibilities, "the existence of the rights themselves, including the imposition of duties upon corporations to protect . . . such rights, seems beyond reasonable doubt" (Donaldson 1989, 50). Once he has established that these bodies do have moral personality and responsibilities, he is able to argue that a list of basic rights is so essential to human welfare that no organization can ignore them and still claim to be acting ethically.

Recall from chapter 1 that Berle and Means, writing on the growth of large corporations in American society, wondered how these corporations and their newly independent managers would handle the responsibility placed in their hands (Berle and Means 1932, 2; also see Galbraith 1973, 252–303). The increasing power of large organizations means that more and more aspects of modern life are affected by decisions made by their managers; they develop stakeholders among owners, employees, consumers, and even those affected by pollution and other externalities. "Because of its economic power and the scope of its influence on almost every facet of the lives of individuals," Frederick Sturdivant writes, "one serious student of business has concluded that 'the great corporation *is* our way of life'" (Sturdivant 1985, 23; emphasis in original). To the extent that bureaucracies in modern society are fulfilling the responsibilities traditionally left to family or to governments—everything from regulating the economy to caring for the elderly—they take on responsibilities and obligations that go beyond the traditional business creed of increased efficiency. The position of the most influential and active international organizations is similar; in some situations at least, they have either supplemented or displaced government authority in very real ways.

Power, in other words, cannot legitimately be used without reference to its social context. And this is particularly true in the case of IGOs—for there is no appeal to higher authority in the international realm. IGO staff members can and do claim that their activities, driven by technical and scientific considerations or by economic logic, are separate from moral considerations and are ethically neutral. In reality, most powerful organizations, whether domestic or international, *have no choice* in the matter, and they must accept the reality of their position as powerful moral agents. This might seem like morals by default, which is not the most satisfactory basis for a system of ethical criticism; but the failure of these institutions to truly act in a neutral manner makes it imperative to consider how to control and guide their decision making. IGOs and other international organizations, including multinational corporations, must recognize both the need to shoulder moral responsibility and their obligation to do so, by virtue of their influence over international public policy and the lack of any viable alternative.

Recognizing the human rights implications of these agencies' activities is an important first step in determining what they ought to be doing with their power. This has both positive and negative connotations: They should refrain from harming rights but should also think about how their activities positively affect such basic rights issues as freedom, equality, personal security, and subsistence. Simply declaring that such concerns are part of their operational paradigm is not enough; positive organizational changes are necessary to control their activities and to make certain that rhetoric and reality converge. This might encompass activities ranging from giving NGOs a greater voice within IGOs, to changing hiring and promotion practices, to rethinking basic mission statements. The important issue is to recognize that modern IGOs can and do act on their own—that they are important sources of new ideas as well as of funding and physical resources. Scholars of international relations increasingly recognize that when IGOs act, they are difficult to control and may have their own set of priorities. What is needed is more attention to the question of what they *ought* to be doing.

# Notes

## Chapter 2

   1. Anonymous interview, New York, February 24, 2004.

   2. Anonymous interview, New York, June 14, 2004.

   3. Anonymous telephone interview, October 1, 2004.

   4. Anonymous interview, New York, June 14, 2004.

   5. Anonymous interview, New York, July 7, 2004.

   6. Anonymous interview, New York, June 14, 2004.

## Chapter 3

   1. Anonymous interview, Washington, November 2, 2005.

## Chapter 4

   1. Anonymous interview, Geneva, September 16, 2003.

   2. Anonymous interview, Geneva, September 16, 2003.

   3. Anonymous interview, Geneva, September 16, 2003.

   4. Anonymous telephone interview, Geneva, September 16, 2003.

   5. Anonymous interview, Geneva, September 18, 2003.

   6. Anonymous interview, Geneva, September 16, 2003.

   7. Anonymous interview, Geneva, September 16, 2003.

   8. Anonymous telephone interview, Geneva, August 5, 2003.

   9. Anonymous interview, Geneva, September 17, 2003.

  10. Anonymous interview, Geneva, September 17, 2003.

  11. Anonymous telephone interview, August 10, 2006.

  12. Anonymous interview, Geneva, September 15, 2003.

# References

Advocacy Project. 2002. The World Bank and Human Rights: A Debate Organized by the Georgetown Human Rights Forum under the Joint Sponsorship of the Institute for the Study of International Migration (Georgetown University), and the Advocacy Project. November 24. www.advocacynet.org/news_views/news_240.html.

Alfredsson, Gudmundur. 2002. The Usefulness of Human Rights for Democracy and Good Governance. In *Human Rights and Good Governance: Building Bridges*, ed. H.-O. Sano and G. Alfredsson. New York: Martinus Nijhoff.

Allen, Charles. 1950. World Health and World Politics. *International Organization* 4, no. 1:27–43.

Alston, Philip, and Mary Robinson, eds. 2005. *Human Rights and Development: Towards Mutual Reinforcement*. New York: Oxford University Press.

Ascher, Charles S. 1952. Current Problems in the World Health Organization's Program. *International Organization* 6, no. 1:27–50.

Ascher, William. 1983. New Development Approaches and the Adaptability of International Agencies: The Case of the World Bank. *International Organization* 37, no. 3:415–39.

Ayres, Robert L. 1983. *Banking on the Poor: The World Bank and World Poverty*. Cambridge, Mass.: MIT Press.

Barnett, Michael N., and Martha Finnemore. 1999. The Politics, Power, and Pathologies of International Organizations. *International Organization* 53, no. 4:699–732.

———. 2002. Beyond Delegation? Paper presented at Program on International Organization and Change, Park City, Utah, May 3–4.

———. 2004. *Rules for the World: International Organizations and Global Politics*. Ithaca, N.Y.: Cornell University Press.

Bartkowski, Maciej. 2003. Analysis of Change within International Organizations. Paper prepared for European Consortium for Political Research Joint Sessions Workshops, Edinburgh, March 28–April 2.

Beetham, David. 1974. *Max Weber and the Theory of Modern Politics*. London: George Allen & Unwin.

Beitz, Charles. 1979. *Political Theory and International Relations*. Princeton, N.J.: Princeton University Press.

Bellamy, Carol. 1998. Guidelines for Human Rights-Based Programming Approach. Report CF/EXD/1998-04. New York: UNICEF.

Berle, Adolf A., and Gardiner C. Means. 1932. *The Modern Corporation and Private Property*. New York: Macmillan.

Biersteker, Thomas. 1992. The "Triumph" of Neoclassical Economics in the Developing World: Policy Convergence and Bases of Governance in the International Order. In *Governance without Government: Order and Change in World Politics*, ed. J. Rosenau and E.-O. Czempiel. New York: Cambridge University Press.

Bissell, Richard E. 1997. Recent Practice of the Inspection Panel of the World Bank. *American Journal of International Law* 91, no. 4:741–44.

———. 2003. The Arun III Hydroelectric Project, Nepal. In *Demanding Accountability: Civil-Society Claims and the World Bank Inspection Panel*, ed. D. Clark, J. A. Fox, and K. Treakle. Lanham, Md.: Rowman & Littlefield.

Black, Maggie. 1986. *The Children and the Nations: The Story of UNICEF*. New York: UNICEF.

Blustein, Paul. 2001. *The Chastening*. New York: Public Affairs.

Bradlow, Daniel D. 1996a. A Test Case for the World Bank. *American University Journal of International Law and Policy* 11, no. 2:247–94.

———. 1996b. The World Bank, the IMF, and Human Rights. *Transnational Law and Contemporary Problems* 6, no. 1:48–90.

———. 1999. Precedent-Setting NGO Campaign Saves the World Bank's Inspection Panel. *Human Rights Brief* 6:7–27.

Brodnig, Gernot. 2001. *The World Bank and Human Rights: Mission Impossible?* Cambridge, Mass.: Carr Center for Human Rights.

Brown, Bartram. 1992. *The United States and the Politicization of the World Bank: Issues of International Law and Policy*. New York: Keegan Paul.

Brundtland, Gro-Harlem. 1998. Address on the Fiftieth Anniversary of the Universal Declaration on Human Rights, December 8. Paris. www.who.int/director-general/speeches/1998/english/19981208_paris.html.

Bryn, Robert J., et al. 2005. In Faint Praise of the World Bank's Gender Development Policy. *Canadian Journal of Sociology* 30, no. 1:95–111.

Bull, Hedley. 1966. The Grotian Conception of International Society. In *Diplomatic Investigations*, ed. H. Butterfield and M. Wight. London: George Allen & Unwin.

Burki, Shahid Javed, and Guillermo E. Perry. 1998. *Beyond the Washington Consensus: Institutions Matter*. Washington, D.C.: World Bank.

Camenisch, Paul F. 1983. *Grounding Professional Ethics in a Pluralistic Society*. New York: Haven Publishing.

Carr, E. H. 1939. *The Twenty Years' Crisis 1919–1929.* 2nd ed. London: Macmillan.

Carroll, Archie B. 1986. *Ethics and Stakeholder Management.* 3rd ed. Cincinnati: South-Western College Publishing.

Cernea, Michael, ed. 1985. *Putting People First.* New York: Oxford University Press.

Cernea, Michael, and Scott E. Guggenheim, eds. 1993. *Anthropological Approaches to Resettlement: Policy, Practice, and Theory.* Boulder, Colo.: Westview Press.

Clark, Dana. 2002. The World Bank and Human Rights: The Need for Greater Accountability. *Harvard Human Rights Law Journal* 15: 205–26.

———. 2003. Understanding the World Bank Inspection Panel. In *Demanding Accountability: Civil-Society Claims and the World Bank Inspection Panel,* ed. D. Clark, J. A. Fox, and K. Treakle. Lanham, Md.: Rowman & Littlefield.

Cohen, Cynthia Price. 1993. The Developing Jurisprudence of the Rights of the Child. *St. Thomas Law Review* 6, no. 2:1–96.

Cook, Rebecca J., and Bernard M. Dickens. 2001. *Advancing Safe Motherhood through Human Rights.* Geneva: World Health Organization.

Cox, Robert. 1969. The Executive Head: An Essay on Leadership in International Organization. *International Organization* 23, no. 2:205–30.

———. 1987. *Production, Power, and World Order: Social Forces in the Making of History.* New York: Columbia University Press.

Cox, Robert, and Harold K. Jacobson. 1973. *The Anatomy of Influence.* Cambridge: Cambridge University Press.

Crawford, Gordon. 1995. *Promoting Democracy, Human Rights and Good Governance through Development Aid: A Comparative Study of the Policies of Four Northern Donors.* Leeds, U.K.: Leeds University Press.

Crawford, Neta. 2003. The Slippery Slope to Preventive War. *Ethics & International Affairs* 17, no. 1:30–36.

Crossette, Barbara. 1997. UN Health Official, Opposed By U.S., Won't Seek Re-election. *New York Times,* April 30, 5.

Dakolias, Maria. 1996. *The Judicial Sector in Latin America and the Caribbean: Elements of Reform.* World Bank Technical Paper 319. Washington, D.C.: World Bank.

Darrow, Mac. 2003. *Between Light and Shadow: The World Bank, the International Monetary Fund and International Human Rights Law.* Portland, Ore.: Hart Publishing.

Davis, Gloria. 2004. *A History of the Social Development Network in the World Bank, 1973–2004.* Social Development Paper 56. Washington, D.C.: World Bank.

Davis, Shelton. 1993. The World Bank and Indigenous Peoples. Paper presented at Denver Initiative Conference on Human Rights, Denver, April 16–17.

De George, Richard T. 1985. *The Nature and Limits of Authority*. Lawrence: University Press of Kansas.

Diehl, Paul, ed. 2001. *The Politics of Global Governance: International Organizations in an Interdependent World*. 2nd ed. Boulder, Colo.: Lynne Rienner.

Dijkzeul, Dennis, and Yves Beigbeder. 2003a. Introduction: Rethinking International Organizations. In *Rethinking International Organizations: Pathology and Promise*, ed. D. Dijkzeul and Y. Beigbeder. New York: Berghahn Books.

———, eds. 2003b. *Rethinking International Organizations: Pathology and Promise*. New York: Berghahn Books.

Donaldson, Thomas. 1989. *The Ethics of International Business*. New York: Oxford University Press.

Donnelly, Jack. 1999. Human Rights, Democracy, and Development. *Human Rights Quarterly* 21, no. 3:608–32.

Dubin, Martin David. 1995. The League of Nations Health Organisation. In *International Health Organisations and Movements, 1918–1939*, ed. P. Weindling. Cambridge: Cambridge University Press.

Dunkerton, Kristine J. 1995. The World Bank Inspection Panel and Its Effect on Lending Accountability to Citizens of Borrowing Nations. *University of Baltimore Journal of Environmental Law* 5:226–61.

Economic and Social Council. 2003. United Nations Commission on Human Rights: Fifty-Ninth Session—Written Submission by the World Health Organization. Report E/CN.4/2003/122. January 30.

Edstrom, Judith. 2002. Indonesia's Kecamatan Development Project: Is It Replicable? World Bank, Washington, March.

Einhorn, Jessica. 2001. The World Bank's Mission Creep. *Foreign Affairs* 80, no. 5:22–35.

Finnemore, Martha. 1996. *National Interests in International Society*. Ithaca, N.Y.: Cornell University Press.

Foot, Rosemary, S. Neil McFarlane, and Michael Mastanduno. 2003. *US Hegemony and International Organizations*. New York: Oxford University Press.

Forsythe, David P. 1989. *Human Rights and World Politics*. 2nd ed. Lincoln: University of Nebraska Press.

———. 2000. *Human Rights in International Relations*. New York: Cambridge University Press.

Fox, Jonathan A. 1998. When Does Reform Policy Influence Practice? Lessons from the Bankwide Resettlement Review. In *The Struggle for*

*Accountability: The World Bank, NGOs, and Grassroots Movements,* ed. J. A. Fox and L. D. Brown. Cambridge, Mass.: MIT Press.

Fox, Jonathan A., and L. David Brown. 1998a. Introduction. In *The Struggle for Accountability: The World Bank, NGOs, and Grassroots Movements,* ed. J. A. Fox and L. D. Brown. Cambridge, Mass.: MIT Press.

————, eds. 1998b. *The Struggle for Accountability: The World Bank, NGOs, and Grassroots Movements.* Cambridge, Mass.: MIT Press.

Franck, Thomas M. 1992. Emerging Right to Democratic Governance. *American Journal of International Law* 86, no. 1:46–91.

Freeman, R. Edward. 1984. *Strategic Management: A Stakeholder Approach.* Marshfield, Mass.: Pitman Publishing.

Friedman, Milton. 1970. The Social Responsibility of Business Is to Increase Its Profits. *New York Times Magazine,* September 13, 17–20, 32–125.

Friedrich, Carl J. 1958. Authority, Reason, and Discretion. In *Authority,* ed. K. J. Friedrich. Cambridge, Mass.: Harvard University Press.

Gadamer, Hans Georg. 1981. *Reason in the Age of Science.* Cambridge, Mass.: MIT Press.

Galbraith, John Kenneth. 1973. *Economics and the Public Purpose.* Boston: Houghton Mifflin.

Gellman, Barton. 2000. Death Watch: The Global Response to AIDS in Africa. *Washington Post,* July 5, 2000, 1.

George, Susan, and Fabrizio Sabelli. 1994. *Faith and Credit: The World Bank's Secular Empire.* Boulder, Colo.: Westview Press.

Goodin, Robert. 1995. *Utilitarianism as a Public Philosophy.* New York: Cambridge University Press.

Gordenker, Leon, Roger A. Coate, Christer Jonsson, and Peter Soderholm. 1995. *International Cooperation in Response to AIDS.* New York: Pinter.

Gostin, Lawrence O., and Zita Lazzarini. 1997. *Human Rights and Public Health in the AIDS Pandemic.* New York: Oxford University Press.

Greenwood, Ernest. 1983. Attributes of a Profession. In *Moral Responsibility and the Professions,* ed. B. Baumrin and B. Freedman. New York: Haven.

Griffiths, Thomas, and Marcus Colchester. 2000. Report on a Workshop on "Indigenous Peoples, Forests, and the World Bank: Policies and Practices." Forest Peoples Program and Bank Information Center. www.wrm.org.uy/actors/WB/IPreport.html.

Gruber, Judith. 1987. *Controlling Bureaucracies: Dilemmas in Democratic Governance.* Berkeley: University of California Press.

Gruskin, Sofia, and Daniel Tarantola. 2002. Health and Human Rights. In *Oxford Textbook of Public Health,* ed. R. Detels, J. McEwen, R. Beaglehole, and H. Tanaka. New York: Oxford University Press.

Haas, Ernst B. 1990. *When Knowledge Is Power: Three Models of Change in International Organizations.* Berkeley: University of California Press.

Haas, Peter. 1992a. Introduction: Epistemic Communities and International Policy Coordination. *International Organization* 46, no. 1:1–35.

———, ed. 1992b. *Knowledge, Power, and International Policy Coordination.* Columbia: University of South Carolina Press.

Hall, Rodney Bruce. 2003. The Discursive Demolition of the Asian Development Model. *International Studies Quarterly* 47, no. 4:71–99.

Hardin, Russell. 1988. *Morality within the Limits of Reason.* Chicago: University of Chicago Press.

Hawkins, Darren G., David A. Lake, Daniel L. Nielson, and Michael J. Tierney, eds. 2006. *Delegation and Agency in International Organizations.* New York: Cambridge University Press.

Hazelzet, Hadewych. 1998. The Decision-Making Approach to International Organizations: Cox and Jacobson's Anatomic Lesson Revisited. In *Autonomous Policy Making by International Organizations,* ed. B. Reinalda and B. Verbeek. New York: Routledge.

Head, John W. 2004. For Richer or For Poorer: Assessing the Criticisms Directed at the Multilateral Development Banks. *Kansas Law Review* 52, no. 2:241–325.

Heald, Morrell. 1970. *The Social Responsibilities of Business.* Cleveland: Press of Case Western Reserve University.

Henderson, Hazel. 1996. Changing Paradigms and Indicators: Implementing Equitable, Sustainable, and Participatory Development. In *Development: New Paradigms and Principles for the Twenty-first Century,* ed. J. M. Griesgraber and B. G. Gunter. East Haven, Conn.: Pluto Press.

Himes, James. 1993. *The United Nations Convention on the Rights of the Child: Three Essays on the Challenge of Implementation.* Florence: UNICEF International Child Development Center.

Hirschman, Albert O. 1945. *National Power and the Structure of Foreign Trade.* Berkeley: University of California Press.

Hodgkin, Rachel, and Peter Newell. 2002. *Implementation Handbook for the Convention on the Rights of the Child.* New York: UNICEF.

Hunt, Paul. 2003. WHO Workshop on Indicators for the Right to Health: A Background Note. May 15. World Health Organization, Geneva.

International Development Association. 1960. IDA Articles of Agreement, International Development Association, 1960. http://siteresources.worldbank.org/IDA/Resources/ida-articlesofagreement.pdf.

Jonsson, Christer. 1996. From "Lead Agency" to "Integrated Programming": The Global Response to AIDS in the Third World. In *Green Globe Yearbook 1996,* ed. H. O. Bergesen and G. Parmann. Oxford: Oxford University Press.

Kahler, Miles. 1990. The United States and the International Monetary Fund: Declining Influence or Declining Interest? In *The United States and Multilateral Institutions*, ed. M. P. Karns and K. Mingst. Boston: Unwin Hyman.

———. 2001. *Leadership Selection in the Major Multinationals*. Washington, D.C.: Institute for International Economics.

Kaiser, Kai. 2006. Decentralization Reforms. In *Analyzing the Distributional Impact of Reforms: A Practitioner's Guide to Pension, Health, Labor Market, Public Sector Downsizing, Taxation, Decentralization and Macroeconomic Modeling*, ed. A. Coudouel and S. Paternostro. New York: World Bank.

Kapur, Devesh. 2002. The Changing Anatomy of Governance of the World Bank. In *Reinventing the World Bank*, ed. J. R. Pincus and J. A. Winters. Ithaca, N.Y.: Cornell University Press.

Kapur, Devesh, John P. Lewis, and Richard Webb. 1997. *The World Bank: Its First Half Century*. Vol. 1. Washington, D.C.: Brookings Institution Press.

Kardam, Nuket. 1991. *Bringing Women In: Women's Issues in International Development Programs*. Boulder, Colo.: Lynne Rienner.

———. 1993. Development Approaches and the Role of Policy Advocacy: The Case of the World Bank. *World Development* 21, no. 11:1773–86.

Koehn, Daryl. 1994. *The Ground of Professional Ethics*. New York: Routledge.

Kraske, Jochen. 1996. *Bankers with a Mission: The Presidents of the World Bank, 1946–91*. New York: Oxford University Press.

Krasner, Stephen D. 1981. Power Structures and Regional Development Banks. *International Organization* 35, no. 2:303–28.

Kratochwil, Friedrich, and John Gerrard Ruggie. 1986. International Organization: A State of the Art on the Art of the State. *International Organization* 40, no. 4:753–75.

Landell-Mills, Pierre. 1992. Governance, Cultural Change, and Empowerment. *Journal of Modern African Studies* 30, no. 3:543–67.

Lawyers Committee for Human Rights. 1995. *The World Bank: Governance and Human Rights*. New York: Author.

Leary, Virginia. 1994. The Right to Health in International Human Rights Law. *Health and Human Rights* 1, no. 1: 24–56.

LeBlanc, Lawrence J. 1995. *The Convention on the Rights of the Child: United Nations Lawmaking on Human Rights*. Lincoln: University of Nebraska Press.

Lewin, Elisabeth. 2000. Supporting the Change of National Frameworks to Meet the Demands of the CRC: The Role of UNICEF. www.unicef.org/evaldatabase/index_14414.html.

Linklater, Andrew. 1982. *Men and Citizens in the Theory of International Relations*. New York: St. Martin's Press.

Lyne, Mona, Daniel L. Nielson, and Michael J. Tierney. 2006. A Problem of Principals: Common Agency and Social Lending at the Multilateral Development Banks. In *Delegation and Agency in International Organizations*, ed. D. A. Lake, D. L. Nielson and M. Tierney. New York: Cambridge University Press.

MacKay, Fergus. 2005. The Draft World Bank Operational Policy 4.10 on Indigenous Peoples: Progress or More of the Same? *Arizona Journal of International and Comparative Law* 22, no. 1:65–98.

Mann, Jonathan. 1988. AIDS: Discrimination and Public Health. Paper presented at IV International Conference on AIDS, Stockholm, June 12–16.

————. 1999. Human Rights and AIDS: The Future of the Pandemic. In *Health and Human Rights*, ed. J. Mann, S. Gruskin, M. A. Grodin, and G. J. Annas. New York: Routledge.

Marmorstein, Victoria E. 1978. World Bank Power to Consider Human Rights Factors in Loan Decisions. *Journal of International Law and Economics* 13:113–36.

Marquette, Heather. 2003. *Corruption, Politics, and Development: The Role of the World Bank*. New York: Palgrave MacMillan.

Martin, Lisa. 2002. Agency and Delegation in IMF Conditionality 2002. www.people.fas.harvard.edu/~llmartin/imfconditionality.html.

Martin, Lisa L., and Beth A. Simmons. 1998. Theories and Empirical Studies of International Institutions. *International Organization* 52, no. 4:729–57.

Mertus, Julie A. 2005. *The United Nations and Human Rights: A Guide for a New Era*. New York: Routledge.

Meyer, John W., and Brian Rowan. 1991. "Institutionalized Organizations: Formal Structure as Myth and Ceremony." In *The New Institutionalism in Organizational Analysis*, edited by W. W. Powell and P. J. DiMaggio. Chicago: University of Chicago Press.

Mihevc, John. 1995. *The Market Tells Them So: The World Bank and Economic Fundamentalism in Africa*. Atlantic Highlands, N.J.: Zed Books.

Mikesell, Raymond. 1972. The Emergence of the World Bank as a Development Institution. In *Bretton Woods Revisited*, ed. A. L. K. Acheson, J. F. Chant, and M. J. F. Prachovny. Toronto: University of Toronto Press.

Miller-Adams, Michelle. 1999. *The World Bank: New Agendas in a Changing World*. New York: Routledge.

Mingst, Karen A. 1990. The United States and the World Health Organization. In *The United States and Multilateral Institutions: Patterns of Changing Instrumentality and Influence*, ed. M. P. Karns and K. A. Mingst. Boston: Unwin Hyman.

Moore, David B. 1995. Development Discourse as Hegemony: Towards an Ideological History—1945–1995. In *Debating Development Discourse:*

*Institutional and Popular Perspectives*, ed. D. B. Moore and G. Schmitz. New York: St. Martin's Press.

Moravcsik, Andrew. 1999. A New Statecraft? Supranational Entrepreneurs and International Cooperation. *International Organization* 53, no. 2:267–306.

Mueller, Dennis C. 1989. *Public Choice II*. New York: Cambridge University Press.

Muldoon, James P. 2004. *The Architecture of Global Governance*. Boulder, Colo.: Westview Press.

Murphy, Craig. 1994. *International Organization and Industrial Change: Global Governance since 1850*. New York: Oxford University Press.

Murphy, Josette L. 1995. *Gender Issues in World Bank Lending*. Washington, D.C.: World Bank.

———. 1997. *Mainstreaming Gender in World Bank Lending: An Update*. Washington, D.C.: World Bank.

Narayan, Deepa. 2002. *Empowerment and Poverty Reduction: A Sourcebook*. Washington, D.C.: World Bank.

Nardin, Terry, and David R. Mapel. 1992. *Traditions of International Ethics*. New York: Cambridge University Press.

Nelson, Paul J. 1995. *The World Bank and Non-Governmental Organizations: The Limits of Apolitical Development*. New York: St. Martin's Press.

Ness, Gayl D., and Steven R. Brechin. 1988. Bridging the Gap: International Organizations as Organizations. *International Organization* 42, no. 2:245–73.

Newman-Black, Marjorie. 1991. Introduction. In *The Convention: Child Rights and UNICEF Experience at the Country Level*, ed. M. Newman-Black and P. Light. Florence: UNICEF.

Newman-Williams, Marjorie. 1999. How Things Changed. *UN Chronicle*, Summer, 38–39.

Nye, Joseph. 2001. Globalization's Democratic Deficit: How to Make International Institutions More Accountable. *Foreign Affairs* 80, no. 4:2–12.

O'Brien, Robert, Anne Marie Goetz, Jan Aart Scholte, and Marc Williams. 2000. *Contesting Global Governance: Multilateral Economic Institutions and Global Social Movements*. New York: Cambridge University Press.

Oestreich, Joel. 1998. UNICEF and the Implementation of the Convention on the Rights of the Child. *Global Governance* 4, no. 2:183–99.

———. 1999. Liberal Theory and Minority Group Rights. *Human Rights Quarterly* 21, no. 1: 108–32.

———. 2004. The Human Rights Responsibilities of the World Bank: A Business Paradigm. *Global Social Policy* 4, no. 1:55–76.

Pais, Marta Santos. 1999. A Human Rights Conceptual Framework for UNICEF. UNICEF International Child Development Center, New York, May.

Prasada, Charulata. 2001. *Case Study: Operationalizing Rights-Based Programming, UNICEF Nepal.* New York: UNICEF.

Rawls, John. 1971. *A Theory of Justice.* Cambridge, Mass.: Harvard University Press.

———. 1993. The Law of Peoples. In *On Human Rights,* ed. S. Shute and S. Hurley. New York: Basic Books.

Raz, Joseph. 1990a. Authority and Justification. In *Authority,* ed. J. Raz. New York: New York University Press.

———. 1990b. Introduction. In *Authority Revisited,* ed. J. Raz. New York: New York University Press.

Razavi, Shahra, and Carol Miller. 1995. *Gender Mainstreaming: A Study of Efforts by the UNDP, the World Bank and the ILO to Institutionalize Gender Issues.* Occasional Paper 4. New York: United Nations Research Institute for Social Development.

Reinalda, Bob. 2001. Decision Making within International Organizations: An Overview of Approaches and Case Studies. Paper presented at European Consortium for Political Research, 29th Joint Sessions of Workshops, Grenoble, April 6–11.

———. 2004. *Decision Making within International Organizations.* New York: Routledge.

Reitbergen-McCracken, Jennifer, ed. 1996. *Participation in Practice: The Experience of the World Bank and Other Stakeholders.* Washington, D.C.: World Bank.

Renteln, Alison Dundes. 1997. United States Ratification of Human Rights Treaties: Who's Afraid of the CRC: Objections to the Convention on the Rights of the Child. *ILSA Journal of International and Comparative Law* 3, no. 2:629–40.

Rios-Kohn, Rebeca. 2003. Human Rights Based Programming: The Mali Experience. New York: UNICEF.

Risse, Thomas, and Kathryn Sikkink. 1999. The Socialization of International Human Rights Norms into Domestic Practices: Introduction. In *The Power of Human Rights: International Norms and Domestic Change,* ed. T. Risse, S. C. Ropp, and K. Sikkink. New York: Cambridge University Press.

Risse-Kappen, Thomas, ed. 1995. *Bringing Transnational Relations Back In: Non-State Actors, Domestic Structures, and International Institutions.* New York: Cambridge University Press.

Rittberger, Volker, ed. 2001. *Global Governance and the United Nations System.* New York: United Nations University Press.

Rozga, Dorothy. 2001. Applying a Human Rights-Based Approach to Programming: Experiences of UNICEF. Paper presented at Workshop on Human Rights, Assets and Livelihood Security, and Sustainable Development, London, June 19–20.

Ruggie, John Gerard. 1983. International Regimes, Transactions, and Change: Embedded Liberalism in the Postwar Economic Order. In *International Regimes*, ed. S. D. Krasner. Ithaca, N.Y.: Cornell University Press.

Sano, Hans-Otto. 2002. How Does Good Governance Relate to Human Rights? In *Human Rights and Good Governance: Building Bridges*, ed. H.-O. Sano and G. Alfredsson. New York: Martinus Nijhoff.

Sarfaty, Galit A. 2005. The World Bank and the Internalization of Indigenous Rights Norms. *Yale Law Journal* 114, no. 7:1792–1818.

Schechter, Michael G. 1988. The Political Role of Recent World Bank Presidents. In *Politics in the United Nations System*, ed. L. F. Finklestein. Durham, N.C.: Duke University Press.

Schlemmer-Schulte, Sabine. 1999. The World Bank Inspection Panel: A Record of the First International Accountability Mechanism and Its Role for Human Rights. *Human Rights Brief* 6:1–20.

Scott, W. Richard. 1992. *Organizations: Rational, Natural, and Open Systems*. Englewood Cliffs, N.J.: Prentice Hall.

———. 1995. Symbols and Organizations: From Barnard to the Institutionalists. In *Organization Theory: From Chester Barnard to the Present and Beyond*, ed. O. E. Williamson. New York: Oxford University Press.

Shihata, Ibrahim F. I. 1988. The World Bank and Human Rights: An Analysis of the Legal Issues and the Record of Achievements. *Denver Journal of International Law and Policy* 17, no. 1:39–66.

———. 1991. *The World Bank in a Changing World*. Boston: Martinus Nijhoff.

Siddiqi, Javed. 1995. *World Health and World Politics: The World Health Organization and the UN System*. Columbia: University of South Carolina Press.

Sikkink, Kathryn. 1991. *Ideas and Institutions: Developmentalism in Brazil and Argentina*. Ithaca, N.Y.: Cornell University Press.

———. 1993. The Power of Principled Ideas: Human Rights Policies in the United States and Europe. In *Ideas and Foreign Policy: Beliefs, Institutions, and Political Change*, ed. J. Goldstein and R. Keohane. Ithaca, N.Y.: Cornell University Press.

Slim, Hugo. 2002. Making Moral Low Ground: Rights as the Struggle for Justice and the Abolition of Development. *Praxis* 17.

Smyke, Patricia. 1990. UNICEF and the Convention on the Rights of the Child. Unpublished internal report, UNICEF, New York.

Social Development Task Group. 1997. Social Development and Results on the Ground. Social Development Task Group, World Bank, Washington, May 1.

Stein, Howard, and E. Wayne Nafziger. 1991. Structural Adjustment, Human Needs, and the World Bank Agenda. *Journal of Modern African Studies* 29, no. 1:173–89.

Streeten, Paul. 1994. Human Development: Needs and Ends. *American Economic Review* 84, no. 2:232–37.

Sturdivant, Frederick. 1985. *Business and Society: A Managerial Approach.* Homewood, Ill.: Richard D. Irwin.

Tarantola, Daniel. 2000. *Building on the Synergy between Health and Human Rights: A Global Perspective.* Working Paper. Boston: François-Xavier Bagnoud Center for Health and Human Rights.

Taylor, Allyn Lise. 1992. Making the World Health Organization Work: A Legal Framework for Universal Access to the Conditions for Health. *American Journal of Law and Medicine* 18, no. 4:301–46.

Theis, Joachim. 2004. *Consolidation and Review of the Main Findings and Lessons Learned of the Cast Studies on Operationalizing HRBAP in UNICEF.* New York: UNICEF.

Toebes, Brigit C. A. 1999. *The Right to Health as a Human Right in International Law.* Oxford: Intersentia.

Tripp, Aili Mari. 1992. The Impact of Crisis and Economic Reform on Women in Urban Tanzania. In *Unequal Burden: Economic Crisis, Persistent Poverty, and Women's Work,* ed. L. Benaria and S. Feldman. Boulder, Colo.: Westview Press.

Umaña, Alvaro, ed. 1998. *The World Bank Inspection Panel: The First Four Years (1994–1998).* Washington, D.C.: World Bank.

UNICEF (United Nations Children's Fund). 1984. Report of the Executive Board. Report E/ICEF/1984/12, UNICEF, New York.

———. 1985. Report of Meeting on UNICEF's Role in the Draft Convention on the Rights of the Child. UNICEF, New York, July 17–19.

———. 1986a. Children in Especially Difficult Circumstances. Report E/ICEF/1986/L.3, UNICEF, New York, February 27.

———. 1986b. Observations of UNICEF on the Draft Convention on the Rights of the Child: Speech by Tarzie Vittachi. Document MBN/cT-0004Q, UNICEF, New York.

———. 1986c. Report of the Executive Board, April. Document E/ICEF/1986/12, Decision 1986/21, UNICEF, New York.

———. 1987. Handwritten notes of 25-27 November UNICEF Workshop on the Draft Convention on the Rights of the Child, UNICEF, New York.

———. 1989. Report of the Executive Director: Children in the 1990s. Report E/ICEF/1989/2 (part I), UNICEF, New York, March 7.

———. 1994. Government of Bangladesh: UNICEF Country Programme of Cooperation. UNICEF, Dhaka.

————. 1998. A Human Rights Approach to UNICEF Programming for Children and Women: What It Is, and Some Changes It Will Bring. Report CF/EXD/1998-04, UNICEF, New York, April 21.

————. 1999. Programme Cooperation for Children and Women from a Human Rights Perspective. Report E/ICEF/1999/11, UNICEF, New York, April 5.

————. 2002. Adopting a Human Rights Approach to Programming: The UNICEF Tanzania Case. UNICEF, Dar es Salaam.

————. 2003a. Core Course: Human Rights Principles for Programming. UNICEF, New York.

————. 2003b. Report: The Second Interagency Workshop on Implementing a Human Rights-Based Approach in the Context of UN Reform. UNICEF, New York, May 5–7.

————. 2004. Report on the Mid-Term Review of the UNICEF Medium-Term Strategic Plan (2002–2005). Report E/ICEF/2004/13, UNICEF, New York, July 20.

————. 2005. UNICEF Joint Health and Nutrition Strategy for 2006-2015. Report E/ICEF/2006/8, UNICEF, New York, November 15.

————. 2006. United Nations Special Session on Children. www.unicef .org/specialsession/about/followup-national-plans.htm.

United Nations. 1951. *Yearbook of the United Nations—1950.* New York: United Nations Office of Public Information.

————. 1960. *Yearbook of the United Nations—1959.* New York: United Nations Office of Public Information.

————. 2001. *HIV/AIDS and Human Rights: International Guidelines.* New York: UN Joint Program on Aids and Office of the UN High Commissioner for Human Rights.

United Nations Standing Committee on Nutrition. 2000. Report of the Meeting of the Working Group on Nutrition, Ethics and Human Rights. United Nations Standing Committee on Nutrition, New York, April 13.

Uvin, Peter. 2002. On High Moral Ground: The Incorporation of Human Rights by the Development Enterprise. *Praxis* 17.

————. 2004. *Human Rights and Development.* New York: Kumarian Press.

Vaubel, Roland. 1986. A Public Choice Approach to International Organization. *Public Choice* 51, no. 1:39–57.

Verbeek, Bertjan. 1998. International Organizations: The Ugly Ducklings of International Relations Theory? In *Autonomous Policy Making by International Organizations,* ed. B. Reinalda and B. Verbeek. New York: Routledge.

Wade, Robert. 1997. Greening the Bank: The Struggle over the Environment 1970–1995. In *The World Bank: Its First Half-Century,* ed.

D. Kapur, J. P. Lewis, and R. Webb. Washington, D.C.: Brookings Institution Press.

Walzer, Michael. 1983. *Spheres of Justice: A Defense of Pluralism and Equality.* New York: Basic Books.

Weaver, Catherine, and Ralf J. Leiteritz. 2005. "Our Poverty Is a World Full of Dreams": Reforming the World Bank. *Global Governance* 11, no. 3:369–88.

Weber, Max. 1946. *From Max Weber: Essays in Sociology,* trans. H. H. Gerth and C. W. Mills. New York: Oxford University Press.

———. 1947. *Max Weber: The Theory of Social and Economic Organization,* trans. A. M. Henderson and T. Persons. New York: Free Press.

Weiss, Thomas, and Leon Gordenker, eds. 1996. *NGOs, the UN, and Global Governance.* Boulder, Colo.: Lynne Rienner.

Whitehead, Ann. 2003. Failing Women, Sustaining Poverty: Gender in Poverty Reduction Strategy Papers. Gender and Development Network / Christian Aid, London, May.

WHO Executive Board. 2001. Health Systems Performance Assessment. Report EB107.R8. World Health Organization, Geneva, January 15–22.

Wilks, Alex. 2003. *World Bank Social and Environmental Policies: Abandoning Responsibility?* London: Bretton Woods Project. www.brettonwoodsproject.org/doc/env/safeguards.PDF.

Willetts, Peter, ed. 1996. *The Conscience of the World: The Influence of Non-Governmental Organizations in the UN System.* Washington, D.C.: Brookings Institution Press.

Williams, David, and Tom Young. 1994. Governance, the World Bank, and Liberal Theory. *Political Studies* 42, no. 1:84–100.

Williams, Douglas. 1987. *The Specialized Agencies and the United Nations: The System in Crisis.* New York: St. Martin's Press.

Williamson, Oliver E. 1967. *The Economics of Discretionary Behavior: Managerial Objectives in a Theory of the Firm.* Chicago: Markham Publishing.

Wintrobe, Ronald. 1997. Modern Bureaucratic Theory. In *Perspectives on Public Choice,* ed. D. C. Mueller. New York: Cambridge University Press.

Wojcik, Mark E. 1998. Tribute: On the Sudden Loss of a Human Rights Activist—A Tribute to Jonathan Mann's Use of International Human Rights Law in the Global Battle against AIDS. *John Marshall Law Review* 32, no. 1:129–38.

Woods, Ngaire. 2001. Making the IMF and the World Bank More Accountable. *International Affairs* 77, no. 1:83–100.

———. 2003. The United States and the International Financial Institutions: Power and Influence within the World Bank and the IMF. In *US Hegemony and International Institutions,* ed. R. Foot, S. N. McFarlane, and M. Mastanduno. New York: Oxford University Press.

World Bank. 1967. Memorandum of the Legal Department of the IBRD, 22 UN GAOR Annex II. Document A/6825(1967). Washington, D.C.: World Bank.

———. 1979. *Recognizing the "Invisible" Woman in Development: The World Bank's Experience*. Washington, D.C.: World Bank.

———. 1989a. IBRD Articles of Agreement. http://siteresources.worldbank .org/EXTABOUTUS/Resources/ibrd-articlesofagreement.pdf.

———. 1989b. *Sub-Saharan Africa: From Crisis to Sustainable Growth*. Washington, D.C.: World Bank.

———. 1990. *The Social Dimensions of Adjustment in Africa: A Policy Agenda*. Washington, D.C.: World Bank.

———. 1991. *World Development Report 1991*. New York: Oxford University Press.

———. 1992a. Effective Implementation: Key to Development Impact (Wapenhans Report). Washington, D.C.: World Bank.

———. 1992b. *Governance and Development*. Washington, D.C.: World Bank.

———. 1994. *Governance: The World Bank's Experience*. Washington, D.C.: World Bank.

———. 1995a. *Toward Gender Equality: The Role of Public Policy*. Washington, D.C.: World Bank.

———. 1995b. *The World Bank and Legal Technical Assistance*. Policy Research Working Paper 1414. Washington, D.C.: World Bank.

———. 1997. The Strategic Compact: Renewing the Bank's Effectiveness to Fight Poverty. Washington, D.C.: World Bank.

———. 2000. *Advancing Gender Equality: World Bank Action since Beijing*. Washington, D.C.: World Bank.

———. 2001a. *Engendering Development: Through Gender Equality in Rights, Resources, and Voice*. New York: Oxford University Press.

———. 2001b. Integrating Gender in World Bank Assistance. Document 23035. Operations Evaluation Department, World Bank, Washington, October 25.

———. 2002a. The Gender Dimension of Bank Assistance: An Evaluation of Results. Operations Evaluation Department. Washington, D.C.: World Bank.

———. 2002b. *Integrating Gender into the World Bank's Work: A Strategy for Action*. Washington, D.C.: World Bank.

———. 2002c. Reforming Public Institutions and Strengthening Governance: A World Bank Strategy: Implementation Update. World Bank, Washington, April.

———. 2002d. *The World Bank Annual Report 2002*. Vol. 1. Washington, D.C.: World Bank.

————. 2004a. *Initiatives in Legal and Judicial Reform.* Report from Legal Vice Presidency. Washington, D.C.: World Bank.

————. 2004b. Social Development in World Bank Operations: Results and the Way Forward. Discussion Draft. Social Development Department. Washington, D.C.: World Bank.

————. 2004c. *World Bank Operational Manual.* http://wbln0018 .worldbank.org/Institutional/Manuals/OpManual.nsf/05TOCpages/ Operational%20Manual.

————. 2005a. Empowering People by Transforming Institutions: Social Development in World Bank Operations. World Bank, Washington, January 12.

————. 2005b. Evaluating a Decade of World Bank Gender Policy: 1990– 99. Operations Evaluation Department. Washington, D.C.: World Bank.

————. 2005c. *Expanding the Use of Country Systems in Bank-Supported Operations: Issues and Proposals.* Washington, D.C.: World Bank.

————. 2005d. Putting Social Development to Work for the Poor: An OED Review of World Bank Activities. Operations Evaluation Department. Washington, D.C.: World Bank.

————. 2007. Public Sector Governance. http://web.worldbank.org/wbsite/ external/topics/extpublicsectorandgovernance/,,menuPK:286310 ~pagePK:149018~piPK:149093~theSitePK:286305,00.html.

World Health Assembly. 1988. Avoidance of Discrimination in Relation to HIV-Infected People and People with AIDS. Report WHA41/1988/ REC/1. World Health Assembly, Geneva, May 13.

————. 1992. Women, Health and Development. Report WHA45.25. World Health Assembly, Geneva, May 14.

————. 1994. International Decade of the World's Indigenous People. Report WHA47.27. World Health Assembly, Geneva, May 12.

————. 2001. International Decade of the World's Indigenous People. Report WHA54.16. World Health Assembly, Geneva, May 21.

World Health Organization. 1958. *The First Ten Years of the World Health Organization.* Geneva: World Health Organization.

————. 1992. The Global AIDS Strategy. World Health Organization, Geneva.

————. 1995. Paris AIDS Summit. Report EB95.R14. World Health Organization, Geneva, January 16–27.

————. 1998. *Gender and Health: Technical Paper.* Geneva: World Health Organization.

————. 2000a. Informal Consultation on Health and Human Rights. Report HSD / GCP / June 2000. World Health Organization, Geneva.

———. 2000b. World Health Organization Assesses the World's Health Systems. Press Release. World Health Organization, Geneva, June 21. www.who.int/inf-pr-2000/en/pr2000-44.html.

———. 2001a. *Globalization, TRIPS and Access to Pharmaceuticals.* WHO Policy Perspectives on Medicine 3. Geneva: World Health Organization.

———. 2001b. *Transforming Health Systems: Gender and Rights in Reproductive Health.* Geneva: World Health Organization.

———. 2001c. *WHO's Contribution to the World Conference against Racism, Racial Discrimination, Xenophobia and Related Intolerances.* Health & Human Rights Publication 2. Geneva: World Health Organization.

———. 2002a. *Integrating Gender Perspectives in the Work of the WHO.* Geneva: World Health Organization.

———. 2002b. *25 Questions & Answers on Health & Human Rights.* Geneva: World Health Organization.

———. 2002c. Water for Health Enshrined as a Human Right. Press Release WHO/91. World Health Organization, Geneva, November 27.

———. 2003. Leading the Health Sector Response to HIV/AIDS. World Health Organization, Geneva, May.

———. 2006a. Child and Adolescent Health and Development: Child and Adolescent Rights. www.who.int/child-adolescent-health/RIGHTS/cah_work.htm.

———. 2006b. Gender and Reproductive Rights: Rights-Based Approach—Country Pilot Projects. www.who.int/reproductive-health/gender/country.html.

Young, Oran. 1991. Political Leadership and Regime Formation: On the Development of Institutions in International Society. *International Organization* 45, no. 3:281–308.

———. 1999. Comment on Andrew Moravcsik, "A New Statecraft? Supranational Entrepreneurs and International Cooperation." *International Organization* 53, no. 4:805–9.

Zuckerman, Elaine, and Wu Qing. 2003. *Reforming the World Bank: Will the New Gender Strategy Make a Difference?* Washington, D.C.: Heinrich Böll Foundation / Gender Action.

# Index

accountability issues, 198–207; and claim to impartiality, 199; and democratic deficit, 198–99; and focus on what IGOs *ought* to be doing, 200; and freedom of action, 199; and private sector corporations, 200–207; and stakeholder ethics model, 201–9; and World Bank governance agenda, 77–78, 94–95

adaptation of human rights goals, 2, 24, 156–82; adoption of rights agenda, 157–61; definition of rights agenda, 161–64; implementation process, 164–66; implications for the study of international organizations, 179–82; learning and adaptation, 170–73; open systems/interaction with environments, 181–82; power of principled ideas, 173–79, 181–82; principal–agent theory and public choice approach, 168–70; similarities, 22, 23–24, 156, 166–67, 177–78; state control, 167–68, 173. *See also* adoption of rights-based agendas; definition of human rights agendas; implementation of human rights agendas

adoption of rights-based agendas: and consensus, 158; factors explaining, 157–61; and IGOs' humanitarian tasks, 157; and IGOs' idealism, 157; outside/external pressures, 9, 73–74, 78–79, 159; and small groups of champions, 157–58; and top leader-

ship, 160–61; and true believers, 7–8, 11, 146–48, 159–60, 174–75, 177, 178–79; UNICEF, 26–33, 35, 36–37, 57, 60, 157–60; WHO, 119–31, 157–61; World Bank, 67–80, 93, 102, 110, 114, 157–61

agency and IGOs, 1–25; academic studies/research on, 9–10, 12–13, 16–17, 179–81, 183–84; adoption of principled ideas, 5, 7–9, 12, 17–19, 173–79, 181–82; bureaucratic/organizational nature of IGOs, 12–17, 179–80; and epistemic communities, 10–12; explanations for IGO behavior, 6–10; factors separating management from ownership, 13–17, 199; and human rights concept, 19–21; and IGOs' freedom of action, 15–17, 199; IGOs' new priorities, 4–6; IGOs' relationship to UN, 4, 189; member states and IGOs, 6, 11, 21, 22, 186–87; necessity of understanding IGO autonomy, 9–10; practical levels of independence in each IGO, 22; principal–agent dynamics, 9–10, 12–13, 16–17; realist perspectives, 186–87; research design and case selection, 4–5, 21–23; and staffs, 10–11; standard bureaucratic explanations, 6–7; and true believers, 11; two separate purposes of IGO decisions, 11. *See also* accountability issues; ethical responsibilities of IGOs